CHASING THE CHARIOT

CHASING
THE
CHARIOT

How Clive Woodward Won a World Cup,
Changed English Rugby . . . Then Left

MICK COLLINS

MAINSTREAM
PUBLISHING
EDINBURGH AND LONDON

First published in Great Britain in 2004 by
MAINSTREAM PUBLISHING COMPANY (EDINBURGH) LTD
7 Albany Street
Edinburgh EH1 3UG

ISBN 1 84018 882 0

A catalogue record for this book is available from the British Library

Typeset in Bembo and Times New Roman
Printed and bound in Great Britain by
Antony Rowe Ltd, Chippenham, Wiltshire

To Cas, Honor and Amy,
with all my love and thanks.

Acknowledgements

It would have been impossible to write this book without the help, assistance, advice and support of the following people, so beginning with the professional and moving through to the personal, thanks are directed as follows:

To Vernon and the Tigers, Dave Berry and all at Guy's Hospital RFC, Adam Lowles and all at St Columba's, and to Jim Hooley and all who work to make the Daily Mail Schools' Tournament such an uplifting event, many thanks. Cheers to Phil Sandilands of PSA Sport for taking the trouble and buying the drinks. Thanks also to Steve Jones and Mick Cleary, who devoted time, advice and opinions to someone many rungs down the ladder. Oh, and thanks to Ronan, who landed on my head and made my day. I'll explain later . . .

At the highest levels of the game, I was helped by a number of busy people, all of whom generously found the time to deal with my various requests. To Jason Leonard and the ever-helpful Dolores McGinley and Ashley Woolfe at Sportscastnet.com, and Dee McIntosh and Nicki Jupp at the RFU, many thanks for your assistance and patience. The same sentiments apply to Erin Mitchell and Andrew Scoular, along with apologies for leaving you with a soggy office. Finally, to Sir Clive Woodward, who found time to talk despite a schedule already groaning at the seams.

On the personal front, thanks to Bill, Peter, Graeme, Ailsa and Lizzie at Mainstream, for being good at what they do. A particular vote of thanks goes to my editor, Kevin O'Brien, who spent hours chipping my words into shape, and remained calm and invaluable, even through the late, and somewhat unhelpful, resignation affair.

Among my friends, I owe a debt of gratitude (although a pint usually suffices) to, among others, Charlie Connelly, Jeanette Earl, Jo Cantello, Rick Shearman, the Far Canal and all the others who put up with my inability to do a 'proper job'. Many thanks to Andy Spencer, who cured a sick and ailing computer when it was struck by a virus a day before the manuscript was submitted – it'll never know how close it came to going through the window. Thanks also to those who hired me to scribble bits and pieces along the way, without whom 'self-employed' would have been 'unemployed'. Thanks also to William Webb Ellis, sport's finest and possibly most apocryphal historic cheat, who, in a moment of lateral thinking, provided a lifetime of enjoyment for generations to come.

Heartfelt thanks to my family, without whose love and support this wouldn't be possible, and quiet at the back to all those who suggest it might be easier if it wasn't. To Dot and Brian, Dan, Nets and Aidan, Mary and Joseph and Patrick (my Twickenham correspondent), all my love. To Mum and Dad, sincere thanks for your extraordinary help and your subtle and understated advice – it's much appreciated.

Finally, to my wife Cas, and my two perfect, if gloriously argumentative daughters, Honor and Amy, my love, admiration and thanks for all the happiness and delights. Long may it all continue.

Contents

Preface

On 1 September 2004, English rugby took an unexpected turn. There had been a spate of stories about the possibility of Sir Clive Woodward walking away from Twickenham and, amazingly enough, towards a footballing future. The round-ball game had been a lifelong love, he told us through serialised chunks of his book in the Sunday papers, and he seemed to like the idea of a new challenge based on an old passion.

Rugby coaching, we were invited to believe, had always been a staging post – a convenient stopover on the way to his true love. Inconveniently, he was rather good at it, a World Cup win proving quite a distraction from his supposed first-choice career path. It all sounded wildly far-fetched, and my first reaction was to treat the story as another silly-season tale, but first, I thought I'd err on the side of caution.

In the finest traditions of the confused and uncertain, I phoned a friend. He knew Woodward, had as good an idea as anyone of exactly how the tale was likely to unwind, and confirmed that the stories were partially correct. Sir Clive was indeed leaving his job as coach of the England rugby team.

Woodward subsequently held a press conference, at which he distanced himself slightly from football, while letting his old bosses at the RFU have it with both barrels. It was dramatic stuff, headline catching and attention grabbing, but with this book days away from an encounter with the printing presses, I had a potential problem.

Every newspaper in the country carried tales of how, as a result of the resignation, the game was in crisis – how it had been shaken to its core and had no idea what to do next. Rugby's bubble, we were told, had burst.

My problem was simple. I had spent the previous nine months, since the day of the World Cup-final victory, trawling my way through English rugby, from top to bottom. I'd met the Southwark Tigers, who hail from a Peckham housing estate, and I'd visited St Columba's, who compete on public-school playing fields. I'd talked to the Guy's Hospital rugby team, the oldest club in the world, and Jason Leonard, the most capped player in the game. In between this, I'd met coaches, community leaders and development staff, as well as Sir Clive himself. I'd seen the game at all levels, and I knew it was thriving.

More children than ever before played, more people watched the national side and larger crowds gathered to see the top clubs in action. On top of that, the Webb Ellis trophy lived in its new home, at Twickenham, as England luxuriated in the glow of being world champions. The game had just undergone a much-publicised blip at its very top, but if this was a crisis, then I'm not sure how you describe the depths to which the English game has occasionally plunged over the last few decades.

No, make no mistake, the departure of Woodward may have stopped me temporarily in my tracks, and the reaction of the papers may have given me reason to briefly reconsider, but I'd seen the whole picture, over an extended period, with my own eyes. The plans Woodward had put in place wouldn't crumble just because he left his job – his legacy would live on.

This, then, is the story of the nine months following England's capture of the rugby World Cup. I didn't expect it to end amid such acrimony, but I didn't expect it to pass so pleasurably, either. English rugby, at all levels and especially among the younger players, is booming.

If the events of early to mid September 2004 truly do represent a crisis in the game, then, on the strength of what I've seen, it doesn't seem to be suffering all that badly.

I

Just another Saturday morning

To be honest, the reasons for my impending adventure weren't entirely clear. Not when the alarm went off, anyway, and the full coldness of the morning became apparent as I looked out of the window and saw the freezing cold rain hurtling out of a still-dark sky. The plan to have a nice, warm shower and wake gently into the day went up in smoke, in favour of an extra quarter of an hour in bed and a quick splash of water to the face. In retrospect, it was clear that it wasn't going to be an occasion for which you needed to look your absolute best.

Thanks to the whim of a man with an eye for a feature, the task in hand was to watch the people watching the rugby World Cup final. In a pub. At nine o' clock in the morning. In London. A train ride away from my house. A train which, conveniently enough on this bitterly cold and wet morning, left from a station a good 15 minutes' walk away. It wasn't the most promising of starts.

I stood on the platform, performing that trick so beloved of men caught in the rain: hunching my shoulders, trying to become too small a target for the droplets. In doing so, I pondered that it wasn't, as I grew slowly more damp, much of a trick. As a distraction, I wondered who, of the three other people standing alongside me, were likely to be heading off with the same intention in mind.

One of them was a middle-aged black woman, quietly reading a Bible, while standing underneath a floral umbrella. Another was dressed in a Connex Day-Glo jacket, plainly on his way to work on the railway, while the third bore the distinctive hallmarks of a teenager still on his way home from the night before. It was reasonably safe to assume, I assumed (reasonably safely), that I was on my own.

It was never likely to have been any other way. Having grown up with rugby, played it, loved it, watched and understood it, I knew all about the old men in blazers who ran it. More importantly, I knew about the blokes who turned up and just played it – played it because it was what they did, and what they enjoyed. I knew why people still sang about Eskimo Nell (well, I didn't actually, but I knew they still sang about her) and I knew it was unique.

I also, and for the purposes of this trip, most importantly, knew that rugby was a very small club. Not too many people played the game, not that many watched it, and only about half the referees understood the rules, let alone anyone else. Being a rugby fan was like following a small, insignificant band – you had all the albums, the B-sides and the rest of the back catalogue, and you luxuriated in the fact that you were one of a proud minority.

There would be me, a handful of others, some television coverage and a few headlines the next day. Everyone else would be tucked up in the warm, watching it on the couch, if at all, and starting their weekend at a civilised rate. There had been a fair smattering of attention over the course of the previous week, but that was hardly surprising. England never really won anything – in the literal sense, that is, as opposed to doing better than expected but still losing in the end. And certainly not in team sports.

If they won, there would be a bit of fuss, rugby would get its 15 minutes, and we'd be straight back to who beat who in the Premiership and whether David Beckham had changed his hairstyle. That was how it was, and that was how people understood it. To be honest, that was how I liked it: just me and a few others, locked into a private passion, with the rest of the country excluded because they didn't understand what the rules were and what was going on. Nobody was going to hijack the occasion, because nobody knew all that much about it.

Once on the train, I sat down, in order that the nylon-covered seat could better diffuse the water dripping off my coat across my previously dry backside. It was still pitch black, and the steamed-up windows left the outside world a gloomy mystery, made up of occasional streetlights and car headlights.

When we pulled into the next station, the confident prediction that I was the only person in London en route to this particular destination took something of a clattering. As the doors slid open with a satisfying hiss, a man stepped aboard and immediately attracted my attention.

Indeed, it's probably fair to say he attracted the attention of just about everyone. He was, after all, wearing a Father Christmas outfit, at 7.30 a.m., in the pouring rain. Clearly worried that this would not gain him sufficient recognition, he also carried a life-sized cardboard cut-out of Jonny Wilkinson, tucked under his arm, as if he were the most normal travelling companion imaginable.

Attempting not to stare at him, determined to keep this a personal mission unhindered by 'newcomers', I set about affecting an air of calm and composure. We were into a cheery conversation within about 30 seconds. The self-important air of separation and reserve had fallen immediately under the challenge of a Father Christmas outfit and a cardboard cut-out. I asked him if he was going to watch the game, hoping that my straight face would be taken as a sign of cheerful irony. Somewhat disconcertingly, he answered back in the same, serious tone.

'I am actually. In a bar with some friends. We've hired out the basement.'

With the exception of the basement bit, which was a little precise, I could probably have guessed this without claiming the gift of ESP, but it was a start. When I asked if Jonny was going to be accompanying him through the course of the day, he looked at me as if it was the most absurd question he had ever been asked. For the record, it's strangely disquieting, even as a grown man, to have Santa Claus treat you like a fool.

'Of course he will, he's like part of the family now. He's watched every game with us so he couldn't miss the big one. After the game, we're going to take him up to Earls Court to a few Australian pubs, just to show the locals that there's no hard feelings. I think it's the least we can do. They'll love it.'

I had reservations about that, to be honest, but it seemed churlish to raise them. He'd improved my mood just by being there, and as the train pulled into London Bridge station, we got off and strolled down the wet platform, chatting like old friends. Well, old friends who were ignoring a large cardboard cut-out of a rugby player and the gentle tinkling of a bell on the top of a Father Christmas hat. If the day was going to be strange, it had at least started in precisely the way it intended to continue.

The arrangement with Rick, a friend of mine, had been to meet at a café around the corner from the Southwark Tavern – that morning's pub of choice. It's always better to watch a big match with someone else, and to be honest, I was a little scared that I'd be the only one in there otherwise. As much as I was beginning to look forward to it, I didn't want anyone to think I assumed it was normal to sit and drink on my own early in the morning.

I mooched around Borough Market for a while, watching stall holders loading up their carts with fresh, organic fruit and veg, meat, fish, cheese and a hundred other culinary delights. I then headed off to the café for a tasteless sausage sandwich, served on processed white bread, with an anaemic cup of tea. Well, if you're going to be spending the morning wrecking your liver, you don't want to start out by giving it false hopes of nutritious sustenance to come. Better to be honest from the outset, and load your stomach with rubbish from the word go.

I decided to give my dad a call. He was in the stadium, thousands of miles away, waiting to watch the game himself. He complained about the weather, although I could barely hear him for the thudding of rain on the canopy above his head. We agreed to speak later, and the spirit of the occasion was slowly but surely becoming ever clearer. At the table next to me were four blokes in rugby shirts, reading about the forthcoming game in the morning papers. Presuming them to be 'proper fans', I offered forth this nugget of information.

'It's chucking it down in Sydney.'

The roar of delight left the waitress staring on in bemusement and concern. Another piece of the jigsaw was falling into place – I wasn't going to be watching alone, and I wasn't going to be without other people who understood the game. A cheer, just on account of the weather, showed a shrewd appreciation of how it might affect the sides. After aquaplaning past the French in the semi-final, England were seen as the more adaptable of the two. At the first hint of drizzle, in the eyes of these fans at least, Woodward's men were seen as certainties. Kick-off was almost due, and as commentators all over the world were synchronically muttering clichés, it was time for the talking to stop. It had just gone half eight in the morning – the pub beckoned.

To say it was packed would be failing to do justice to the situation.

It was heaving, with people already standing on chairs around the edges of the room, and the bar itself under serious siege. Thankfully, Rick was straight into 'find a space' mode, a talent possessed by only the most valuable of friends, and somehow directed us to the far side of the room, next to the bar. A few feet of space between a pillar and the wall allowed an unobstructed view of a giant television screen.

Pints were ordered, and suddenly, buoyed by the number of other drinkers, the fact that it was 9 a.m. seemed far less important. By the corner of the bar stood a pile of promotional Guinness hats, wide-brimmed Australian spoofs with miniature plastic pints dangling from the edges, hanging in place of corks.

'Some idiot will be wearing one of those by half-time,' Rick predicted. He was, and very smart it looked on him too, despite it being at least ten minutes into the second-half before he donned it, having had to temporarily switch to best bitter while the Guinness barrel was changed, thus slowing his otherwise impressive progress.

After an early Australian try from Lote Tuqiri caused a brief stutter among the nervously drinking masses, Wilkinson, doubtless to the approval of his cardboard-effigy-carrying fan in a basement bar somewhere, set about kicking England back into the lead. Next to us sat a middle-aged man, pint close at hand, half-turned to the bar as he tucked into a huge fry-up. I caught his eye, and he started laughing.

'Bloody heaven, this is! A pint, a fry-up and England winning the World Cup final as I sit and watch.'

As he lowered his fork and raised his glass to toast the sentiment, things went temporarily mad. Or madder, depending on your perspective. Lawrence Dallaglio galloped forwards, contemptuously swiping away tackles as if suddenly bigger than anyone else on the pitch. The ball was slipped inside to Wilkinson, who guided a pass back to the flank into the hands of Jason Robinson. From 15 yards out, Robinson was sliding over the line before words of encouragement had a chance to be bellowed. England were ahead, 14 points to 5, and though we didn't know it at the time, the last try of the 2003 World Cup had just been scored. Prior to the match, the Australian press had asked mockingly of England, 'Hands up if that's all you've got?' After the hour of try-less rugby which followed, it was a query that could just as easily have been directed at their own side.

The air went whatever colour air goes when filled with recently launched beer, as a couple of hundred pairs of pint-bearing hands flew upwards in unison. Robinson's snarling celebration, shouting to the stands and punching the ball high into the air, was utterly out of character, and yet perfectly in tune with the spirit of the moment. The happiest man in the world remained euphoric, despite having just knocked his pint into his fry-up. An Australian in the midst of it all recovered from the cuddles and kisses rained down on him, and offered a tactical opinion.

'The bastard cheated. It's not a try. It's a forward pass. Or something . . .'

He surrendered to his fate, amid more cheering England fans. His mates, also wearing green and gold shirts, laughed at him. People laughed back at them. Not one angry word was exchanged. It was the sort of situation only rugby can offer. Midway through a World Cup final, two sets of fans were drinking heavily, jeering and cheering in turn, and mocking each other's downfall at every opportunity. Had it been football, the place would have been a war zone in minutes.

It was everything you hope sport can be – enthralling and frustrating, vivid and blurred, all rolled into one, muscular frames skidding across a greased, green baize, generating differing emotions with each new passage of play. And, of course, there was a degree of farce, lest it all became too much to bear. England had gone into the tournament wearing new Nike shirts, proudly boasted of as being un-rippable and immune to any sort of mistreatment, tugging or tearing. I wouldn't like to comment on the degree of success attained by these shirts, but Ben Kay in particular appeared to play the game in an off-the-shoulder number. By the end of the game, England looked as if they'd been dressed by Vivienne Westwood in the early days of punk.

And then, just as the clock reached half past ten, England reached the promised land. Except they didn't. The marvellously named Elton Flatley, square jawed, blood streaked and a stereotypical Aussie to his core, slotted home a last-minute penalty to send us into extra time. England hadn't scored a point for the last 45 minutes, and the Australians had timed their recovery to absolute perfection.

Looking back now, it's possible to admire Flatley's kick for what it was. With pressure the like of which few players have ever had to endure, he had shown supreme strength of character and a technique capable of passing the toughest of tests. The kicks he was being offered might have been the fruits of dubious penalties, but the way he was dispatching them was magnificent. If nobody in a white shirt deserved

JUST ANOTHER SATURDAY MORNING

to lose that day, there were a few in gold jerseys who didn't either. As the kick went over, we in the pub just knew who was going to be the first to react.

'Who wants to kiss a bloody convict's arse now, eh?'

Slightly the worse for wear, the victim of the first-half taunting had, as Flatley sent the ball through the posts, become the instigator. To be fair, he'd been warming to it for the last ten minutes. As Joe Roff, the Australian wing, prepared to come on as a substitute, the commentator mentioned that he had an impressive record.

'They've all got bloody records – that's why they're there in the first bloody place!' boomed a Home Counties voice from deep within the throng.

'You're good, mate, you're good,' countered the spokesman for the Australian nation as a whole, 'but Aussie is on your tail. You can't keep a convict down . . .'

He may have got kissed again for that one, but the memory was becoming a little fuzzy by this stage. Rick, who I noted with a degree of concern had started to bang his head on the bar as Flatley's kick went over, had decided to call his dad, to see how he was. Even as grown men, it's nice to know that we're both mature and independent enough to need to phone our dads when things get tough.

Between the two of them, they seemed to have convinced themselves that they'd convinced each other this was merely a delay in the victory, rather than anything more serious. Rick put the phone down, and tried to look like a man reassured by the discussion – he failed. At the other end of the line, I suspected a very similar thing was happening. Reassurance and certainty were going to be in short supply for the next 20 minutes.

In Sydney, Jason Leonard was walking around the England team, nodding, shaking hands, patting people on the back, and generally making sure they were ready for the next dramatic and decisive period. Back in 1966, Sir Alf Ramsey was famously quoted telling his players at the end of normal time that they'd won the thing once, now go out there and do it again. Leonard seemed to be playing much the same role.

The tension, it seemed, was getting to everyone. Drink was arriving and disappearing at a fearful rate of knots, and Rick's Marlboro Lights were being consumed in similar proportions. Resplendent in his new hat, he looked like a black and white chimney, continually announcing the selection of a new pope. With two minutes to go, Flatley squared things once more. This was getting ridiculous.

I'd roughly scribbled down the stuff I needed to file over to the office at the end of the game, even as the effects of the morning left me barely coherent enough to talk to a copytaker. With 30 seconds left on the clock, events conspired to ensure that I drowned out the last hints of sobriety. From the restart, Lewis Moody failed by an inch to get a hand on a hastily sliced Australian clearance kick, leaving England with the throw-in to a handily-placed lineout. An inch closer, and the merest touch of his hand would have left Australia needing only to win their own lineout ball and clear to touch to drag the whole thing into the unbearable prospect of sudden death.

The lineout was duly claimed by a white jersey, no more than 30 yards from the Australian posts. With scores level and seconds left, this was already, in reality, sudden death: who scores, wins. As if in slow motion, Matt Dawson, with his suitably Fagin-esque pickpocket's gloves, lifted the ball from beneath the noses of the gold-shirted pack and snuck away through the crowd into open space. He was reclaimed fifteen yards further on, and a mad scramble of bodies ensued. Leonard acted as bouncer, throwing out a few undesirables from the side of the ruck, while Johnson's heftiest intervention reset the ball, restored some order and allowed Dawson the chance to escape the ruck and send a clean pass to his stand-off.

Wilkinson collected it, took scarcely a glimpse and swung his right foot, sending the ball tumbling through the Sydney sky towards the Australian posts. His arms were aloft the second it left his boot, and Andre Watson followed by raising one of his a second or so later, signalling the kick's success. It was about the only decision the referee had given England all day, and it won them the World Cup.

Chaos reigned. The pub didn't calm down a fraction between the kick going over and the whistle being blown, although given that the gap was only about 20 seconds, that's not as impressive as it sounds. What was impressive were the scenes that greeted the whistle. People leapt about and hugged each other. Someone bought the Aussie a pint in exchange for one last cuddle. Rick, who is three inches and three stone smaller than me, picked me up and bounced around for the best part of a rather surreal minute. Upon closer scrutiny, he was crying his eyes out, quite possibly as happy as he'd ever been. The windows were full of people from outside, looking through and cheering and waving. If Richard Curtis ever writes a rugby film, this is how it will end.

George Gregan went over to Johnson and offered him a handshake and a hug of congratulation. His sporting world had just performed the cruellest of about-turns, but there were standards to be maintained, decency to be displayed, and a captain's duties to perform. It was a deeply dignified gesture, which showed that being a giant on the pitch was about more than just your physical stature.

The extent of the emotion generated, and the degree of adrenalin running through the main players, even after it was over, was demonstrated on television in vivid close-up within five minutes of the final whistle. Dallaglio was asked what it meant to him to answer the critics and claim the prize in Australia, where the hostility had been highest.

'We've taken a lot of crap here . . .' he began menacingly, desperately trying to keep his emotions in check as he was almost overwhelmed with the moment, the satisfaction of thrusting the doubters' words back down their throats. He wasn't going to crack, though, and fought hard to achieve total control, with the vein on his neck giving the only clue as to how hyped-up he remained, even with the result claimed and the game over – it was pulsing like a hosepipe conveying a string of melons.

Similarly, Woodward, the most controlled of them all, was having problems expressing quite what it meant to him when confronted with a television interviewer moments after the final whistle. He may have become hugely experienced at hiding his emotions over the years, but now, in an instant, there was no need, and the freedom, combined with everything else, left him temporarily stunned.

'It's been fantastic. I just want to say thank you to every single fan in this stadium, to everyone watching on television, it's just, I'm, well, speechless. We won, we won, so who cares what I thought? We've won the World Cup – it's fantastic, unbelievable.'

If his finest moment didn't exactly coincide with his most coherent, nobody was going to hold it against him – the cheer when he collected his medal told you all you needed to know about his popularity. Besides, he wasn't alone in struggling to express himself. I went outside, in a vain bid to put over some copy, and slumped quietly in a doorway as the rain made a bluish chaos of the felt-penned jottings collected together during the course of the morning.

Slurring monologue eventually complete, I lurched back into the pub and located Rick, who had again spoken to his dad on the phone, this time so that they could cry at each other for a minute or so. It may not have represented the high point of their relationship, at least in terms of the quality of the discourse, but it's likely that few chats have ever meant more. He was also nursing a freshly purchased bottle of champagne, two more pints of Guinness and few ambitions outside of watching the rerun and reaching oblivion. It was still only about twenty past eleven in the morning.

We managed most of the rerun and achieved the oblivion part of the plan beyond all dispute, before setting off into the rainy afternoon. The market was now full of normal, sober people who seemed delighted to meet those daft enough to have got up early and drunk their side home to victory. I celebrated by buying random items of fruit and veg, in a flawed bid to appear more reasoned and sober upon my return: 'What do you mean, I'm drunk? I've been shopping.' I arrived home with large amounts of tarragon and some red peppers, which, as I'm allergic to one and not fond of the other, singularly failed to fool anyone. Compared, however, to the thought of my chum from earlier heading off to Earls Court with his Jonny Wilkinson cardboard cut-out, in hindsight, I think I was rather restrained.

The day had begun with the firm conviction that I was in a tiny minority of people who were going to watch the final. I ended it unsteady on my feet, but unswerving in my belief that I had watched something remarkable take place. The news bulletins were full of the game, the papers dominated by it, and conversation obsessed with that extraordinary 100 minutes of rugby. This wasn't going to be our little game any more, the one we understood with a few others and held to our hearts almost as a secret we didn't want to share with the world. This had just become very different, in front of our alcoholically skewed eyes.

Rugby had never been quite this big before, but it had enjoyed big moments, gone professional, ushered in a new era, and botched it – it had been run by dusty old men, the '57 old farts', who believed in a feudal, rather than a commercial, world. Now it was about to undergo an upsurge in its fortunes like never before. Where Woodward had rebuilt the playing side of the game, the administrators were about to be given the chance to discover whether they, on the non-playing side, had kept pace.

As the England party had waited at Sydney airport for their flight home, one of their senior members was chatting to a journalist, who suggested that things would never get better than this.

'Don't worry,' he said, 'the blazers could still bugger the whole thing up for us.'

And there was that fear again, put into words. Rugby doesn't run itself very well, and it treats the modern world with deep suspicion. England may be world champions on the pitch, but their performance off the field hasn't always been something to get too excited about. They may not lose money with the reckless abandon of, say, football clubs, but they've not always been run along smooth and considered business lines either.

Staffed by volunteers-laden committees, English rugby had a structure easily as complicated as anything the old Soviet Union could muster. Decisions took months and years to be made, agreed, ratified, passed and enacted, usually just in time to be reversed, as they became outdated the day they came into force. If it hadn't handled being bad, how on Earth was English rugby meant to deal with being good?

If you've got millions of potential new fans, what sort of plans do you have in place to make the most of them? If people are growing tired of the excesses of football, how does rugby intend to promote itself as a viable alternative?

The decision was made. I was going to throw myself into the game, at all levels from top to bottom: mini rugby, veterans' rugby, internationals and Fifth XVs. I was going to ask them, the players and coaches, the managers and volunteers, about the state of the game. Rugby had, throughout the course of its history, made some memorably bad decisions – what was going to stop it doing exactly the same thing, all over again? The game had just won the sporting lottery, and I was going to find out what its governors and practitioners intended to do with the cheque.

It was to be an illuminating journey.

II

The morning after the night before

I wasn't the only one who woke up the following morning with a muzzy, hungover sense of detachment. Equally, I don't suppose I was unique in peering uncertainly at the sports sections of the Sunday newspapers, just to confirm that all had really gone exactly as I remembered it. While it's perfectly usual to have great sports events leaving a sense of 'I can't believe what I've just seen' in their wake, when, like this one, for so many people they were combined with large amounts of alcohol at an unearthly hour of the day, it became almost inevitable.

As it turned out, I needn't have bothered delving through or flipping to the back for the sports sections – without exception, this was designated front-page news. It provided some magnificent reporting, even if, strangely enough, the headline writers somehow failed to rise to the occasion. All right, there was nothing actually wrong with the *Sunday Telegraph*'s 'CHAMPIONS OF THE WORLD', even if it was a little bland and straightforward, but the *Mail on Sunday*'s picture of Jonny Wilkinson celebrating at the final whistle was slightly undermined by a later admission from the player himself.

'WE'VE WON WE'VE WON!' proclaimed the front page, putting words to a picture of Wilkinson leaping in the air and shouting. Unfortunately, Wilkinson informed us later that afternoon that he'd actually been bellowing, 'World Cup, World Cup!' Still, the thought was there, and it was a lot more sensible than the *News of the World*'s 'DROP OF THE WORLD', which bore the hallmark of someone trying much, much too hard . . .

By the time Monday morning had arrived, the *News of the World*'s sister paper, *The Sun*, had opted for the George and Ben Cohen angle, offering us the less than catchy, 'AFTER 37 YEARS IT'S THE GOLD ONE-TWO . . .', while the *Daily Star* was true to its tabloid roots with, 'SCRUM ON HOME'. The *Daily Express* became the first to attempt to consign the result to history and look to the future, with the ever so slightly demanding, 'WE WANT MORE'.

What was extraordinary wasn't the nature of the headlines, but their very existence. Football, for so long the mainstay of tabloid-newspaper life, had been relegated to a few odd paragraphs here and there, largely consisting of David Beckham and Sven-Goran Eriksson offering messages of congratulation. Admittedly, *The Sun* also carried messages from Craig David, Lisa Riley and Toby Anstis (no, me neither), so the hordes of 'A-list' stars may not have been as vast as they'd hoped, but rugby was still maintaining its place at the front of the public consciousness.

One of the problems it faced was that the British public in general, perhaps even the vast majority of them, knew very little about the game at all. Wilkinson was a household face, and Martin Johnson's grizzled features had been shown collecting the trophy from an unforgivably gloomy John Howard enough times to make him instantly recognisable, but few of the other players were especially well known outside rugby circles.

As Johnson stepped forward to meet the unsmiling Howard, collecting a trophy the Prime Minister was evidently only too loath to surrender, several of the faces behind him wearing white shirts and broad smiles were enjoying their final moments of relative anonymity.

Perhaps it was the mistaken belief that nobody was watching terribly carefully which contributed to Howard's performance in setting a new record for gracelessness when distributing medals. Dispensing each golden disc with a backhanded flick and scarcely a nod of the head, it was all the Australian Premier could do not to lob Johnson the trophy itself from somewhere just off stage. As it was, the English captain can look back at the tape and smile at the sight of himself wiping his hands carefully on his shorts in readiness for a handshake that simply refused to arrive.

Had the phrase 'You've got what you wanted, now piss off' accompanied this utterly undignified performance, the words would hardly have been out of keeping with his actions. The victims of Dick Turpin handed over their gold rather more graciously, and Mr Howard's curmudgeonly demeanour will surely be remembered long after his political career ends.

For every ounce of decency, honesty and generosity Australian captain George Gregan managed after the match, the meanness of spirit displayed by his Prime Minister exceeded it a dozen times over. When history suggests Andre Watson's refereeing as the worst individual performance of the 2003 World Cup final, it would do well to remember the contribution of John Howard. It might just save the official's blushes.

It was also worth remembering, however, the scale of the task Australia had undertaken in hosting the tournament, and how brilliantly the nation had risen to the challenge. Contained, as it surely always should be, within a single nation, even from a range of several thousand miles, it was like tuning into coverage of a large party whenever you flicked on the television. If, as appeared likely, the final was going to be considered as one of the great games of all time, it was perfectly appropriate that it acted as the icing on the cake of one of the great tournaments.

It's become all too easy, in the wake of the victory, to consider all Australians and their behaviour during the tournament as being accurately reflected by the headlines and stories carried by a few of their more volatile newspapers. For the duration of the tournament, the Australian media had been hostile to the England side in a way that only, well, the English tabloid media could possibly hope to equal. Each day was the same – choose any two negative adjectives from the list, focus on today's trait and get stuck in. England were boring, predictable, old, slow, dull, arrogant and boorish, depending on which paper you read, and voodoo dolls of Wilkinson were the cut-out of the week.

Try making a case that the English nation as a whole can accurately be summarised by some of the more xenophobic utterances of *The Sun*, however, and you'll rightly be shot down in flames. Adopt a similar approach to the Australian nation as a whole, and you're behaving in exactly the arrogant manner some of their papers complained about in the first place.

After a night spent rehydrating in a way surely approved of by rugby players of old, the side were given another reminder of how their lives were to change. Alongside pictures of the final itself, almost every paper picked up on the fact that Johnson had been unable to find a cab following their celebration night out (John Howard's doing? You decide) and had walked back to his hotel. A few months earlier, it would have been hard to see how this could have been considered in the slightest bit newsworthy, but that was before Johnson became a World Cup winner. Now he was a celebrity, and celebrities didn't tramp back home through dark streets in the rain.

Johnson, however, was a rugby player – not a celebrity. At least, that was how he appeared to view it himself, and the idea of becoming a piece of public property didn't, one suspected, much appeal. Passionate speeches and pre-match assertions can make headlines, but only performances make memories. At the very highest level, when the physical acts on the pitch match even the wildest of expectations, they can sometimes, just sometimes, make history. Johnson only ever asked to be judged on his actions, and they, not the words, cannot be bettered when we look for reasons to pay tribute to him.

Unlike so many British sporting failures, Johnson had no reason to look back and make excuses, but instead could leave people to watch what had happened, safe in the knowledge that the performance could not have been bettered. In the afterglow of the triumph, anything he said, as considered and measured as it tended to be, simply added a sheen to the nature of the achievement. Reviewed with the benefit of hindsight, however, his public utterances showed a clarity of purpose, reinforced by a certainty of action, all combining to provide a memory richly deserved by a modest man, who had become, unquestionably, a British sporting great. He wanted to be judged on actions, not words – to be successful, rather than just quotable. Johnson had asked his team to deliver a performance worthy of winning the World Cup, and the events of the last 12 hours bore testimony to the persuasive powers of a large, contented figure from the East Midlands, tramping back to his hotel through a rainy Sydney night.

They had certainly given a 'good account of themselves', but Johnson's men were unlike so many English sides of old, who repeated that particular refrain by way of comfort, having turned up, been defeated and gone home, without ever seeming terribly surprised at the outcome. Historically, 'giving a good account' had been used as a smokescreen, to help disguise the reality of failure. For this side, there was no hiding and no disguising – it mattered not what others thought, winning was the only outcome they were prepared to accept. His team's preparation ensured performances of a different level to previous sides. When they said that they 'did their best', they did so knowing that their best was good enough to win, rather than a consolation to cling to in the face of defeat.

Within an hour of the final whistle, even in the wake of such an epic contest, the early analysis and first evidence of recriminations were starting to appear. That England won in a photo finish, when they should have triumphed by a far greater margin, was inevitably the subject of debate. Prime among the targets of what little discontent remained in English ranks was the referee, Andre Watson, who, by general consent, had given a performance that was, at best, erratic.

The *Telegraph*'s Mick Cleary, a knowledgeable and respected observer of the game for many years, described the South African official as 'shrill and pompous' and his refereeing of the scrummages as 'an utter disgrace'. Hard words by any standards, but weighted with more meaning when written by someone who understands the intricacies and fine details of the relevant laws. Stephen Jones, too – rugby correspondent of the *Sunday Times* and one of the game's truly great writers – was equally scathing:

'Andre Watson had an appalling match. He incensed England almost beyond words. It was distasteful. Had England lost, it would have been the primary scandal of the English sporting year.'

England had, throughout the course of the tournament, failed to concede a penalty at a scrummage. During the course of 100 Watson-adjudicated minutes, they had, the official concluded, offended four times – all four while competing against a pack of forwards weakened by the loss of Ben Darwin in the semi-final, and having huge problems dealing with a formidable English unit.

In footballing terms, they were continually surging into the area only, according to the official, to choose to kick the keeper rather than shooting at goal. Despite winning a crucial battle, they were choosing, so Watson decided, to needlessly break a law – in effect, shooting themselves in the foot. The referee was later given the chance to justify his decisions in the *Sunday Times* magazine, and sought to do so in intricate detail, one at a time, with Jones responding afterwards.

Watson examined each in turn, and declared himself happy with his work and unable to see any room for complaint. Equally and eloquently, Jones was sticking to his guns.

'Andre Watson asks us to acclaim him. Why? He was arresting old ladies for littering while thugs were committing murder on the other side of the road. He was so busy making random calls on finicky offences on one side of the scrum that he ignored blatant and dangerous cheating on the other – desperate Wallaby actions designed to offset England's scrummaging superiority.'

The logic of the situation, however, rather than the strict interpretation of laws which the vast majority do not understand, will suffice. Common sense dictates that there was no reason for England to cheat in an area of the game in which they were already superior. Whether you understand the small print which governs the front-row union or not, it's hard to see why they would have felt the need to cancel out one of their greatest strengths. Besides, the admission of Australian prop Al Baxter afterwards that he had been getting comprehensively turned over by Trevor Woodman scarcely adds to a case it appears Watson is now fighting alone. Even the Australians aren't trying to defend his decisions any more.

For the sake of the game, though, one particularly wonderful moment involving Watson seems to have gone by unnoticed by almost everyone, partly because it happened at the very end of the match amid scenes of general euphoria, and partly because we wouldn't, as spectators, have expected anything less. As Ben Kay, shredded shirt and all, leapt jubilantly into the air at the final whistle, he looked around for someone to celebrate with, and realised he was standing virtually next to Watson.

Out of sheer instinct and tradition, he reached a hand out, gave a broad beam and said, 'Thanks, Ref'. It wasn't sarcastic in the slightest, and it wasn't meant to be anything other than a polite and sincere gesture, the sort of thing Kay had been doing since he first played the game. It's drilled in – as soon as it's over, regardless of the result or the performance, you thank the referee for making the game possible and you go and find an opponent in order to thank him too. Elsewhere, Jason Leonard and Phil Vickery were delaying their celebrations until they'd located and spoken to the seriously injured Darwin.

Here we were, then, at the end of one of the great games of all time

– a match which was about to change lives – and the players were complying with the unwritten code which made their sport possible. They shook hands, hugged each other and generally conducted themselves with considerable dignity. There was no celebratory taunting of the losers, nor a refused handshake or post-match fracas. Indeed, as the teams finally left the arena, they formed the traditional 'tunnel' for each other on the way back to the dressing-rooms, taking it in turns to clap each other from the field.

John Howard may have no idea of how to conduct himself in a diplomatic fashion on a rugby pitch, but the players of two nations, even while struggling to come to terms with emotions at opposite ends of the spectrum, were up to the challenge. There may already be too many contrasts drawn between rugby and football, but sometimes things happen to make you stop and think. A few weeks earlier, England's footballers had fought their Turkish opponents in the tunnel during the course of a 0–0 draw in Istanbul. England's rugby players, at the conclusion of a contest infinitely more physical, applauded theirs off the pitch, and then had the gesture reciprocated. It doesn't take a genius to spot the lesson that could be learned – being aggressive and brave on the pitch doesn't mean you have to be petulant and fractious as you leave it.

Elsewhere, it was the turn of Eddie Jones, the Australian coach, to offer a few last thoughts about the new champions before, for the first time, they returned to the northern hemisphere as owners of the Webb Ellis trophy. While not going nearly as far as his nation's media, Jones couldn't resist one last dig:

'You slug it out for 100 minutes and get beaten in the 99th – I think that qualifies as a photo finish. England were outstanding – they're the best team in the world by one minute.'

As a way of viewing a game, to say that Jones is putting forward an argument with a few holes in it scarcely does it justice. Sure, it was in the balance to the death, but to attempt to diminish the nature of their victory by claiming that England were the best 'by one minute' is to deliberately and fundamentally misunderstand sport at the highest level. If Jones's view is true, then equally, Ali was the best heavyweight by one punch, Viv Richards only dispatched straight sixes rather than surrendering outside edges by about two inches, and Pelé was, most of the time, within an inch of mis-kicking his way through the 1970 World Cup. The margins among the very best are very slight, and to use that as a method of criticism after a defeat is verging on the dishonest. Had the refereeing been better, England would have walked it, which is one particular 'margin' Jones chose to ignore.

'I like Wilkinson's Adidas commercials,' he offered, with more than a hint of sarcasm. 'They're flash . . .'

Again, the comparisons tell the story of another poorly aimed salvo from the Australian coach. Wilkinson could be flash if he so chose, because he had the talent to back it up. What he achieved on the pitch was wondrous, occasionally taking the breath away, but even in those commercials, what was traded on was his ordinariness, the fact that his ability was without even a hint of the consciously extrovert. If anyone in sport failed to live up (or down) to the billing of 'flash' then Wilkinson was surely the man.

It would, however, be hard to paint Jones as a lone figure as far as sniping comments both pre and post match are concerned. He and Woodward had swapped pointed observations for weeks on end, and the allegations had flown back and forth at a rate of knots. For all his certainty of purpose and clear thinking, Woodward could also be as obdurate and irritable as the best of them, but triumph had inevitably left him painted in the most flattering of lights. To remember Jones as the villain and Woodward the hero, at least as far as their arguments are concerned, is to oversimplify matters, but history, as Winston Churchill proclaimed, is written by the victors. Not, I'd guess, that quoting Churchill is the most effective way to convince an Australian that you don't suffer from an overblown sense of your own superiority.

That rule of thumb does, however, still work both ways. It would be difficult to argue that the subsequent perception of Woodward, publicly at least, wasn't changed by the victory. If England had lost, he was dictatorial, vindictive, taciturn and tactically naive. Victory made him focused, ruthless, measured and tactically assured. He was the same man, win or lose, but as with Jones, history would remember him according to the result, not the person.

Despite that, to try to stand in judgement over the relative merits of Jones and Woodward is surely to become enmeshed in the detail while neglecting to consider the fuller picture. Between the two of them, they had brought two very different sides to a peak at precisely the right time, helping create a match to live forever in the memory. Let them snipe away all they like; if the end result is always going to be as good as this, the verbal jousting is a small price to pay.

By now, though, the process of looking back was being swiftly overtaken by a desire to look forwards – to calculate how best to celebrate the return of a squat, gold cup and the men who claimed it. It was a process that removed all doubt from the players as to the impact they had caused 'back home'.

Six thousand people waited at Heathrow Airport at 6 a.m. to greet them – another early start, another raucous crowd. Baggage handlers may regularly cause similar numbers of people to hang around an airport terminal at such an early hour, but they've never caused quite as much happiness. As the players walked out into an arrivals hall packed to its limits with cheering fans, it was easy to spot the slightly stunned expressions sweeping across their faces. Journalists and friends alike had spent the past couple of days telling them what it was like back in England, but few of them could have imagined this. If ever they doubted the scale of their achievement, something as surreal as this was impossible to ignore.

A fortnight later, just as they might have thought they were returning to normal – several of them had even played for their club sides in a bid to get 'back to everyday life' – they were given another extraordinary reminder of what their achievement meant to the country. Through the London traffic, even at its most congested, it shouldn't take an hour and a half to get from Marble Arch to Trafalgar Square. If you've got a World Cup to show off, though, even with the temperature dipping below freezing, you're going to draw a bit of a crowd – three quarters of a million of them, to be imprecise.

On an open-topped bus, the squad made their way along Oxford Street, down Regent Street and into Trafalgar Square amid scenes the like of which London has not seen for many years. Shop staff, office workers, men on scaffolding in hard hats and thousands upon thousands of people who just felt the desire to relive the glory of that November morning, swarmed to watch and cheer, with pavements packed tight with crowds.

The players were interviewed in the shadow of Nelson's Column, and received the freedom of the City of London from Ken Livingstone, the Mayor. Quite who was going to stop them from entering town in any event was a point nobody thought to ask, but on a day like this, even a publicity-hungry politician was not going to dampen the mood.

A quick stop at Buckingham Palace followed, where Johnson attempted not to look like an ogre when bending way, way down to shake the Queen's hand, and failed. It's often difficult to watch the Queen in action when talking to sportsmen and suppress the thought that she rarely has any idea who they actually are. Unless they arrive in full silks, whip in hand and thoroughbred tethered at the door, you suspect they're of limited interest to her. She'd plainly been told, however, that they were all about to get awards of varying kinds, and that they'd given her grandson a nice new shirt. Oh, and the tall, scary-looking one had brought back the cup she'd given to that other tall, scary Australian chap a dozen years earlier, so she smiled away.

Then it was on to Downing Street to meet the Prime Minister, who could, if you looked closely, be seen mentally counting the votes that his handshakes with Johnson, Woodward, Wilkinson and the rest might realise. Once an avowed football fan, heading the ball around the back garden with Kevin Keegan and greeting David Beckham like an old friend, and previously welcoming Oasis and the rest of the 'Brit Pop' era, Tony Blair had decided it was now rugby's turn. On a day when London cheered a group of men on a bus, it was hard not to raise a rueful smile at people jumping onto a bandwagon and attempting to bask in a bit of reflected glory. The fewer playing fields that got sold off, it occurred to me, the greater the chances of enjoying a repeat performance a few years down the line.

The players all spoke of the wonderful experience and the lifelong memories the day had doubtless brought, but it would be hard to hold it against them if minds were not turning to the final engagement of the day. Dallaglio had, with stupendous timing, managed to get his testimonial year in full swing, and a celebration dinner rounded off the day. Even given the professionalism and preparation of this particular group of athletes, the prospect of a pint after a day like that must have been taking on almost mythical status.

With one last wave to the crowds and cameras, they made their way from their bus and into the sanctuary of a marquee in Battersea Park. Almost a million people over the whole course of the day had watched 30 of the people least appropriately built to wearing Paul Smith designer suits parade the spoils of their efforts. Despite looking like a combination of defendants, nervous best men and nightclub bouncers, they remained dignified throughout the day. When England's football team returned defeated from the 1990 World Cup, Paul Gascoigne opened his tracksuit top to proudly display a pair of (presumably) false breasts. It was somehow hard to imagine a repeat performance.

As Jason Leonard, looking more than a little uncomfortable in his team-issue jacket, took the trophy into the tent and out of sight, it wasn't difficult to imagine the tie, the knot of which rested somewhere below his left ear, being loosened, a jacket removed and a beer sought.

They had deserved it. The day had removed any doubts as to the way they had entered the public consciousness, but it had confounded expectations to a degree beyond which anyone seriously expected. If this is what it was going to be like from now on, sitting down to have a bit of a ponder over a pint didn't seem to be a bad idea at all.

III

January 2004

Typically enough for a man who was about to get knighted for his ability to remain focused under pressure, Clive Woodward's measured reaction to the continuing outpouring of delight every time the Webb Ellis Cup was produced was reasonably easy to predict. As far as Sir Clive, who received notification in the New Year's Honours List that he was to be celebrated in the same way as that other World Cup winner, Sir Alf, was concerned, the sooner they got the trophy shut up in a cabinet somewhere, the better.

There were things to be won, life to be got on with, and something just didn't feel right about the continual glancing backwards over the shoulder at a job completed when there were other challenges still remaining. With the World Cup having been won and a work ethic almost beyond compare, it was no surprise that the preparations for its defence appeared to start within weeks of the prize returning home. Given the appetite for improvement instilled by the England coach into his squad, several of them were doubtless already imagining how much improvement they could manage in the space of the next four years.

For the captain, however, it was time to call a halt to one of the great international careers. If anyone needed confirmation that rugby had penetrated the national consciousness in a way it had never managed before, the events of Saturday, 17 January 2004, less than two months after victory in Sydney, did the job rather emphatically.

At about 5.30 p.m., with football reports coming in thick and fast, with Wolves beating Manchester United and the Premiership title starting to look destined for Highbury rather than Old Trafford, *Sports Report*, Radio Five Live's flagship programme, headed off to Welford Road, home of the Leicester Tigers. At a press conference attended by rather more journalists than usually turn up at such affairs, Johnson explained that he had played internationally for the last time.

As parting gestures go, holding aloft a World Cup isn't a bad way to depart, and as with almost every other rugby ambition he had ever harboured, it was duly achieved. Besides, for a man whose drive, bravery and single-mindedness ensured his place in the list of the finest sporting, let alone rugby, captains of them all, going out at the top was the only acceptable option. His comments that day, as the flashbulbs exploded on his freshly bloodied features following an afternoon in battle for his club against Ulster, revealed something of what makes him tick.

'There have been many highlights,' Johnson reflected, reading from a statement and, you suspected, wondering how many of the assembled throng were ever going to be able to understand exactly how he felt. 'The Grand Slam, winning the World Cup – but most of all, I will remember the moments together as a squad, just before and just after matches, in the changing-room.

'I would like to thank Clive and the other coaches who have worked with me since I made my debut, the guys I have played with and the fans who have followed us around the world.'

To the end, as well as being a captain of quite extraordinary ability, Martin Johnson was a players' player, never happier than when surrounded by the colleagues who knew how it felt to suffer the knocks and the discomfort that went with the joy of victory. It was a rugby epitaph, for rugby people. If there was a choice between a formal dinner and a few beers with the men who made it all possible for him, you knew exactly which option he would take. Indeed, he had quietly mentioned to someone a few weeks earlier that the whole experience since the victory was beginning to get a bit surreal.

'I've been to a couple of dinners in the last few weeks when they've brought the Cup in on its own, and it's got a standing ovation. The Cup

– not with a player or Clive or someone holding it, just on its own. The world's gone mad.'

Having already been awarded an OBE, Johnson became a CBE, and duly handed over the captaincy to Dallaglio. There may be people in the sporting world who need an award in order to tell of their achievements even less than Johnson, but the list will not be long. If opposition forwards thought that the departure of a grizzled and driven warrior from the international scene would make their life easier, the sight of Dallaglio was not one to cause them too much cheer. If they broke the mould when they made Johnson, they retained a remarkably similar back-up for the creation of Dallaglio.

Elsewhere in the world of rugby, attention was focused on Jonny Wilkinson's car crash (he'd suffered bigger impacts in Australia, but the tabloids still loved it), Wilkinson's shoulder and neck (broken, bruised or trapped nerve, depending on the paper and the day), Wilkinson's love life, Wilkinson's dress sense, Wilkinson's diet and Wilkinson's family. In general, I think you get the picture. He was going where only Beckham had been before, and while remaining desperately polite and affable, it was hard to resist coming to the conclusion that he could do without it all.

So, with Johnson retired, Wilkinson looking set to need an operation, Dallaglio waiting to have his captaincy confirmed and the domestic season welcoming back its returning heroes, English rugby was ready to see what differences the achievements 'down under' would bring.

In the heady world of Kent League Division One, Guy's Hospital were making their bid for the top, with victories over Sheppey and Askeans. Their surge benefited from a spare set of shirts (supplied by a local bar and evidently very handy on the mud-swept plains of Sheppey) and a Johnson-like strengthening of attitude. They may not, I accept, have come to your attention all that frequently up to this point in time, but that is an omission which will be addressed.

Post World Cup, while the views and actions of the stars of the game were informative and interesting, they still didn't tell the whole story. Even among the game's more casual followers, a delicate balancing act between the upkeep of tradition and the firming of attitudes was underway. While Sir Clive, Jonny (and shoulder), Johnson and his memories and other heroes and their views will feature in due course, it is to a level fractionally below the international arena we now head.

When England tramp back to the dressing-room at the end of play, they gulp down Lucozade and slide into an ice bath. In order to discover something of the traditional spirit of the game, however, we need to meet men to whom such behaviour borders on the offensive.

From isotonics and ice baths to best bitter and communal baths, the journey to rugby's heartland starts here . . .

IV

The men in white coats

Joe Hamilton was an amiable hulk of a man, about as wide as he was high, with painful-looking bruised ears clinging to a painful-looking bruised head. His left eye was gently discolouring, doubtless in preparation for swelling tightly shut, while there appeared to be a few trickles of fresh blood running away from just below the hairline at the side of his head.

The image was not improved much by the events of the next 30 seconds. Placing a muddy finger to the side of each nostril, one at a time, before blowing hard, Joe sent a stream of nasal debris down the front of his shirt. A large snorting noise followed, before what seemed to be about a quarter of a pint of phlegm was deposited onto the mud and grass in front of him.

An enthusiastic breaking of wind, and trust me, you wouldn't describe anyone breaking wind as 'enthusiastic' unless you were absolutely sure, completed the ablutions. A shake of the head from side to side, followed by a couple of slaps delivered to his chest, and Joe was grabbed by two other similarly sized men, both with similar features and, at the risk of libel action, similar habits.

Another mud-streaked and bloodied head pushed its way through from behind, appearing between the legs of Joe and the man next to him, muddied and bloodied and clinging on tightly. After a momentary pause, they surged forward, collapsing into eight men of similar appearance, before someone slipped, a couple of muffled shouts filled the air and a man with a whistle attracted their attention, telling them all to get up and try again.

The world of student rugby was as mucky and grim as I remembered it, and the men of Guy's Hospital seemed proud to be maintaining the tradition. The un-muddied figure out on the wing, staring across at the chaos caused by two packs of tired forwards, looked decidedly unsure of his chances of seeing much of the ball throughout the rest of the afternoon. Judging by his demeanour, that wasn't a prospect that caused him too much distress, either.

The man clinging to Joe's shirt was now kneeling, gingerly massaging his left calf through his mud-caked sock, and causing yet another delay.

'Leg's fucked, I think,' he muttered to the referee by way of explanation, without waiting to be asked about the precise nature of his problem. I made the first of many a mental note to avoid having an accident anywhere near him, at least until his diagnostic skills became a touch more sophisticated.

Joe, for his part, is a medical student, who will one day, exams and collapsed scrums permitting, just like most of his colleagues, become a doctor. The ones who don't opt to spend their careers trying to fix your body are destined to be let loose on your molars. I made a second mental note, the ink scarcely dry on the first, to brush my teeth extra thoroughly tonight. He looked forbidding enough as it is – put a stethoscope around his neck or a drill in his hand and dress him in a white coat, and he becomes a figure of genuine terror. Even with the blood cleaned off him.

Guy's were playing against the Royal United Medical School, known to all, it would seem, as 'RUMS', in the semi-final of the United Hospitals' (UH) Cup. I put aside thoughts of the World Cup being impressively long-standing at 16 years of age, and gloried in the fact that this is the oldest knockout rugby competition in the whole world, and it was being partially contested by Guy's, the oldest rugby club in the world.

'We were around years before anyone else,' said a man on the sideline, swigging from a bottle of port, which had, I later understood, been designated the spectators' 'drink of the day'. It occurred to me to ask exactly whom they played against for those lonely seasons, but the sight of a man trained to use a scalpel, finishing off a bottle of Cockburn's persuaded me to keep the observation to myself.

All around, things were happening which, even without the benefit of a bottle of fortified wine, couldn't help but leave me with a pleasantly warm feeling about the day. Silly things, really, and not all that unexpected when I came to consider them, but cheering nonetheless. When a centre managed to twist awkwardly after a tackle, for example, there was a virtual queue of players waiting to offer a diagnosis as to exactly what might have happened to him. Normally, packs of forwards get involved in fights over, well, whatever occurs to them at the time, but here they had purpose – they were more likely to engage in fisticuffs over the misdiagnosis of a sprain.

A ginger-haired figure on the touchline was clasping a notepad, wearing a Guy's Hospital Rugby Club tracksuit top, and offering the odd tactical gem to his charges on the pitch, sandwiched between some rather more basic expressions of frustration. Dave Berry will never play at Twickenham, never drop a goal in a World Cup final, and would be struck dumb if he ever came to meet Clive Woodward. Despite all of this, rugby means as much to him as anyone who took their turn to hold up the Webb Ellis Cup on that November evening. In fact, given that he doesn't get paid to play, crams his rugby around his medical studies and yet still organises and runs a side about which he feels passionately, it's fair to say that it might just mean even more.

Dave is the Guy's club captain – a role which involves rather more in the way of mundane and trivial tasks than might be faced by his England counterpart. If there are shirts to be washed and distributed, fixtures to be arranged, training to be organised or travel plans to be finalised, Dave, as far as I can see, gets landed with the responsibility. While international captains are off talking to the press or meeting sponsors post-match, Berry is piling muddy kit back into a bag and trying to make sure someone has bought a jug of bitter to get things going.

Another part of Dave's job which is unique to captaincy at this level is to leave all his contact details on his club's website, thus making himself a one-stop shop for potential new players, interested parties and authors looking for a student rugby team to follow. I don't mind being accused of the second on the list, and hold my hands up to the third category, but, having seen them warming up, really didn't fancy the first at all. Having spent their week curing the sick, they appeared hell-bent on acquiring first-hand knowledge of medical injuries over the course of the next 80 minutes, giving themselves something to treat over the course of the following days.

On the surface, all of them, and in this particular case the opposition as well, represent something of the intellectual elite of the country. They are the crème de la crème of the caring professions – the sort of people they write Saturday evening dramas about, who save lives and expect little more than a manly nod and a shake of the hand by way of thanks. Dave offered a thought on the nature of the calf injury, and left my daydream in tatters:

'It's gay leg syndrome, I'm afraid. Definitely gay leg syndrome. Nothing much wrong with it, but he needed a rest and a sit down, so he gave his calf a bit of a rub and waited to get his breath back. Very shabby, very shabby indeed.'

I giggled away at the diagnosis, but it wasn't just on the pitch that they made me laugh. The goings on via the Guy's website also told an entertaining story. Now, personally, I'm not all that comfortable with the idea of every single rugby club getting itself a website, although almost all of them seem to have done so. I thought urban myths of props side-stepping and second rows throwing long spin-passes were best left to develop over pints of bitter in run-down clubhouses, and I'm quite certain that the internet doesn't allow stories to be told in quite such a convivial way. Then again, these days props do side-step, and second rows can spin-pass, so perhaps it's me who's out of date?

Whatever the case, the message board on the Guy's site provided a perfect stage for some of the very best (and all of the very worst) aspects of student medical humour. The night before the game, someone had posted a message with a decidedly panicky tone:

'Woke up this morning with a temp of 40°C, a colicky pain in the abdomen and decreased concentration. Need diagnosis and suitable medication before able to play in game.'

The response was short and to the point, and arrived from someone calling himself A. Doctor. I'm not a detective, but I have a feeling it may be a pseudonym:

'I have considered your symptoms. My diagnosis is that you are nervous. Pull yourself together and stop acting like such a tart.'

There were also some unexpected gems from the fulsome minutes of their committee meetings, which were diligently put online every month. Take, for example, this snippet about the club dinner, and ponder what exactly might have gone on:

'Terry Gibson thanked Tim Price [of Guy's, King's and Thomas's (GKT)] for his work in organising last year's UN Dinner. The food, wine, speeches and singing received general approval. Unfortunately, we were not given our deposit back.'

And, of course, many suggestions were wonderfully rephrased before being inserted into the minutes. An entry in relation to a proposed tour to the south of France illustrates the point as well as any:

'Roy Turner is in discussion with Marc Cabasse, our local man on the ground. The lure of Marc's sisters, fine wines and a spot of rugger in the sun were appealing to the committee.'

In retrospect, that was one of the more intelligent offerings. By the end of the season, they had descended to putting a picture of a drunken Dave, waving inanely at the camera while slumped against the counter of a kebab shop, on an American site where people vote about how good looking you are. The last time I checked, he was a very respectable 7.3 out of 10, which tells you either that internet polls are very easily rigged, if all your mates log on and vote for you, or that Americans have strange tastes. As you can see, our nation's future health is in safe hands.

I really hadn't known what to expect when it came to the game. Did the air of chumminess pervade through everything? Was it to be an afternoon of back slapping and mutual appreciation, with a bit of running rugby thrown in for good measure? These were intelligent people – there obviously wasn't going to be anything silly going on.

On close inspection, things appeared to be going somewhat differently. The players were bickering a bit, the sense of all being medics together just playing a game seemed to be entirely absent, and the fans lined up in the finest territorial fashion along opposite sides of the pitch in order to better hurl abuse at each other. It wasn't exactly an Old Firm derby, but the respective sides didn't appear all that pally, either.

Dave would normally be rather more active, but a sore hamstring had got the better of him so he was forced into non-playing duties, as coach for the day. This, as I learned, meant striding up and down the touchline, staring at a notebook as if the secrets of the rugby-playing universe were lurking within its pages, and trying and failing not to look too nervous.

Within five minutes, I discovered why. Guy's watched an early penalty go sailing over their posts and then found themselves hopelessly carved apart as a wonderful, direct run from the RUMS winger saw him leave a string of would-be tacklers stranded on the right flank. Touching down in the corner, he sent his side eight points clear, as the resultant kick spiralled away on the breeze to leave the try unconverted.

Dave caught my eye, and I muttered something about the Guy's scrum-half releasing the ball very early and the lack of composure it seemed to be spreading throughout his side. He shrugged, pulled a thoughtful expression, and examined his notebook briefly: 'Could be, but then again, it could just be that we always have a really, really shit start.'

It was a statement that resisted all attempts at a response. My scintillating tactical analysis and shrewd eye for the game had been rebutted with a chilling blast of common sense. I decided not to fall into the trap of playing the pundit any further.

You couldn't help but be reminded of the occupations of the two sides, though, as all around me were small (and not so small) signs that this was a game featuring medics. When a loose forward went down holding his finger at the sort of angle that made my stomach churn, a whole bunch of people wanted to have a go at popping it back into place. Some of them were probably training to be dentists, so quite why they needed to practise this particular skill is beyond me, but nobody, including the patient, strangely enough, seemed to object.

'That'll make his eyes water,' said an elderly, softly spoken Welsh voice beside me. I made sympathetic noises and we chatted for a while about the match, the game in general and other peripheral pleasantries. I enquired as to whether he lived locally and popped down often, and he explained that he'd been watching Guy's for a long time, and liked to get down to these Cup games whenever he could. He'd worked at Guy's for a number of years, and now he was enjoying semi-retirement as a tour guide at Twickenham.

I mentioned the reasons for my visit, and as the conversation developed, it became clear he was very knowledgeable about the game. He might have been supporting his side, but he wasn't someone with a blind loyalty to one club or team as much as someone who had obviously been in love with the game for years and enjoyed discussing it with anyone who gave him the opportunity. Poor old man probably didn't get much chance to have a proper conversation any more, so I humoured him – might have patted him on the head, come to think of it.

It wasn't until a couple of days later that I attempted to assign a bit more of an identity to Hywel, my new chum on the touchline, the chap to whom I'd spent a while explaining how complicated it could be to write a book, the man for whom I'd tried to simplify my explanations, lest it got a bit complicated. Hywel, the amiable old buffer who chatted about the good old days and how things had changed.

Yes, through my efforts to explain in simple language what I was doing there, I'd made a friend of Hywel. Or, as he's also known, as I discovered when I looked him up, Hywel Thomas, PhD FIBiol CBiol, Dean of Basic Medical Sciences, Senior Lecturer in Biochemistry, United Medical and Dental Schools of Guy's and St Thomas's Hospitals, London.

Glad I kept it simple, then, just in case he couldn't keep up. Oh well, if you're going to make a patronising fool of yourself, I figured, you might as well share it with the rest of the world, just in case anyone out there still hasn't made up their mind about you. I really enjoy talking to clever people – lawyers, doctors and the like, who are generous enough with their time and sharp enough with their intellects to make complicated things sound simple. People who, regardless of the subject, leave you with a sense of awe as a result of their ability to grasp the finer points of an argument while retaining a view of the wider picture, all at the same time.

I just wish the more modest and unassuming ones, a category into which Hywel fitted perfectly, could give the rest of us some warning that they're super intelligent before we open our mouths and prove that we're not. I'd known it was a different sort of sporting experience at the time, and now I'd stumbled across further evidence to prove it. With the benefit of hindsight, the memory of my conversation with Hywel, when I deliberately didn't go too fast so as not to confuse the old chap, left me holding my head in my hands with embarrassment. There I was, surrounded by doctors, and it never dawned on me that he might actually be a rather senior one. I've always had a good nose for a story.

Behind me, sitting on the bottom step of the deserted main stand, was a substitute, stripped down to the waist and asking for a little help in taping up his shoulder. Medics descended upon him like vultures preparing to devour a particularly fresh and succulent cadaver. Within five minutes, he looked like the sort of figure you find lurking within a sarcophagus. 'One more strip and you're done,' reassured one of the elite bandaging squad as the substitute disappeared beneath another layer of Elastoplast. If he ever got on, he'd pose little danger when trying to charge down a kick, because his arms seemed unlikely to get above shoulder level for quite some time.

As it transpired, Guy's had little need of him. Dave was right, their start had been awful, but as soon as they settled down and began to play the game in a way which evidently felt more familiar to them, they had very little to fear. Far too strong in the forwards for their opponents, Guy's claimed a couple of penalties to steady the ship, and then grabbed two neat tries in the run-up to the break, sending them off to their oranges 18–8 up.

On the sideline, bottles of port were beginning to collect at a fair old rate, and a few hardy souls had made their way into the pavilion in order to claim a pint with which to further blot out the cold during the second half. RUMS landed a penalty within the opening five minutes of the half, thus confirming that it wasn't just the start of the game when Guy's suffered, but the start of each new half. I made a further mental note never to let another doctor wander off, no matter how briefly, during the course of treating me. On this evidence, if he trained at Guy's and played rugby, I could be long dead by the time he'd got back up to speed.

As another forward hit the deck, so another small group of men gathered around him, forming a mud-streaked diagnostic committee. Judging by their request, made at the end of fully three minutes of discussion, they weren't all that keen on anything too technologically demanding: 'Can we have a bucket, please?' Suffice to say, the injured party made a swift recovery, rising to his feet shortly before a couple of gallons of freezing water could be tipped over him. In hindsight, maybe they knew what they were doing all too well. I think it's known as preventative medicine.

As had been the pattern of the first half, once stung into action, Guy's remembered that they were quite a lot better than their opposition, and with the extrovert but wonderfully taken addition of a long, late drop goal, they emerged winners by 31–11. They had a small, squat fly-half called Pete Gretton, who stood out as the best ball player on the pitch by a country mile, and a scrum-half, Sam Rigg, who baited the opposition too much and passed the ball too little – to be fair to him, just like every other scrum-half in the world. In the pack, apart from Joe the self-diagnosing hooker, Guy's had a gangling and boisterous, ginger-haired back-row forward by the name of Matt Morgan, who seemed to take a troubling degree of delight in any form of physical conflict. He looked well capable of playing at a higher level one day, providing he doesn't get distracted by something pointless, like medicine.

Glancing back at the pile of empty port bottles, I saw they had now been joined by a sprinkling of empty, plastic pint glasses and a few similarly drained cans of cider. It was a collection that was destined to grow considerably before the post-match debrief came to an end, and I knew I'd never again listen to a doctor offering advice on sensible levels of alcohol consumption. As you can see, it was an illuminating sort of day.

I wandered back into the pavilion and hung around for a bit, where I could admire the numerous posters and leaflets affixed to walls and noticeboards, requesting support for half a dozen different candidates in forthcoming student elections. Jugs of beer were being poured behind the bar and the unmistakable smell of a post-match pie and baked-bean meal was wafting across the hall. Dave was still deep in the changing-rooms with his victorious side, and I decided to leave him to it and catch up with him later. He'd been friendly, a bundle of information, and as good an ambassador as any side could hope to have, but this was his day, with his mates, and I didn't want to gatecrash.

I sent him an e-mail of congratulations later that night, and got a response the next day. 'Sorry you couldn't hang around,' it read, 'but I guessed you'd have other places to be.' It was a guess that made me sound far more busy and important than I was, but having driven over there, leaving early proved to have been a reasonably wise choice. 'To be honest,' Dave continued, 'we had a few pints and things got a little bit messy.' I'll bet they did. A few pints was one thing, but when they were set down on a small ocean of port, the fact that the end result was 'a bit messy' wasn't a vast surprise. I'd made a timely departure.

The win sent Guy's into a final against St Mary's, who were, so the experts seemed to think, the best team in the competition. In a soggy gale at Old Deer Park in Richmond, home of London Welsh, they set about proving it. Dave could have slipped another couple of hundred pages of tactical gems into his notebook and it would have made little, if any, difference. Having dominated RUMS in the pack, Guy's were now suffering much the same fate. If the diagnosis was bleak after the first few set pieces, by the time they emerged from a first half with a near hurricane behind them and no points to show from it, matters had become considerably more serious.

To a crowd of just over a thousand, which in itself was fairly impressive given the state of the weather, the result, if I'm being completely honest, seemed to be something on which their enjoyment of the day didn't entirely hinge. Port shares were presumably up once more, and having a liberally lubricated afternoon seemed to be the order of the day for most of the spectators. By the time a St Mary's second row piled over the Guy's line in the last minutes of the contest, his side were already home and dry, and the final score of 20–0 was a bit unfair on Dave's men.

I was reminded of Woodward's words about the way to treat success and failure – the dangers of analysing defeat too closely, when you might as well just go straight down the pub. I had extreme doubts as to whether it was the far-reaching influence of the England coach that was making the Guy's players head off in the immediate direction of the bar, but maybe his reach extends even further than I'd thought?

Whatever the case, they seemed keen to follow a course of action that could be argued, albeit somewhat loosely, had been advocated by him. Whether what followed was drunkenness 'as endorsed by Sir Clive Woodward' or drunkenness through sheer force of habit, it was achieved with relish. A final mental note was added – never let them treat me the day after a game. If they can't focus on the patient, the odds surely aren't great on them identifying the illness.

'The port thing is a bit of a tradition,' Dave grinned, as we chatted, oddly enough, in a pub, a couple of weeks later. 'You have to take the cork out and throw it away as well, just to make sure that the whole bottle disappears in one sitting.' Of course you do. Drinking just half a bottle of port before getting stuck into a few pints would be positively abstemious, and would represent no sort of challenge at all. In an age of Lucozade and video analysis, visual awareness coaches and critical non-essentials, Guy's were a glorious throwback to the way rugby used to be.

In the same way that you find yourself looking twice when you see someone smoking on television in a 1970s rerun, or telling the sort of joke that wouldn't be acceptable in these supposedly more enlightened times, Guy's were like taking a step back in time. There's nothing wrong with taking your rugby desperately seriously, training religiously and dedicating your life to the game, but equally there's nothing wrong in deciding not to. These were people with careers to follow, important things to achieve and a vital role to play in society. They were taking enough things seriously without worrying about what they did on Wednesday and Saturday afternoons. At least they weren't drinking aftershave. Yet.

'We have a lot of fun, because we love playing the game, and there's nothing better than playing it with your mates and people you work with and are surrounded by on a daily basis. At the same time, being successful is very important to us. We play for our hospital, and there's a huge amount of pride involved in getting results for them.

'It wasn't so long ago that the national press reported on hospital rugby on a regular basis. Once upon a time, they didn't pick the first England team for the Five Nations until after the UH Cup had been played, because they wanted to see which players were going to feature in their plans.'

As well as the Rugby Football Union (RFU) and the England selectors paying close attention to the Guy's side, in the present-day world it seems that allegiances run deep, and loyalty to the cause lasts well beyond the end of someone's playing career.

'I was phoning around a few people earlier this year, checking on availability for our Saturday side, and one of the props said he couldn't make it because he had too much work to do. He said he had an essay to finish, and if he went out and played rugby it would lead to a few beers and he wouldn't get onto it until Sunday, and then it would never get finished, blah, blah, blah – you know the story.

'Anyway, I asked him who the essay was for, and it turned out to be someone who'd played for us a few years earlier. I called him, explained the situation, and he said he'd sort something out. Next thing I know, I get a call back from my prop, telling me that he has had an extension on his essay, and he's able to play. In fact, he told me that he was ordered to play, and told that if he didn't, his essay was going to have to be twice as long. That's the sort of support you need as a captain.'

I don't remember seeing that scene on *Holby City* or *Casualty*, but maybe I was looking the wrong way. Then again, maybe the writers rejected it because it sounded too far-fetched – a bit too *Carry on*

Doctor. Behind the seriousness, however, there was obviously an admirable sense of the absurd just waiting to escape. Like all stressful professions, they seemed to exist by a work hard, play hard ethos which, as I was to discover, occasionally veered more towards *Animal House* than *Doctor Kildare*.

'There's an ongoing tradition that on the night before the UH Cup final, each side tries to do something to the other, and it's been going on for years and years. We had our sentries out around Guy's with eggs and flour, waiting and ready, but they never showed up to try anything. They never kept a proper lookout on their own school either, though, and that's why it got out of hand.

'Some of our lads apparently managed to cement a boat to the floor of Imperial College medical school, which, you've got to accept, is a magnificent gesture by anyone's standards. A boat! Cemented to the floor!

'Then it got silly, though, because they sent us an invoice for removing it, which is just a completely ridiculous reaction. I mean, this is a tradition, it's been going on for years, and suddenly they want to start invoicing people for it.'

Dave kept a straight face, and I failed to discern whether he was pulling my leg or not. Through the efforts of concealing my giggles, however, I still couldn't help but express my admiration for a bunch of people who could cement a boat to the floor of a medical school. More to the point, a group who then claimed, seemingly seriously, that the unreasonable ones were the ones who invoiced, rather than those who affixed a sailing vessel to their marbled halls. Suddenly, drinking aftershave seemed positively tame.

Even amid the jokes and the stunts, however, it was clear that rugby came first, and the drinking, clowning and laughter followed behind. As with many people I met on my travels, Dave's interest in Woodward bordered on a fascination. Had I met him yet? What did I reckon he was like to talk to? What must it be like to be coached by him?

'What I don't understand is, if he can grab a team and turn it around so it starts to win things and then ultimately becomes the World Champion, why can't other national coaches do that in this country? He seems a fascinating bloke, and there's something really meticulous about the way he goes about his job.'

And that's probably the strongest connection I would find between one of the sides I met for this book and Woodward, I thought to myself.

If anyone understands the benefits of a scientific approach, ruling minor changes in or out depending on the improvement they helped to create, then it's a bunch of medics – scientists with a human side. Woodward had started out like a keen junior house officer, full of ideas and theories, but with the 'powers that be' unwilling or unable to fund each and every development, even if they could see the potential benefits. A bit of success, however, and he'd gone private, and now all the little details, the famed 'critical non-essentials', had been taken care of. As a theory, it still needed a bit of polishing, perhaps, but in a world of rugby-mad medics, it seemed fairly close to the mark.

'The World Cup was a great day. We had breakfast at the clubhouse with a few beers, watched the win, and then went down to Lordswood, who were the league leaders, and won! Maybe we should prepare like that all the time. Could get interesting.'

The game might have moved on over the course of the last few years, and the top tier might be moving away from the others at an ever-increasing rate of knots, but Dave and his side are more than just a link back to a past generation. They're not all about warm beer and meeting that prop from Esher Extra 'A's you had a beer with at Twickenham last year. History might make it hard not to use them as an unofficial litmus test of the game's progress, but their expectations and ambitions stretch beyond being just a measuring stick.

'We had our last England international in 1970, but we did have someone here a year or so ago who played for Sri Lanka, so we still pop up in some unexpected places. We also had more than 80 people training with us this year during the UH Cup run, so it's clear that not only is the game popular, but the importance of playing for your medical school is very much in the front of people's minds.'

Guy's had just about come to the end of their season, with only a sevens tournament or two to complete, while Dave, thanks to the pulled hamstring which had badgered him throughout the year, had most definitely reached the end of his. It had been a good year for Guy's on the pitch, but off it, as I'd discovered, and as Dave explained almost despairingly, things were looking a lot bleaker.

About 20 years earlier, the Guy's medical school had merged with St Thomas's Hospital, and a joint side had been born. It hadn't had much effect on the side from a historical perspective, it seemed, with the addition of one more letter to their name to form GTHRFC (Guy's and St Thomas's Hospitals Rugby Football Club), and the kit and colours of the previous Guy's side still worn as before. This was a far smaller change than was taking place at other clubs throughout the game, so tradition was not offended and there seemed to be little cause for concern.

A few years ago, King's College Medical School also amalgamated with the two institutions, and the funding for the various sporting and social clubs came under the control of the King's Student Union. So far, so uncomplicated, but huge changes were afoot. An initial decision not to adopt the King's name into the already extended club title seemed to have put a few noses out of joint and, armed with the power of grant distribution, an unholy row broke out.

Guy's were told that their grant was to be slashed by half, with the reason being, in part at least, that their Saturday side wasn't truly a student side, so the funding previously offered was not to be continued. Dave put some meat onto the bones of the tale.

'They said that our Wednesday side was a student side, but that our Saturday team couldn't be classed as such. They said we had non-students playing and that they wouldn't be able to offer us any money as a result.

'It's total nonsense, as any reasonable person will tell you as soon as the full facts are explained. We do have a handful of non-students playing for us, maybe three or four, but the fact is that they were students until a couple of years ago, when they qualified and went off to work in hospitals elsewhere. They'd always played their rugby with their mates at Guy's though, so they carried on doing so.

'It's not like we play in a student league on a Saturday, so it's not as if we were doing anything even slightly underhand, but it's being used as an excuse to cut our funding and make our life difficult. They even want us to pay to play at our own ground next season, despite having cut our grant to shreds.

'It's about to get legal, so it's not as if it's just going to resolve itself and go away either. This is our future on the line, and we're going to fight for it.'

Dave wasn't wrong. I went away and had a look back through the minutes of the committee meetings. In between finding cures for cancer, saving lives and the other peripheral activities doctors occasionally indulge in, there were some very senior and very angry people going on the record with all manner of furious statements.

Demands to get better media coverage for their campaign were made with reasonable frequency, while the president of Guy's, Dr Terence Gibson, discovered that the King's women's football team runs an old girls team, while receiving a grant from the university to support it. It didn't take a genius, thankfully in my case, to spot that there were some serious double standards at work and that, as a result of this spat, someone on the King's Student Union was playing at politics and putting at risk the future of the oldest rugby club in the world. Compared to this, downing bottles of port was far from the daftest piece of student behaviour I'd seen.

As the students battled on, senior figures also joined the fray, in many cases with an impressive degree of gusto. Professor Challacombe described the treatment of the club as 'scandalous', and demanded a written statement from King's explaining why they were withholding the money. King's responded that they were legally unable to fund a side containing non-students, which seems a little at variance with their treatment of women's football, and the legal profession were on the brink of being called in by the medical.

If it sounds as if the situation annoys me, then I don't apologise for the fact. Guy's represent something vital in the rugby world, an irreplaceable link with its very earliest days. While someone indulges in a petty piece of junior-common-room politics, they could yet cease to be, and the position is unacceptable. As Woodward's England revolution continues, I'd always imagined the blazers who threatened its progress were on the backs of elderly dinosaurs who objected to progress with the same vehemence with which they once rued the collapse of an empire and the birth of the 'permissive society'. Now I learned that a new breed, 57 more old farts in the making, were donning those blazers and putting a core component of the game's history at enormous peril.

I hope and trust that common sense wins through, and that Guy's continue a proud tradition with the spirit and love for the game which plainly exists among them. From senior academics who stroll along touchlines, to freshers with a nose for enjoyment and a nod to their heritage, all of them understand what the game is really about.

Doing battle with the establishment is obviously not a challenge limited to the very highest tiers of the sport.

V

Lunch with a legend

With typically exquisite timing, I found myself writing to Jason Leonard, asking about the possibility of an interview, just two days after he'd announced his retirement from international rugby. I tried to envisage the queue, pondering its other inhabitants, and working out how far I was from the front. Pessimistically, I concluded there was unlikely to be anyone standing behind me.

Two short days later, a letter, on Harlequins notepaper, popped through the door. My immediate reaction was to curse quietly, because something so short, arriving back so swiftly, could only be a bog-standard, photocopied, pre-prepared reply, expressing regret and offering best wishes with the project. I know the signs – as you may have spotted, I've been knocked back before.

Having opened it, I was quite stunned. There was a three- or four-line note, penned by Leonard himself, apologising for being really busy at the moment, but promising that he'd be happy to help in any way he could. The most capped rugby player in history and recent recipient of a World Cup winners medal, had replied with dizzying speed. The assertion on behalf of many parts of the sporting media that someone had displayed a moment of 'class' may be used with far greater frequency than honesty and accuracy demands, but in Leonard's case, it seemed just about spot on.

As we sat, squirreled away in the corner of a restaurant, I tried to offer some tentative thanks for the speed of his response and the donation of a few hours of his time. Self-effacingly, characteristically so, as I was to discover, he played down the gesture.

'I'm not the most organised person in the world, because my life's very hectic, but I get things done when I can, because that's the way I am. You wrote to me, it wasn't a big deal, just a chat. I could fit it in, so here we are. It's no huge inconvenience to me, and it helps someone out a bit, so why not do it? That's the way I look at things. It's a very small price to pay back for what I've got from the game.'

Common decency and good manners – it was a theme to which he returned several times during the course of a fascinating chat with a man who lives up to every pleasing preconception you ever had. Built like a semi-detached house and issuing forth tales and opinions gathered during a career in which he'd played international rugby more times than anyone else in the history of the game, Leonard is heaven's own interviewee. Sometimes, no matter how you might subsequently try to make it sound like hard work, it really does drop in your lap.

He first came into contact with the game in Barking, two decades and 114 international caps ago. Even as a youngster, his build and energy ensured this burly, beaming figure was neither destined nor suited to play anything else.

'It started off as organised mayhem, it really did. To be told that I could charge round at 100 mph and slam into people and not get into trouble for it, well, that was music to my ears. I mean, I played all my sport like that, I played football like that, but rugby was the only one that actually encouraged me to do it. My football team was a good one, because I come from a part of the world where they take their football very seriously.

'We had kids getting apprenticeships to professional clubs, even the goalkeeper was a county player, and then there was me, standing there and looking to get as involved as I could. In the end, they told me that if a player got past everyone else, all other nine outfield players, it was my job to kick them up in the air. I'd be worth millions if they changed the rules.

'It's corny, but it's true that there's a role for everyone in a rugby side, people of all shapes and sizes, and that's why I settled into the game. I loved smashing about and thumping into people, and rugby had this position ready made for someone of my size and shape. You know what it's like – the big, lanky one gets put in the second row, the nippy runners go in the backs and the short, wide one goes in the front row. I looked like I was grown in a bucket so there it was, decided, and I never played anywhere else.'

It's a wonderful phrase – 'grown in a bucket' – and very apt. Leonard is solid, in a way that isn't conveyed through a television screen, or even from a seat in the stands. He may or may not actually have a neck; the dimensions are such that it's hard to distinguish it from an average person's shoulders. As he relaxes in his chair, he reminds you quite why the phrase 'barrel-chested' was born, while his forearms protrude from his T-shirt like an extra pair of thighs, but with hands on the end.

To gain a true picture, rather than the television-generated one, of the power of modern-day front-row forwards, you have to put yourself in their company. I'm slightly bigger than average build, yet felt much smaller, sitting in the company of this human land mass. If you want to remind yourself why your belief that you could have been a top-class sportsman is mere fantasy, a trip to watch them train will generally do the trick – the pace, touch and power bring you swiftly back down to earth. If you want to remind yourself why you couldn't play as an international front row, simply being in their presence achieves much the same aim.

Now that a top-class scrum had formed around him for the last time and it was all over, though, I floated a suggestion. He'd always struck me as the sort of man who might still enjoy the odd game with the lads, the occasional Saturday run out with some friends, followed by a pint and a reminisce. Did the idea of going full circle appeal to him? Would he be quietly heading back to Barking, now the serious stuff was over, back to basics for the hell of it?

'It would be impossible, sadly, although I'd love to. The problem I'd have is that you've got some up-and-coming players out there; they'd all want to have a bit of me. I know what I'm like. I wouldn't have that, so I'd be fighting every week, getting sent off. It just wouldn't work.

'At the level you're talking about as well, I mean, some of the Premiership referees are pretty poor, although they're getting better, but at that level they can be really poor. I'd be bound to say something, make a comment, I can just see it, or they'd have a pop. They'd want to be able to say they'd marked my card a little bit, and would give me a little lecture every week about who's in charge. No, sadly, I can't see it happening.'

Don't be taken in by the smiling exterior. Leonard, as you'd expect from a man who survived and prospered so long at the highest level, possesses an inner drive every bit as fierce as ever it was. Behind all the humility, there's a realism and a justifiable sense of pride. He stepped out while at the top, and neither he nor anyone else is going to remember it ending any other way.

Rugby fans, old-time ones especially, have taken Leonard to their hearts, more so, perhaps, than anyone else from Woodward's World Cup-winning side. Even if they've never spoken to him, they think they know what he's like – he's one of them, 'our Jason', the sort of bloke you meet in clubhouses all over the place. Better, of course, much better, but never feeling the need to remind you of the fact. His record stands before him, and accompanying that is something genuine, rather than a falsely constructed persona. Falseness is not the way he does things, and out of that sense of propriety and decency has been born an extraordinary relationship with the rugby public all over the world.

'I think people feel they have something in common with me, and I'm very lucky in that regard. I think you can put it down to a few different reasons. I don't come, or I didn't come initially, from an area where people really played rugby very much. The East End is a football part of the world. There's also a class thing, which maybe started to fade out when I first got into the England team.

'When I got picked, there were people like Wade Dooley, Peter Winterbottom, Mike Teague and Paul Ackford. Well, maybe Ackers was a bit public school, but you know what I mean. He'll kill me for that! Lots of them came from backgrounds that hadn't really fed too many players up to the top ranks before. It's also the case that people like to see players who enjoy their rugby, and I always have done – that's why I do it.'

It's clear Leonard enjoys the lifestyle and camaraderie of the game and, in this new world of professionalism, perhaps the most refreshing aspect of his character is the link he provides to a lost era, when pre-match preparation was less important than post-match celebration. It's not a contrived or deliberate stance, though, but just the way he is. For him, the two sides of the game, the social and the professional, are simply impossible to separate.

'I like to meet people, have a chat, have a few drinks. That's what I love about the game, and if you took that away from it I wouldn't enjoy my rugby any more, so people tend to draw a few parallels with themselves when they see that. They've also seen me play for a long time, so there are old props in the clubhouse who can say that they've seen me playing as a kid and they've watched me come through. It's also really nice that people hold you up as a bit of an example to the kids, telling them that I've done it, so they can too.

'Truth is, it's not something I work at either, because it's just the way I am. If you try to pretend to be something you're not, people see through you, especially when you've been around as long as I have. There's no point faking anything, because you wouldn't be able to keep the act up, and in the end, people would work you out and think a bit less of you because you were putting on an act.'

In an age where English rugby has produced a myriad of heroes, Leonard stands alongside the best of them, but still seems to hold that little bit extra in terms of people's affection. Born out of a recognition of what drives him, what makes him tick, he's the closest the game has had, over recent years at least, to a folk hero. People who have never met him think they know him, and people who have met him have a strange habit of elevating the briefest exchange to the most meaningful of discussions. Not always, he laughs, without incident.

'I hear stories about me all the time, and often they're not very accurate. I mean, I don't complain, because I'd say 99.9 per cent of the time they're saying nice things, so I'm lucky, but things get exaggerated to the point where you can't recognise what really happened. Often it's someone who has had a pint with me, or was in the group with me, or in my company, and slowly it's changed as they've told it and told it.

'I'll give you an example. There was a bloke the other week who was telling me that we'd met before, just after the World Cup final. I asked him where it was, you know, Sydney, Manley, where I was at the time, and he told me it was at Twickenham. Now that couldn't be true – that was a bit much, but he was insistent, and he started telling me that Winterbottom was there as well, having a pint, and he was with the pair of us. It turned out that he was talking about 1991!

'I mean, firstly, it was thirteen years ago, secondly, we'd just lost a World Cup final, and thirdly, I was probably off my face, given what had happened. He got quite narked when I couldn't remember him, really sort of taking offence. You can't please them all.'

Neither are the stories exclusively domestic, as he explains. Foreign tours have brought, as long as they have been embarked upon, a wealth of tales. Once upon a time, it was the players and a list of alcoholically fuelled horseplay, the details of which were repeated like a solemn mantra throughout rugby bars and pubs whenever people gathered to drink and chat. As time has progressed, professionalism has curtailed the misdeeds of the players, leaving the fans to take centre stage.

'There was one time, out with the British Lions in New Zealand in 1993, when me and Peter Wright, the Scottish prop, went out for a beer one night. Now, obviously you don't wear any of your gear, and we were tucked quietly away in a corner, but the waitress must have heard our accents, and she asked if we were there for the rugby. You can't say you're a player, because that's a bit nauseous and self-important, so we said we were there watching the tour.

'She said we must know the two guys her and her friend were chatting to at the bar then, and we looked over and saw these two blokes in kilts. Peter asked who they were, and she told him that her and her friend were being chatted up by Rob Andrew and Jason Leonard. Peter cracked up. I almost lost it with laughter, but we asked her to buy them both a beer, and then point out it was from us, saying thanks for all the entertainment they'd given us on the pitch.

'She went over, poured their beer, and then pointed over to us as she gave it to the two blokes. They looked up and, honestly, the look on their faces was probably the funniest thing I've ever seen. They'd sold this girl a bit of a tale, things were going along quite nicely, despite the kilts, and we probably weren't what they needed to see at that point. We gave them a little wave and let them get on with it. That was priceless!'

It's an old-fashioned sort of story, relying for its punch line on an old-fashioned sort of fear, that of being caught out pretending to be something you're plainly not. It's told in an endearingly fresh manner, however, without smacking of the sort of tale that's been dragged through a hundred rugby-club dinners, like so many similar tales.

The old-fashioned rationale is a recurrent theme of Leonard's, part of a seemingly deep-rooted desire to make sure that the best bits of the past are not forgotten. If he can do something to help someone out, especially if it comes as a result of the position he's reached, Leonard doesn't view it as a chore, as much as a responsibility which comes along with a privilege. The game, he feels, has given him a lot, and giving something back is just part of the deal. Standards, decency and manners – doing things right. You can take the old man out of the East End, but you can't take the old East End out of the man.

'Some people, and maybe a lot of them are footballers, maybe not, but it's not in their background to do it. They'll get told about it and just think "sod it" and not bother, but that's not how I was brought up, not the way I am. If I haven't had time, I don't think people have thought I couldn't be bothered. They'd accept that I would have done it if I could, which is true, and it's nice that they see that.

'There are manners in rugby, and that's the way we got brought through the game, with older players making sure the etiquette was observed and carried through, if you like, into the next generation. These days, the young players in the game have gone to their clubs straight from school, without getting any real experience of life, and as that process carries on, I do worry about that side of things, the handing down of standards and traditions, getting left behind a little bit. You need the standards of that generation to carry on through, for players to get a little slap on the wrist and be told "you do say please and thank you, you do remember your manners", because that's what makes the atmosphere surrounding the game special.'

He pauses for a minute, has a gulp of his coffee, and reflects. That sounded like I was having a pop at footballers, you can see him thinking, and that's not entirely fair. I'm not trying to use them just to make my point, not trying to make headlines, so I'll qualify that – put it right. Can't be ill-mannered in making a point about manners. In truth, the real politeness, the real display of good manners, is in the thought he gives to his answer. When it's been reasoned and rounded, with the odd concession thrown in, an argument is so much more persuasive.

'Now, I know some of the football boys, and they're good lads, but all too often, something happens. I don't know if it's an agent or what, but they get a voice in their ear saying "you're bigger than this, better than this" and they don't think the manners are important any more. Now, let's be honest, if you're getting 50 grand a week, your sense of reality goes out of the window a little bit.

'The important thing about rugby is that there are good people out there. Not all of them, that would be a daft claim, but most of them are decent, and they won't tell you what you want to hear, puff you up, suck you dry and then move onto the next person. It's not like that, and that's why it's got the feeling about it that it has. The day we lose that ethos, it will be everyone's loss, and getting it back will be very difficult.'

Another pause, another mouthful of coffee, and a decision. It's been left a bit unbalanced. He's gone too far the other way. There's nothing wrong with being fair to football, but not at the expense of his own game. If the point is going to be made properly, it needs to be made fully. One more observation. An elbow is lifted onto the table, finger on chin, while a final search for the right words is completed. He continues.

'I don't want it to sound like I'm having a pop at football, because there are a lot of fantastic things about it, and it's been around as a professional game for a very long time. What we need to do, though, is look carefully at it, take the good things and make sure we leave the bad things behind. We can learn from it, learn a massive amount from it, but we've got to make sure that it's the right stuff we keep and the bad stuff we dump.'

I hazarded the thought that the press had a role to play as well – that footballers were generally under greater scrutiny than rugby players and, while that was beginning to change, they remained more closely monitored. It was starting to change, though – long lens shots of the England fly-half were hardly going to make the front page of *The Sun* when Leonard first made his international debut. Could he see that sort of development causing a problem in the future?

'I don't blame the press, because you learn when you've been around for a bit that it's just about selling papers. It's a bit of a shame, though, because once it was only the footballers, but now even the rugby players don't pick up the papers, and that's because of the back pages, let alone the front. I just think, "Am I really bothered about that? Do I really need to know what David Beckham's missus is doing every single day?"

'There's a different mentality entering the game since the World Cup, although I do think our press, our rugby press, is very good. When you look at Cleary, Jones, Ackford and that lot, they know what they're talking about, they understand the game, so when they offer an opinion it's worth listening to. Even if you don't agree with it, it's valid, because it's from someone who understands what they're watching.'

It was a good job I agreed with him, because from my less than lofty position as a pundit, framing an objection to someone who'd played more internationals than anyone else in history would have been tricky. As Lester Piggott once replied to an impudent questioner, 'Well, I have won nine Derbies . . .' Leonard could, if he felt so inclined, make a very similar point.

In the wake of an opinion or a serious point, however, as I was starting to learn, came a tale. I recounted to him the conversation I'd had with a steward at Twickenham when I was watching the *Daily Mail* tournament. The steward's son had played at Harlequins as a child and moved through the club over the course of the next ten years or so. Throughout his time there, a newsletter had been sent home on a regular basis, and on the back, in the early days at least, an advert for Leonard's talents as a carpenter had appeared. It's an extraordinary barometer of how fast the game has developed – a World Cup winner who once touted his services with hammer and chisel in order to make ends meet. The mention of it caused far more laughter than I'd expected.

'I'll tell you exactly what that was all about. When you joined Quins, they were well known for being able to find people jobs in the City. Everyone did it: Winterbottom went from being a pig farmer to a Eurobond dealer inside about a week and a half; Brian Moore went to a big City firm of solicitors, and they all got good jobs as a sort of perk.

'Well, I wasn't going to work in the City, had no interest in it at all, and didn't fancy wearing a suit and tie, because that just isn't me. I said to them that I was a chippy by trade, so I'd take any chippy work they could put my way and that would do me nicely. Now, they must have thousands of people on their database, and they sent out this advert, God knows how many times, saying that if people needed any carpentry done, get in touch with me and I'd be able to sort them out.

'So, from all those thousands of people, City high flyers and the rest, I got the grand total of one call. It was from an old girl, must have been about 90, who wanted to know if I could come and fix the gate at the end of her garden because it was a bit creaky. Winterbottom's playing the money markets, Moore's off to the High Court, and I get some dear old Doris asking if I can fix her gate. Terrific. To this day, people say to me "but Quins find everyone jobs" and I think, well, they never found me any!'

The days of top-ranking sides having to offer jobs as inducements appear to have largely gone – these days, playing for such a side is your job, and with that development are other, equally valuable changes. The RFU, once hell-bent on defending a skewed version of amateurism where the talent worked for nothing and everyone else benefited, is professional, progressive and, by and large, enlightened.

Leonard's efforts, and the achievements of him and his colleagues, have left the game's governing body with an opportunity to develop the sport to previously unprecedented levels. I offered the opinion that, based on what I'd witnessed on my travels, it was a chance on which they seemed well equipped to capitalise. Having seen life as an international under the RFU's old and new incarnations, how did he feel they were doing?

'The RFU, in its new form, has been working really hard to make the most of this, of the interest in the game, and they're going about it the right way. When we played the World Cup final of 1991, kids, teenagers, adults, they all started playing the game, the figures shot up by a huge amount, but they didn't know how to deal with it. Back then, the RFU just thought they deserved it, thought that everything deserved to drop into their laps through some sort of divine right, and while it had a good couple of years after that, soon after, they'd lost all that momentum and loads of those players.

'Now, with a professional attitude, people here are still remembering the mess they made of it back then and making sure that it doesn't happen like that next time around. If you watch what they do now, the roadshows, the community stuff, the inner city stuff, it all makes sure they keep hold of the players they attract.

'The idea of all of this is to find the next Jonny Wilkinson, the next Martin Johnson, God forbid, the next Jason Leonard. It is an absolute joy, from my perspective, having played the game, and now having finished, to walk into a rugby club on a Sunday morning and see it loaded full of kids. That's the lifeblood of the game, what it's all about, but to make it happen, people need to know what they're doing. The administrators have to be professional, the coaches and helpers need to be trained properly, and that's what we're starting to get right.'

Tellingly, the discussion of how the game develops, where it goes from here and why it needs to be handled carefully and professionally provoked the most passionate outburst of our whole conversation. His career, his friendships and his experiences were largely described with a smile and the occasional chuckle, but the future of the sport plainly matters hugely to its most capped player.

The obsession with planning and preparation, the need to plot each new move more carefully than the last and the desire to see things built on solid foundations has been used whenever someone tries to sketch out a pen picture of Clive Woodward. Here was evidence that it exists just as clearly, given the right subject matter, among his, until recently, most senior player.

'Look at it this way, junior clubs survive on their income from stuff like this. Suppose I'm in charge of a rugby club, and on a Sunday morning I've got 200, maybe as many as 400, kids coming down, what with my own side and the opposition combined. Most of those kids are going to want a juice, or a Coke, and, let's say, a burger – that's what, three quid?

'OK, so let's say Mum and Dad come along, and the old man has a pint and Mum has a gin and tonic – that's a tenner. Now, say you spend fifty quid and throw down a load of Sunday papers in a back room, cook up a load of bacon sandwiches and a bit of breakfast – Dad can't get there quickly enough, another few quid, and suddenly you've got money coming in all over the place.

'You spend that on kit, shirts, shorts, socks, balls, whatever you need, and fairly quickly, everyone's having a great time and the club's got a new generation of players, learning from people who know what they're talking about, using decent equipment. There are clubs all over the place now who have got that off to perfection – the whole thing. That's a real benefit to the game, that's how we win another World Cup.'

As he was talking, my first reaction was that it was a laudable sentiment, an inspirational rallying call if you like, delivered by someone who knows his audience will listen to what he has to say. On reflection, though, it's more than that. Leonard has thought about this long and hard – the examples, the figures, the possibilities – and decided that it's the right thing to do, and the best way to get there. His willingness to look back at where it once went wrong, especially having been there as it was backfiring, adds even greater credibility to his opinion.

'The RFU have worked overtime to make the most of winning the World Cup, and I really think they've seen that this is their window of opportunity to increase the status and the popularity of the game. It's good – it's the way it should be.'

I flicked through my mental checklist, the topics I'd hoped to get him to discuss, and made a decision. When the whole World Cup story is replayed, when all the articles, books, videos and programmes are digested, only one sour note stands out. Only one episode from the whole tournament continues to cause English rugby fans real irritation. Amid all the celebration and delight, the glory and the triumph, one man still prompts people to express genuine annoyance.

The disputes with the Australian media, the minor controversies and the rest, all pale into insignificance alongside the actions of the World Cup-final referee. Did Leonard, I queried – trying and failing to look innocent – as a recently retired, not bound by a code of conduct, no skin off his nose any more player, have any thoughts about Andre Watson?

I waited for the flat bat, the gentle prod down the pitch. I waited for, potentially, the interview to end. I even put on my best 'don't worry, I know you won't answer that' face, in readiness for the briefest of responses. What I got was a fascinating insight into one of the most controversial episodes in recent rugby history. My initial feeling, that sometimes things just dropped into your lap, was reinforced with each successive phrase.

I'd heard everyone's view of Watson, from the generally held and publicly expressed view of the players and management (we won, there's no need to comment), through to the scribes who knew the game best. Cleary's charges of 'shrill and pompous' and 'an utter disgrace' through to Jones's laments of 'appalling' and 'distasteful' told the story, or so I presumed. At worst, I'd get nothing, at best nothing new. Oh well, once more into the breach . . .

'To be honest, that all got a little bit out of hand. We've had him a load of times, and I might be wrong, but I really don't think we've ever lost with him in charge of us. He's tough; he's a real disciplinarian and won't take any backchat at all, so it's like anything else, you've got to work with the referee. If you're not playing the game to the way he sees it going, and that might not be the way anyone else sees it, you're not going to get going at all.

'What did us was our inability to change to what he wanted, or perhaps, our inability to listen to what he was saying, and to say, "Hold on, this is turning into a farce, what do you want me to do?" Even if I desperately disagreed with him, and the way he was running the game, what did he want us to do to stop getting penalised every five minutes?'

This may represent a new level of professionalism, beyond which even someone like Woodward has yet to venture an opinion. Just about everyone whose view I respected and valued had concluded that Watson had been awful, just terrible, and here was the man, literally at the centre of things, telling me that it was possible that the team could have done more about his refereeing, and maybe, just maybe, it was their fault. He went on.

'When you look at our side, there are some very vocal people who love speaking to referees. Matt Dawson, Johnno, Lawrence Dallaglio, they all love to have a chat, a little word here and there, and you could also see the two props, Trevor Woodman and Phil Vickery, penalised for taking their opposite numbers to pieces, and they needed to have a word with him as well. In the end, Andre just shut up shop, stopped listening, because I wouldn't be surprised if there had been a few sharp words exchanged.

'I wasn't told to diffuse the situation when I went on, or not to scrummage, but just to make sure I didn't give away any more penalties. I jogged on, and just ran past him and said, "Look, you know what I'm like, and you know how I scrummage. I won't go up and I won't go down. I might go backwards and forwards, but you won't have any bother with me, all right?" and he said, "That's all I'm asking, thanks, Jason."'

Whatever anyone feels about the performance of Watson, it's impossible to argue with Leonard's account. Firstly, he was there and we, at least to the same proximity, were not. Secondly, he wasn't penalised when he came on, and seemed to find a way of quelling the penalty count just at the point where it was getting completely out of hand. He has no reason to curry favour either, with his career at an end, and the idea that he'd be better off backing a South African referee than the English media seems laughable. This was a genuinely held view, from the man best positioned to give it. And he wasn't finished.

'You're not going to kid a referee of that standard. You've got to find his wavelength, get onto it, and make sure he's not seeing any of those things that are winding him up and making him give penalties all over the place. After a couple of scrums, and they were tidier because we decided not to give him a chance to penalise us, I jogged past him and asked if it was all going a bit better now. He said, "Thanks, Jason, much better," and we had no more bother.

'The whole thing could have really kicked off if we'd lost, but we didn't, we won. Clive and the other coaches were very gracious, and they made a real point of saying, "Look, we won the World Cup, we're not moaning about things," and waited for it all to fade away.'

Having given a compelling account of his view of his responsibilities on the field, he went on to explain how a task of similar proportions awaited him and his teammates on the sidelines, once the game was over.

'There would have been a great opportunity there, a great media opportunity, for someone, one of the players, to put their foot in it and say, "I think he's a right this, that and the other," but it didn't happen. To be honest, I actually think the truth was that the players weren't thinking about it. We'd just won the World Cup, we were cock-a-hoop, and we weren't going to turn round and start slagging off the referee. We've had that referee before, and he's not a bad ref, he's quite good.

'The other side, of course, is that we're going to have him in the future as well, so you start making a rod for your own back. Everyone just went up to him and said thanks, and even the Australian boys couldn't moan about him, so there was nothing said. It was more by other people than by the players who were involved. Andre's fine: he'll hang around for a beer with you, he's not stand-offish, he's a very nice fella.'

I pondered those phrases again: 'shrill and pompous', 'random calls on finicky offences', 'ignoring dangerous and blatant cheating'. There didn't seem to be, in hindsight, much of a need for anyone to put their foot in it, as the experts had reached a unanimous decision without any assistance from that quarter. Absurd as it may sound, my opinion, from a position less well informed than either side enjoys, is that they're both right.

Watson lost control of vast chunks of the game, acted exactly as described, and the World Cup final deserved better – much better. From Leonard's point of view, though, such excuses are firstly, by dint of victory, unnecessary, and secondly, by dint of his attitude, unacceptable. The referee was a problem, an unpredictable one, in the same way a strong wind or a wet pitch can be, and if you don't moan about them, you can't moan about him. Of all the utterances I heard throughout the course of my journey, his was, intentionally or not, the one which revealed the greatest degree of professionalism.

And that, as much as anything I could distinguish, was the most beguiling part of Leonard's character, and probably the reason people have taken to him in the way they have. Part of him drives onwards, physically, mentally and, well, literally. He trains in a way we'd all love to, with a dedication to which anyone who's ever played the game aspires, all the while knowing it won't happen. Another chunk of him, though, reminds us that, in so many ways, he's just the same as you and me, laughing at the same things and enjoying the game to its fullest extent, in all departments. The perspective of the man in the street, coupled with the determination of the man on the podium – it's a rare combination. Even his memories of the day of the final come tinged with amazement at what it was like at home, as you suspect he would have given anything to have been in two places at once – winning in Sydney, and watching the reaction in England.

'My missus told me that she'd gone round to some friends of ours to watch the game, partly because the kids could play with their kids and keep themselves busy during the morning. She's popped round there from time to time when I've been away on other trips, because we haven't got Sky. I won't have it, because I'd just sit there in front of anything, all day long, so it's for the best. I'm not allowed it – saves arguments!

'She said the whole place was like a ghost town, the old tumbleweed drifting across the street and nobody around anywhere. Until she went past the pubs, that was, because they were crammed, packed solid, and on the way back, people were dancing on the pavement outside them and all sorts. She said it was really, genuinely strange.

'You don't expect, because you're involved in it, that people are going to react like that.'

If he didn't expect it then, the reaction when he returned to England with the rest of the squad soon left him in no doubt as to the magnitude of what they'd achieved. In fairness, few people in England knew that the celebrations from that glorious, good-humouredly drunken morning would live on to such an extent either. Of all the people who arrived at Heathrow to welcome the squad back, few suspected they would be joined by quite so many others.

Thousands of people had woken up early to have a quiet, personal celebration, only to find themselves herded together with thousands of others, for one more huge, early-morning jolly. Not that they need, I suspect, any confirmation that their efforts were worthwhile, but the effect it had on the players looks set to live in their memories for a long time to come.

'We had no idea at all when we were out there what it was going to be like. We didn't really see the sports pages that were sent over, and we just didn't know what to expect. We had no reason to believe that there was going to be anything special going on, let alone what we finally walked back into. That was just unbelievable, like nothing I've ever seen before.

'To this day, I still laugh at the thought of coming through Heathrow, and all those people hanging off the roof and God knows where, just to see us walking back through the arrivals hall. I thought it was a wind-up, but then we drove out of the airport and you could see the chaos. People had driven up to see us, got stuck in traffic at four in the morning, or whatever time it was, and left their car in the road, or on the roundabout. Just to make sure they didn't miss it!

'If there was a traffic warden bothered to get up at that time of the morning, they would have had all their birthdays and Christmases rolled into one. We all just started laughing at the scale of it as we drove out, because it looked like the end of the world had arrived. That was probably the first time we really saw anything that warned us what it was going to be like, and none of us were expecting anything like that. Not even close.'

As the nation now remembers, the airport was just the start. A few days later, the RFU announced a victory parade through the streets of London. Held on a bitterly cold December morning, absurdly enough in midweek, rather than a weekend, thus denying thousands of schoolchildren the chance to attend, the fear was that this would show how the bubble had burst, that they'd get a decent showing, but nothing to really prove to them the emotion and celebration that had been created while they were away. So much for predictions.

Some watched it on television, almost a million others made it to the route itself, while a lucky few got into Trafalgar Square. When you realise you're talking to a man who stood on the bus, though, one of the ones they all came to see, it's probably best to let him tell his own story of the day.

'That parade was great, it really was, but the one thing I would have changed, if it could have been done, was to have held it at the weekend so that the kids could come along. We all got letters as players, individually from people, saying it was a real shame, because they would have loved to have taken their kids up there.

'I spotted people I knew on the route, like the wife of someone I used to play rugby with at Quins, who was standing there with all her workmates. I gave her a big wave and she went mad, cheering away like a lunatic. I was laughing, because she didn't even like rugby when I last spoke to her, but it got to people like that. I looked up at one of the balconies and I saw a mate and his missus, so I gave them a big wave as well, and they went berserk too. It was unbelievable.

'By the time we got to Downing Street, I swaggered up like I owned the bloody place, but with my tie round under my ear, looking like a right mess. In loads of cabs that I've caught since, the drivers end up asking for an autograph and then tell me they won't accept any money for the ride, which is always a really nice touch. Thing is, those cabbies come from the same sort of background as me. They're ordinary lads and they just want to say well done and have a bit of a chat, so it means a lot in a funny sort of way.'

As the celebrations came to an end, however, so did Leonard's career, though it wasn't announced until later. He stayed around for the Six Nations championship, determined to play for as long as he was enjoying it, but the pressures were beginning to mount. After months on the road, despite the most magnificent and glorious of distractions and diversions, home was calling.

'I never pondered packing up when I was at the World Cup, and I can say with certainty that that's the case for everyone else who has since retired as well. We were just too focused on what we were trying to achieve. The thing with me was that I played the World Cup final, and literally, within a week, having landed on the Tuesday, I was playing for Quins on the Saturday. I was on a natural high after we won, then after I got back I was on another high because I was meeting up with all my mates from the club again, so I really never had a chance to think it through properly.

'We then had a strange sort of start to the Six Nations, and it really brought it home to me that I was missing the kids and not seeing enough of the family. I'd been away for the best part of six months, and then we went pretty much straight into camp for the Italy game, which was on Sunday. After that, we went back and prepared for the Scotland game on the following Saturday and by the time I got back from that, I'd been away for another fortnight.

'I just thought, hold on a second, the New Zealand tour is four weeks. Now, I've just about managed two weeks, but there's no way I'll do four. I'm going to be away from home, I won't be happy, and if I'm not happy, I won't be any use to anyone, and anyway, that's the reason

I play – to be happy. There's no point in any of this if I'm not. I had a word with Clive, told him what was on my mind, and he reassured me that the New Zealand trip wasn't actually four weeks. Then he paused, and said, "It's three and a half." As I said to him, for the sake of three days, we'll call it four weeks, I think.

'He was very open with me, said he wanted me to tour, but also that he'd respect anything I wanted to do. I wanted to be open with him, and I didn't want to play the Six Nations and then announce I wasn't going on tour, giving it the big farewell speech bit, because that wasn't fair on Clive and the boys. I could have coped, but I wouldn't have enjoyed it, and I'd decided that, when that day came, it was time to pack up.'

And, as with his whole career, he was as good as his word. Suddenly, after a lifetime of certainty and schedules, fixtures and planning, he's having to look up and ponder where to go next. There will be no shortage of offers and options – Woodward has made it clear he'll welcome him into the fold in a coaching role, but Leonard is biding his time.

'I haven't even gone all that far down the road of looking at what I want to do next. Rest, I suppose. That'll do me for the moment, more mentally than anything else. It's been a hell of a last two years, and it takes it out of you.

'It's now a case of stepping back and trying to take stock of everything. I've got so many opportunities in front of me, which is great, but it's really a case of deciding which way I want to go. What I do know for sure is that, having been wrapped up in the game for such a long time, I don't need or want to tumble straight into something. If I do something, I'm going to stand back, decide to do it, and then set about doing that properly.

'I need to re-acquaint myself with my family a little bit, and then decide, right, that's the thing for me. It's a bit like giving up rugby: you don't do that lightly without thinking it through. I thought about it for a while before coming to the decision that it was time to call it a day.'

Revealingly, despite all the hours of pain and torture that Woodward must have put him through, both directly and not, it was to the subject of the England coach that Leonard returned, as if aware that he hadn't handed out sufficient credit for the high point at which he enabled Leonard's career to end. Jason's decision to retire would have been made much earlier, and in less auspicious circumstances, had the nature of English rugby not changed so much over the course of the last few years.

'You can't go over the top when you're trying to assess what Clive did for English rugby, because he set out what he was all about, told people what he wanted to achieve, and just got on and did it. When he came in, there was a lot of opposition from certain places because he was bringing in all these new ideas, costing them money and telling them that it would all work out in the end.

'I wouldn't have played in the team that I did without him – none of us would – because he made sure the side reached a level that we wouldn't have been able to dream about once upon a time. There are coaches all over the place, forwards, backs, kicking, throwing, you name it, but you can only judge people by their results, and he landed the biggest prize of the lot.

'Obviously, we all put in the work, lots of hard work, to do it, but there's no point pretending that all that set-up just fell naturally into place, because it didn't. It needed someone in there who knew what he was up to and who could have the arguments and stand his ground in order to get it. Clive took a long-term view, and put things together so that if we did things right, applied ourselves and concentrated on what we were doing and where we were going, we could become world champions. He did his job, the team did theirs, and as a unit, we were good enough to do it.

'There's a bond between all of us who played in that side, because we'll always have what we achieved. Also, not one of us is afraid to share the credit around where it's due, because that's the sort of thinking we had to have to get where we did. You give the credit, you take the blame, you all work together and hopefully, as in our case, it will all work out as you want it to. It took a lot of vision and determination for Clive to set all that in motion, though – an awful lot. They call him Sir Clive now, but I bet he was called other things along the way, and people shouldn't forget that. It wasn't always going right, but you've got to get through the rough to enjoy the good times and to make them happen.'

With the record put straight on just about everything that matters, I set about packing up, and he asked if everything was all right, if there was anything else I wanted to ask. In keeping with a public image which I can only report seems to match perfectly the man himself, if he's going to do something, he'll do it properly.

Whatever he opts to do next, you know that Jason Leonard is going to do all right for himself. Sport confers hero-hood far too lightly these days – score a goal in a cup tie, have a decent round at the Open or even, on a slow news day, play snooker rather well and you'll get lauded as such, but they are all transitory investitures. Leonard has made history. In a game for hard men that has become fiercer than ever before, he hasn't just hung around, but saved his best for last. He's one of this country's sporting greats, and deserves to be treated and remembered as such. Lots of sportsmen achieve a moment of glory, but greatness takes a bit longer to come around, and Leonard didn't just last the course but sprinted down the straight.

I left him as he got ready for his next appointment. He was meeting someone to discuss the results of his farewell dinner, which was staged as a tribute to him and as a last chance to collect a nice pay cheque from the game. Instead, all the proceeds were going to a trust fund in memory of Richard Langhorn and Nick Duncombe, two young and talented Harlequins players who died, tragically, far too young. To the last, he was doing what was right.

As he said, manners are all important. When we lose them, the game's in a whole load of trouble. I pondered it as I strolled back down the road. Jason is possibly the best-loved, and certainly the most capped, player in the world, and he was sitting down to discuss a farewell dinner from which he'd handed the proceeds to the memory of people of similar mind, denied the chance to enjoy life as much as him. He is proud, and rightly so, of the work the game is doing in order to prosper in the professional era. He should also be proud, not that he'd be so presumptuous, of his role in ensuring its spirit is similarly protected.

VI

February 2004

While most of the rugby world was concentrating on the start of the Six Nations championship, the owner of England's most famous damaged shoulder was continuing to learn a lesson about his new-found status as a media hero. Despite escaping off to a Caribbean beach for a few days' holiday with his girlfriend, Diana Stewart, while he recovered from his operation, Jonny Wilkinson was still a gift from the gods as far as the tabloids were concerned.

Front-page pictures dominated *The Sun*, while a double-page spread inside showed a string of long-lens snaps, not of drinking binges, nightclub brawls and womanising, but paddling, reading a book and, shock horror, giving Diana a kiss. Fame had clearly turned his head to be acting in such an unnatural way and, a generation on, a story about an English rugby star kissing someone called Diana scarcely seemed newsworthy at all.

On the domestic front, the heroes of the month, and indeed possibly the whole season, were the gloriously named Pertemps Bees from the Midlands. Playing against Premiership champions Wasps in the quarter-finals of the Powergen Cup, they hurled the form book to one side, coming back from a 19–11 half-time deficit to claim an extraordinary scalp with a 28–24 victory in front of a part-delirious, part-stunned home crowd.

What made it especially memorable, however, was another one of those moments rugby seems to save for the big occasion, just in case you had started to think it was forgetting itself a little bit. With just a point between the sides, as the game entered its final quarter, Bees' fly-half Mark Woodrow launched a drop goal which appeared to have sent them four points clear.

Paul Honiss, the New Zealand referee, however, could not see clearly, and as neither touch judge could help him out, he had no option but to rule against the effort, thus leaving Wasps with a clear, if unmerited, path back into the game. To the Bees' credit, it was swiftly closed once more by a Woodrow penalty which was seen by the official, but the reaction afterwards spoke volumes for the spirit of the game.

'To be honest, I was kicking into the sun, and the ref was looking the same way, so neither of us could really make out where it went exactly,' Woodrow explained. 'Obviously, our crowd were going potty, but you can't give a decision based on the crowd's reaction, so there was no option but to rule it out. That's the way it goes, isn't it?'

It was generous and honest, and despite being uttered in the wake of victory, rather than defeat, smacked of sincerity. A couple of hours later, football staged the Carling Cup final in Cardiff, with Middlesbrough beating Bolton Wanderers and a couple of potentially contentious decisions made along the way by referee Mike Riley. Sam Allardyce, the Bolton manager, opted for a rather different tack to the one Woodrow had taken.

'We have paid the price in a major cup final for decisions not being given in our favour.

'I will always look back at the major decisions and Mike Riley was poor. We had our concerns about him before the match and he lived up to his reputation as far as we're concerned. I've never liked him as a referee for us and he has cost us the chance of winning.'

And there, with all the grace of a hippo in quicksand, was football's reaction to a similar situation. While there's no need to keep drawing the comparisons out between the two games, sometimes they're just too blatant to ignore.

As if to stress that there was something that they shared in common, though, the story which followed the Bees' victory harked back to the good old days of blazers, committees, and bloody silly decisions. Pertemps were not in the Premiership, and the Powergen Cup rules had been written without pondering that such a minnow could possibly reach such an exalted level. As a result, they were entitled to none of the financial rewards associated with progress in the competition. They were playing for nothing.

Had they gone out in the first round and reached the semi-final of the plate competition, they would have earned upwards of £30,000, but for winning, not losing, they had surrendered such a reward. It was a blast from the past – a reminder of what chaos the game could cause when it didn't turn its mind to something. Allardyce would have been threatening writs by the bucket-load. Thankfully, nobody asked him for an opinion.

VII

A little local difficulty

After conquering the world, Woodward and his men returned to competitive action midway through February, seeking to add a consecutive Grand Slam to their list of accomplishments. Having arguably played their finest rugby as a side in destroying Ireland at Lansdowne Road at the end of the previous season to attain their first Six Nations clean sweep under Woodward's guidance, expectations were high as their defence of the crown came under starter's orders.

The general view before the start of the tournament was that several obstacles, of varying degrees of potency, lay in their way. France, having lost out in a rain-drenched encounter in the World Cup semi-final, were clearly a side in the ascendant, and had been quietly tipped by more than one pundit to be the form horse of the competition. With a back row packed with athletes capable of replicating the greatest traits of French rugby over the years, and Frederic Michalak blossoming into a more complete fly-half with each international outing, there were compelling reasons to believe the claims that this might be their year.

Having lost Martin Johnson through retirement, Jonny Wilkinson courtesy of a shoulder operation and with increasing doubts hanging over the international futures of Neil Back and Jason Leonard, among others, Woodward was playing with a significantly weakened hand from the one he used to such dazzling effect just three months earlier. England were going to have to show that they possessed strength in depth, that the planning and preparation had left them with reserves of genuine quality and that there was a side within their ranks ready to grow and, ultimately, defend the Webb Ellis Cup.

In addition to the threat of the French, the Irish, under the leadership of Brian O'Driscoll, and the Welsh, who had used the World Cup to showcase possibly the most thrilling return to form of the whole competition, were both considered decent outside shots. If nothing else, there was plentiful evidence to suggest that either of them, if they enjoyed 'one of those days', could prove just too much of a handful for any of the other five nations.

Woodward knew the importance of facing both sides at Twickenham, where his men had not tasted defeat since 1999, when South Africa ended their World Cup dreams amid a flurry of drop goals in a remarkable quarter-final game. In the intervening years, the ground had become a true fortress, hosting 22 successive unbeaten performances and seeing everyone in world rugby sent home empty handed.

England had often benefited at 'HQ' from a passionate home crowd getting behind them, cranking up the atmosphere to extraordinary levels. With the record Woodward's men had created there, it was more than just mere fancy to suggest that, in a close game, and there had been plenty of those, the level of noise generated by their supporters could be the difference between victory and defeat. If you could rob the Irish and the Welsh of their support off the pitch, you'd be a fair way towards making their life more difficult on it.

Before the arrival of the Irish, however, who doubtless presented England's largest challenge since Sydney, there were the small matters of Italy and Scotland, both away from home. England were back to where they had been at the start of the World Cup campaign – trying to make the easy games sound as challenging as the simple ones.

True enough, Wilkinson was ruled out – not just for the Italian episode, but for the entire tournament – as he prepared to undergo surgery on a trapped nerve in his neck. Nevertheless, a weekend in Rome was never likely to unsettle Woodward's side, and so it proved.

Having been worn down by the English pack, the Italians had no reply to the spring-heeled Jason Robinson, who played at centre, at least according to the team-sheet, while waltzing and skipping down either flank, through the middle or from full-back, depending on his mood. Unstoppable, Robinson danced home three times, leaving England to collect a 50–9 victory which barely saw them emerge from second gear.

Much of the talk in the week before the game had been about who would replace Wilkinson, with Paul Grayson, a man who in another era might already have collected dozens of caps, getting the nod. In the event, Woodward could have opted for Larry Grayson for all the pressure he had to withstand from the Italian back row, as the Northampton stand-off notched 20 of England's points.

A week later, and Scotland went the same way as Italy, this time by a margin of 35–13, achieved in the manner of a superior heavyweight boxer settling for a comfortable points win, rather than risk a cut going for a late knockout. The game had started amid a shower of silver paper, fireworks, bagpipers and other nonsense, as the Scottish RFU sought to make the occasion 'one to remember'.

With the debris left on the pitch throughout the course of the next 80 minutes, the overwhelming memory was one of players looking like they were trying to play an international rugby match in Stringfellows. Every time someone stood up, they found themselves spitting out bits of silver foil and trying to remove it from delicate places. The fans might have been singing about sending back 'Edward's army', but Scotland's opponents ended up looking more like muscular glam rockers. Very surreal, and if the rugby on display was more scrappy than spectacular, you couldn't help but reflect that the oddness of the occasion had been set about 10 minutes before either side even got out of the tunnel.

And so the first week of March arrived, and a Six Nations tournament which had yet to throw up anything in the way of a real surprise arrived at Twickenham, as the Irish came to town. Having underperformed in their first outing of the competition, getting comprehensively mauled by the French in Paris, they had warmed up for England in spectacular style with a 36–15 trouncing of Wales in Dublin the previous week.

The win had featured two tries from an irrepressible O'Driscoll and a pair from the long-haired hooker Shane Byrne, who was showing signs of taking up the mantle of Irish forward talisman following the retirement of Keith Wood. If Wood had become much admired and loved for his bald head and committed forward surges, Byrne was proving to be almost a carbon copy in terms of his playing style. As far as personal style went, however, he was posing some rather different questions, with what can only be described as a 'mullet' lurking on his head. Short at the sides, and swept back down his neck, it went where only Chris Waddle had dared to go some years earlier on the football pitch. The fans, inevitably, loved it.

As Wood and Johnson took up their seats in a television commentary box, looking far from comfortable in their new surroundings, Woodward and his men set about showing that the retirements and injuries had not made a significant difference to their ability to produce a home victory on demand. It was a compelling contest, and a truly memorable day.

For all its minor-public-school affectations and middle-class leanings, there are few places quite like Twickenham on the day of a big international, and when one of the home nations is visiting, it becomes more special still. When, and background and ancestry may make me somewhat biased, the visitors happen to be wearing the green of Ireland, it is at its very best. And yet, in among the humour, the banter and the booze, there was an undercurrent of complacency, certainly among sections of the crowd – a self-confidence that bordered on the arrogant. It was not a mood of which Woodward, you suspected, tucked away somewhere with his team, would have approved.

There is something remarkable about the dynamics of a rugby crowd gathering at Waterloo Station on a match-day lunch-time. It is quite unlike the atmosphere you encounter on the way to a large football match, where the passage from station to stadium can all too often feel like a trip through enemy territory, under the direction of a particularly suspicious army. An avenue of police, with their horses and dogs, awaits you, in equal parts threatening and threatened, simply because the opposing fans on the other side of the line may prove to be distinctly damaging to your health.

Once at the ground, the joys of watching football become more apparent still, as you're herded into the 'away end' and kept, under closed-circuit scrutiny, away from anything as dangerous as an alcoholic drink until kick-off time is reached. Having endured the poorest view in the place for the duration of the game, the process is reversed, amidst much hanging around, being threatened and frequently getting cold and wet, all interspersed with a bit more hanging around before being herded back onto a train and shunted out of town. Outside the world of the dominatrix, it's hard to think of another way to pay quite so much in order to be treated quite so badly.

Rugby does things rather differently, and it adds hugely to the whole experience. In return for providing a lifetime's evidence that they won't try to maim each other as soon as the forces of law and order turn their backs, rugby crowds are left alone to do pretty much what they want. What they want, on the evidence of a few thousand people milling around Waterloo, is to have a pint, tell stories that have been refined over the course of a million previous recitals and sing splendidly childish songs in preparation for the game ahead.

The dress code is, to say the least, eccentric. Barbour jackets, corduroy trousers, brogues and replica rugby shirts appear to make up about three quarters of the sartorial inelegance on display – if you were to cross Hackett with the worst replica excesses of the RFU shop, you'd probably end up with something fairly similar. Indeed, the combination of wax jackets and new, nylon England rugby shirts makes this lot about as waterproof a bunch of people as you could ever hope to see. If they all popped off for a swim, ten minutes later only their wet hair would give you a clue as to what they'd been up to.

In fact, the new, streamlined kit seems to have done very little to dissuade Twickenham man away from the perils of donning a replica shirt. If Neil Back had trouble in the World Cup slipping the tight, nylon garment over his muscular torso when his original top got shredded at the bottom of a ruck, the problems facing a fan of, say, heavier build, with cheeks as red as the stripes on his shirt, are just as immense and considerably less aesthetically pleasing. So, a thousand nylon-clad guts hang over a thousand pairs of brown, corduroy trousers, while their owners dispose of the pints which help them maintain their shape.

The Irish, it has to be said, are no closer to getting a request to come and put a catwalk show together. Green, Day-Glo nylon wigs appeared to be the order of the day, with the occasional exception of green and white jester's hats, and in one startling case, the two were combined to form a foot-high mass of lurid nylon, topped off with a selection of bells. The replica shirt was also worn proudly, with a fair number of London Irish jerseys, complete with a large pint-of-Guinness motif affixed to the front.

It was, even by the cosmopolitan standards of city life, an engaging spectacle, and as they stood and chatted, drank and sang, the good-natured atmosphere became ever more apparent. By the time the train was displayed on the indicator boards around the concourse, a large, multi-coloured throng was cheerfully pouring itself into carriages more used to carrying the serious early-morning faces of the Surrey commuter belt into Central London. It also became immediately clear that an unofficial contest was on to find the best one-liner of the day, as every incident, regardless of its triviality, was accompanied by a bellowed comment.

'This is the Reading train, calling at Vauxhall, Clapham Junction . . .' The announcement was cut short by a booming English voice from further down the carriage. 'Bugger Clapham bloody Common, just take us all to Twickenham and don't spare the horses.'

It was greeted with a roar, some applause, and a refusal to take too seriously the sergeant-major-like tones he had adopted for his outburst. The Irish took up a chorus of the 'Fields of Athenry', which has become an unofficial anthem in place of the passion-free drone of 'Ireland's Call', which the authorities play in place of the 'Soldier's Song', lest anyone finds it offensive. Personally, regardless of the words, I find 'Ireland's Call' far more offensive because it's just such a bloody awful dirge, but each to their own.

The English retaliated with a burst of 'Swing Low, Sweet Chariot', the songs leaving people on the platform with decidedly puzzled faces as the 13.02 singing service rattled its way through a suburban station. A man with his face painted green and a fluorescent green, white and gold wig, launched into the 'Soldier's Song', and the English came back once more with 'Swing Low'. By the time the Irish had got through the first two renditions of 'You've only got one song', the point had been made amid much laughter and slapping of backs. This was going to be a remarkable afternoon.

At Clapham Junction, with the train unable to safely accommodate a single extra person, about a thousand of them got on.

'Has anyone got a spare ticket,' boomed another Home Counties voice, 'for a chap from New Zealand, who would like to come and see how rugby is really played?'

The English half of the carriage roared with laughter, in a way that was just starting to sound a little too sure of itself. The Irish, for their part, kept smiling, trying to conceal the sort of nervousness which only grasps you when you know you've actually got a chance of claiming a result. The rest of the journey was spent in the armpit of a man from Meath, who was evidently feeling slightly warm. Twickenham Station has never looked, or, for that matter, smelt, so welcoming.

Walking to the ground, two of the features of modern-day Twickenham internationals, food and ticket touts, were immediately obvious, with one rather more welcome than the other. It was impossible to take more than three strides without someone coming up to you and asking if you had a spare ticket. The police looked on aimlessly, as if determined not to notice the display before their eyes as fan after fan was assailed by tout after tout, some working in packs, some alone, and all equally unpleasant.

One of them, with a three-quarter-length leather coat and a tweed cap, looking like the sort of man who nobbles horses on his day off, approached a pair of huge, green-shirted figures just in front of me. Both had Irish club jerseys on, one with the number four on the back, which had plainly seen reasonably recent action judging by the man's build, with him inside it. The tout was either unconcerned, which was somewhat naive, or didn't care, which was downright stupid.

'I'm paying good money, boys, big money if you've got spare tickets you want to let me have,' he smarmed, looking up expectantly at the figures ambling along as he shuffled quickly backwards so as to remain facing them. There was a silence as the request was considered briefly, and I found myself willing them not to surrender to his request. I needn't have worried.

'My tickets aren't spare,' the man in the Ireland shirt announced, before leaving a slight pause, which saw the tout on the brink of launching into his follow-up sales pitch. He never got round to it, as the giant figure in front of him finished his sentence: 'so feck off'.

I was still snorting with laughter as the tout glared at me before disappearing back down his hole, and the two of them turned to me with a smile in response to my ill-disguised chuckles. 'Did you hear the cheeky little fecker? Like anyone's going to sell their ticket now!' I looked past him and smiled, as the corner of the stadium came into view. He was right – of all the places to try to buy your ticket, this close to the off, with the ground in sight and the atmosphere building, was possibly the worst to choose.

At this point, he stopped, in order to enjoy the other half of that match-day double act – the food. On the walk between Twickenham Station and the ground, a brief stroll of about 400 yards or so, I will confidently predict that you can buy more sorts of food than anywhere else in London. People either rent out their front gardens to companies offering their wares, or, in several entrepreneurial cases, dust off the barbecue and set up their own cottage industry for the afternoon.

Within the space of about 200 yards – I counted, and have the ketchup-stained notebook to prove it – there were stalls offering bacon sandwiches, pies, peanuts, burgers and kebabs. I then looked towards the other side of the road and realised I'd better wipe the notebook clean and start again. This time, I spotted curries, pasties, more burgers, pizza, crêpes, sausages in rolls and biltong (it's South African, and personally, I wouldn't if I were you – it looked and tasted like my belt). One of the less practical young businessmen was offering cans of beer for £2 each, or six for £10. Expensive at the best of times, and when you're situated 30 yards from an off-licence selling them at normal price it's maybe not the cleverest marketing strategy, but doubtless he'll learn from his mistakes.

There were also stalls offering more nylon hats, flags, shirts, T-shirts, pictures, horns, banners and other such delights, along with my favourite item of the day – sunglasses with a red rose affixed to the lens through which you could, by some miracle of science, see. In the future, if anyone accuses English rugby fans of wearing rose-tinted spectacles, I can not only agree, but identify their place of purchase.

Twickenham could easily represent the typical leafy suburb, with its little lanes, quirky shops and tree-lined streets, were it not for the stadium which lives at the edge of town. Having grown stage by stage over the course of the last decade or so, the home of the RFU is arguably the finest stadium in the country.

Holding 75,000 people, the ground has plans to grow larger still, as the south stand awaits the start of a development that will bring it together into a huge, sweeping bowl. It probably still won't hold enough people to put the touts out of a job, but we can live in hope. As a result of the existing developments, the area directly surrounding the ground becomes completely swamped with fans every time England play at home, in a way that you see hardly anywhere else. Both Old Trafford and the Millennium Stadium are built in more open, less densely populated areas, which allow the crowds approaching them to spread out more effectively. The masses forced through the narrow, residential streets from Twickenham Station to the ground seem, as a result of their cramped surroundings, larger still.

A LITTLE LOCAL DIFFICULTY

The mood here was one of almost unshakeable English certainty that the white-shirted fans were turning up not to watch a rugby match, but to participate in an extended victory parade. The first competitive home match since Sydney was not being treated as potentially competitive at all as far as the spectators were concerned, and for the second time in half an hour, I was left wondering what Woodward would make of the attitude.

In addition to the deserved accolades and plaudits, the knighthoods, honours and rewards, victory had brought with it a new level of expectation. Indeed, at its peak, it almost went beyond this to an unshakeable belief that their side were destined to sweep aside anyone who stood before them, regardless of the circumstances. Woodward's greatest triumph had brought him his largest problem to date – how to encourage confidence without the fans mutating it into arrogance.

As the previously clear skies turned dark and a dramatic storm lashed the stadium for the last half an hour before kick-off, an English fan at one of the concourse bars held forth. His words demonstrated, in a way that left me more certain than ever before, that the supporters were getting a little carried away with matters.

'Well, if it gets slippery, we'll just turn them over in the pack instead. Not a problem, let it rain all it likes, swing bloody low.'

He got another little round of applause and we made our way to our seats to watch England try to put his prediction into action. From the first minutes, it was clear that things were not going to proceed in quite the straightforward way he had anticipated. Ireland's pack were on fire, scavenging around to collect the loose ball, dominant in the lineout, and ready to drive and disrupt the English whenever the opportunity arose.

A series of long, raking kicks into English territory saw the Irish spend much of the opening 20 minutes deep in the opposition's half, and the 6–0 lead Ireland held until the half-hour mark looked like a poor return on their territorial dominance. Suddenly, however, with an Irish slip, a hack forwards and a neat, flicked pass from Paul Grayson to Matt Dawson, England appeared to have played their 'get out of jail' card at a time when they needed it most. The scrum-half scampered over the line, touched down close to the posts, and Grayson's conversion saw England claim an unlikely looking 7–6 lead, which soon stretched to 10–6 with a Grayson penalty. The masses were still too confident to express anything approaching relief, and phrases revolving around the theory that you 'can't stop real class' started to boom out. England, their fans had decided, were merely playing a game, lulling the Irish into a false sense of security and then stepping things up when needed.

It was a far from compelling argument, as the Irish lineout continued to operate to perfection and England hooker Steve Thompson had trouble throwing the ball anywhere near one of the towering white shirts leaping in front of him. Time after time, grateful green arms closed around a misdirected throw, leaving the visitors to enjoy the bulk of possession. Two English indiscretions later, the second on the stroke of half-time, left Ronan O'Gara to stroke home a pair of penalties which saw his side reach the break 12–10 ahead.

Less than a minute into the second half, Twickenham saw one of the key moments of the whole tournament, and one which placed more doubts in English minds than any other. Ben Cohen launched himself for the corner, and referee Paul Honiss, enjoying a video replay he had been denied at Pertemps Bees a week earlier, ruled out the try for a double movement. With a fair chunk of the crowd still in the bars finishing their half-time pints, the first they saw of the action was a huge video screen displaying the legend 'NO TRY'.

In an instant, or so it seemed, England's fans realised that they were not guaranteed a route back into the lead. For the first time all afternoon, the home fans were getting nervous, while in inverse proportion, the Irish were beginning to believe. Ten minutes later, as Girvan Dempsey rounded off the best move of the day by sliding into the corner for a famous Irish try, the mood was reinforced dramatically.

I was struck by two things. Firstly, the shock of seeing the England defence carved open in such a thrilling and flowing fashion, and secondly, a man in a green jersey, who had been sitting behind me, landing on my head as his celebrations saw him take briefly to the skies.

'Sorry 'bout tha'. I took off,' he said, which, for some reason reduced me to absolute fits of laughter. He picked himself up, and offered me a hand: 'I'm Ronan. Howaya?'

Even if I had been upset by his actions, which I hadn't, the anger wouldn't have lasted beyond his introduction. Even when he jumps straight on top of your head, it's very hard to feel put out by a large man called Ronan who goes on to introduce himself in such a pleasant manner.

As Ronan took his seat once more, I watched his namesake O'Gara slot home an imperious conversion from the touchline, and Ireland held a 19–10 lead, which nobody could argue hadn't been earned. I braced myself, but Ronan plainly only goes flying for tries, not kicks. I decided not to sit in front of him when Ireland next played Romania.

With 20 minutes left, it looked as if England might have dragged themselves back into the contest as Mark Regan launched himself into the corner, only for Honiss to once more request a replay. As the big screen showed all too clearly, the replacement hooker's foot brushed the line under the weight of a desperate tackle from Malcolm O'Kelly, the Irish lock, and his shoulder thudded into the corner flag on his way to the line. The try that never was, wasn't, and the reaction around the ground told its own story.

Regardless of whether they were holding pints, pies or programmes, 75,000 pairs of arms flew into the air. White-clad versions stopped at head level, palms opened to the sky in a gesture of questioning and bafflement, while their green counterparts continued upwards, punching the air and celebrating furiously. Woodward looked truly desperate, his head hitting his hands as the big screen showed Regan's shoulder hitting the corner flag.

It was all over. Grayson notched another penalty and England enjoyed some late pressure, but they'd been beaten at home for the first time in four years, and well beaten with it. They hadn't played with the over-confidence the crowd had exhibited, nor had they played with an excess of nerves. In fact, they hadn't played at all. They were shut out in the set pieces, beaten up in the loose and left woefully bereft of ideas or plans out wide. England's bid for successive Grand Slams had been dealt a mortal blow. The tournament's bid to secure its status as the greatest annual competition in world rugby had received an enormous, extraordinary boost.

Ronan, the incredible flying fan, was shaking the hand of the man next to him, who was looking decidedly bemused in his England scarf and hat. 'Cheer up! Jeez, you're supporting the second-best team in the world.' If they don't pick up Ronan soon, the Irish diplomatic service will never know what it's missed.

And then, just as they had arrived, so they left. Trooping out of the ground together and heading off in search of a pub to discuss the afternoon's events. White and green together, and hundreds of years of turbulent history almost put to one side in the name of an afternoon at the rugby. Woodward said all the right things, as did Dallaglio, his captain, while the Irish, if they felt like mocking the once overly confident crowd, resisted the temptation.

There were still a few more issues to contend with, of course, as is inevitable with so many people flooding out into the streets at the same time. The Barmy Arms, located down on the riverfront, a ten-minute walk from the ground, ran out of beer shortly after 9 p.m., leaving grown men on the brink of tears, while the station platforms groaned under the weight of thousands of bodies, but there was never a hint of trouble. The pubs were packed beyond their limits until late in the night, doing a month's trade in a day, and it was time to head home and reflect.

As with all intriguing days, the journey back still held one or two gems, and I found myself listening in fascination to a well-dressed couple on the train offering their own, well spoken, version of events.

'Was the referee Antipodean?' the woman queried, 'because a lot of them favour the Irish, you know.' Her husband shrugged, and muttered that she might well have a point. I was left with the suspicion that it was a conversational tactic he might just have used before during the course of their married life. To be fair, she had an air about her with which only the brave or daft would choose to meddle.

We were a couple of stops outside Twickenham when two young lads got onto the train, hooded jackets pulled up tightly, and proceeded to light a joint. It was a classic teenage thing to do, designed as it was to shock and annoy, and it reminded me that my day out, amid the alternative culture that is a rugby international, was at an end. I was wrong, it had one last hurrah. A man opposite, complete with Irish scarf, and possibly the worse for drink in the most amiable of ways, sniffed at the air, took his head out of his programme and looked around.

Spying the two lads, he eased himself from his seat, wandered over and extended his arms, before removing the offending article neatly from between the lips of one of the youths and flicking it straight out of the window. 'See that sign there? It says no smoking – and especially not that shite. Behave yourselves.'

He sat back down, and left the two lads looking stunned. He wasn't a huge bloke, but there was something about his demeanour, and possibly the smell of recently dispatched beer, which left them unwilling to challenge him. As he returned to his programme, I smiled to myself. The chariot might have been thoroughly derailed, but the game, and its standards and traditions, were healthier than I'd dared think. I might have been only at the very tip of it, but with this number of people enjoying it this much, things couldn't be that bad.

A fortnight later, and Woodward's side were back at Twickenham. Having become unpleasantly reacquainted with the notion of defeat, they were trying to put to the back of their minds the shattered walls of their carefully constructed fortress, and seeking to return to winning ways against a Welsh side still trying to decide if it was resurgent or not. The World Cup had seen them involved in marvellously brave, if losing, performances against England and New Zealand, and the return to form of Steve Hansen's side was noted by several observers, trying to avoid the obvious choice, as their highlight of the tournament. Since then, however, it would be fair to say that Wales' recovery had not been entirely plain sailing.

They launched their domestic campaign with a victory over Scotland which told us little or nothing about their form. Having been on a gentle downward slump for several years, Scottish rugby was sitting at the bottom of the heap, the sick man of the Six Nations. The rumours that they were giving away victories over the Scots free with every half-dozen Cornflake tokens was perhaps a touch harsh, but it wasn't all that far from the truth.

As a barometer of Welsh hopes for the rest of the Championships, it was like predicting great things for Paula Radcliffe on the strength of watching her outrun Vanessa Feltz. Their subsequent trouncing by the Irish, and yet another battling but futile display against the French proved, yet again, that nobody provided a false dawn as readily as the Scots.

The Welsh dragon had seen its heart ripped out a few years earlier, as administrators with no feeling for the game had changed the club structure beyond all recognition in order to embrace a new, professional system. Thousands of fans lost their connection with the game and with it, inevitably, their interest. It might be a spurious theory, but since the WRU swapped passion for pounds, their national side seems to lose, rather than win, the really close games.

Who knows what a difference the extra sense of belonging could have had on the team, but is it so hard to imagine that a man from Pontypool might tackle harder playing for the town of his birth rather than, say, the Neath-Swansea Ospreys, where the economics of the game have forced him to go?

As with so many times before, Twickenham saw the Welsh come close – very close – but end up with nothing more than a sense of what might have been. Ben Cohen, bigger than flankers used to be and faster than wingers ever were, claimed two tries that only the most highly physically prepared player could ever hope to score. The first involved sweeping onto the end of a rangy passing movement and heading for the corner, regardless of the presence of Welsh full-back Gareth Jones, who was attempting to block his route.

Cohen took one glance at the situation, maintained his line, and was rewarded by the sight of Jones stepping backwards, as if to buy time for a decision. It was akin to taking a second to decide whether to halt a juggernaut with your right or left shoulder, and Jones joined Cohen in a tumble over the line. Coming from the side, Jonathan Thomas launched himself around Cohen's shoulders in a bid to quell his momentum, and found himself joining Jones for the ride as the wing crashed to the line, before squirming around, shrugging off Welsh objections, and plonking the ball neatly down for a try. It was the sort of try a sixth former scores when playing against the third year. By the end of the season, ironically, Cohen was on the receiving end of the same sort of treatment. Form, as we were beginning to see, can be a fickle thing.

Olly Barkley, in at fly-half for the injured Paul Grayson (who had a strained calf to go with the bruised pride suffered against Ireland), converted, and despite an exchange of penalties throughout the remainder of the half, England went in 16–9 to the good at half-time. A year earlier, England would have moved slowly but certainly out of sight, but like a middle-distance champion short of full fitness, when they searched for that extra gear, it refused to engage.

Wales ran the ball at them like Welsh sides of the past and claimed a thrilling reward. Gareth Thomas slid into the right corner after Mark Taylor had botched an overlap on the far side, only to make amends shortly afterwards by claiming the right option and sneaking a score into the corner he should have sent his wing five minutes earlier. Stephen Jones banana-kicked one of the conversions over, and Wales were 21–16 in front.

Woodward was opting for his best poker face, but with the sense of 'oh no, not again' sweeping over him, his abilities as a card player fell short of those he enjoys as a coach. He looked twitchy, nervous and unhappy, and his side were communally managing a fair reflection of their leader's body language. After a burst of sustained pressure, however, Cohen reclaimed the initiative for his side with an opportunistic and bustling dart from close range, taking another couple of Welsh defenders with him as he sneaked over to level the scores.

Barkley converted to send England in front, and when a promising situation for the Welsh evaporated with a loose ball bouncing kindly for Robinson, rather than into the arms of the Welsh, the pendulum had swung for the last time. The Welsh pack transgressed in front of their own posts to allow Barkley to add a further kick, and in the dying seconds, Joe Worsley crossed in the corner to leave England 31–21 winners.

How to view it? That was a problem that plainly confused more experienced observers than myself. Some saw it as a sign of a continuing Welsh revival, some of English decline, and some both. It was difficult to say, but I thought England won without playing well, which is, as football managers like to tell you, the sign of a good side. Then again, if they're a good side, why aren't they playing well? Football managers never get round to explaining that bit, I've noticed.

Over in Dublin, earlier in the day, the Irish had managed to stay just about upright in a horrendous gale in order to beat the Italians in a game made all but unplayable by the wind, while the following day, the French beat the Scots 31–0. In the last minute, the Scots found themselves on the French line, although whether by accident or design wasn't clear. The commentator was almost urging them on: 'Can they claim a score, just to send the crowd home with half a smile on their face?' That was where Scottish rugby had reached – getting beaten 31–5 would have been a reason to skip away from Murrayfield, whistling that things were starting to look up. Having hit the bottom, they'd started to dig.

The results left the championship on what someone described that evening as a 'three-way knife edge'. I hope they never carve my Sunday roast for me. On a Saturday night, which is a bloody stupid time to stage a Six Nations game, although slightly better than a Sunday lunch-time, which is just obscene, the title would be decided.

Of course, television had made the decision, in advance of the tournament, based on what they assumed would be a Grand Slam decider. If for no other reason than he'd upset the plans of a television executive who thought it OK to tinker with tradition, I'll always remember Girvan Dempsey's try fondly. As he slid into the corner to beat England, a large chunk of the reason for having the game at eight in the evening slid out of the window.

So, mathematically at least, any one of three sides could have ended up lifting the Six Nations trophy. Ireland needed to beat Scotland by some bizarre margin and rely on England winning by less than seven points, or some such quadratic equation, so they were long shots, but if England won by more than eight and Ireland failed to deliver, Woodward and his men hoisted the cup. If they fell short, or if the French claimed victory, the trophy was coming to Paris with the England team and staying there.

Personally, I wanted everyone to feel as confused by this points-scoring system as I did. In a perfect world, the Irish would win by about 49, England by 7 and the whole of the Stade de France would be left waiting and bemused as to who got the trophy. Eventually, a little man with a calculator could arrive on the pitch and lift the arm of the winning captain, as if announcing a points decision after a closely contested boxing match.

Part of the equation went tumbling down in late afternoon when the Irish claimed their first Triple Crown for almost 20 years, brushing aside a Scottish side which continued its woeful tournament by subsiding 39–16. The margin was insufficiently large to leave Brian O'Driscoll's men at the top of the final table, but the result ensured that two of rugby's most famous and revered prizes were handed out straight after the game. In addition to Ireland's prize, the Scots collected the wooden spoon, which was just reward for a season where they looked short of inspiration and genuine class from the first moment to the last.

It left the focus on the evening kick-off, as the French went in search of World Cup revenge, a Grand Slam and the adulation of a nation, while the English went in search of the form which had eluded them for much of the campaign. The months since Sydney had seen Woodward's side battle to rediscover the resilience they had shown to take them to the top of the world, with retirements and injuries robbing them of key figures. There was also the issue of tiredness, both mental and physical. Returning to England and playing again within days was much commented upon when the side first returned home from the World Cup – almost in a stiff upper lip, no point in complaining style.

The papers enjoyed having new, clean-cut sporting heroes, and their insatiable work ethic was all part of the image created for them.

In reality, though, it was inconceivable that some kind of tiredness, some level of fatigue, wouldn't end up affecting them – if nothing else, emotionally. They had been forced to mount unofficial defences of their title within a couple of months of winning it, and the exertions of that were still all too evident. The French, by comparison, were driven by the memory of failure. A team on the way to their peak, they viewed England, rightly or wrongly, as a side sliding down the other side. The Six Nations was their opportunity to demonstrate how badly they had short-changed themselves in that semi-final defeat.

In the commentary box, as, in addition to the 80,000 in the stadium, a Saturday night audience waited to watch the contest in homes, pubs and bars, Eddie Butler was gently limbering up. As Beethoven's 'Ode to Joy' reached the end of a short refrain, the former Welsh forward offered his first attacking flurry of the night:

'Beethoven's "Ode to Joy". Well, it'll be anything but joyful out there. A hundred years ago, England and France signed the Entente Cordiale, a pact of non-aggression. It will be anything but cordial out there as well.'

Compared to the preparation I suspect went into Eddie's Anglo-French play on words, even Woodward's meticulously prepared troops looked like they were doing it off the cuff. His co-commentator, Brian Moore, who glories in the memory of previous front-row battles with the French, was saving his entry into the world of wordplay for a little later – a full 55 seconds after the opening whistle, in fact. As a move broke down, Lawrence Dallaglio found himself exchanging shoves and stares with the French number 8, Imanol Harinordoquy.

'Here we go!' Moore announced, breathless with excitement at what was the most minor of disagreements. Indeed, in many of those pubs and bars showing the game (and possibly some of the homes) there were probably more serious affrays taking place as he spoke. 'It's all kicking off, and Alain Rolland is going to try to bring sense to it. Oh, it's Harry Ordinary, as Lawrence Dallaglio likes to call him.'

If Dallaglio does have a penchant for playing games with the names of his opponents, this wasn't one of his more inspired choices. Olly Barkley missed the resultant penalty, France, through the sheer power of their pack, grabbed the game by the scruff of the neck, and Lawrence was kept rather too busy to come up with any more engaging nicknames. Dimitri Yachvili, who enjoyed a stunning evening at scrum-half for Bernard Laporte's side, knocked over a penalty after 20 minutes to send France ahead, before creating a try as crisp in execution as it was impudent in conception.

As the ball was recycled back on the left-hand edge of the English 22, Yachvili stepped into the fly-half role and swung a punt over to the far corner. English heads spun to watch it skid out of play, to be greeted with the sight of Mr Ordinary, having ghosted from a point a yard onside, standing and waiting in the furthest corner of the in-goal area. Harry allowed the ball to bounce, summoned it to his midriff like an owner calling for an errant puppy, and put it down with the minimum of fuss. As someone pointed out, he would have had time to autograph it first. Such was the timing of the operation, he probably could have added a dedication.

As the French pack rumbled relentlessly on, Yachvili added a couple more penalties before conjuring up another moment of footballing genius to bring the stadium to its feet. Barkley had just stroked over a penalty with what looked set to be the last score of the half, before making a hash of the restart and allowing the French to trundle the ball to within yards of the point where the first try was born. As the ball popped back, the scrum-half eschewed the opportunity to send it cross field and opted for a dart down the blind side. With a jab of the foot, the ball bobbled into the in-goal area, and with Jason Robinson hopelessly out of position at full-back, Yachvili scampered after his prize, landing on it to earn, in the shadow of the interval, the second French try of the half.

A gloriously flighted conversion sent the home side in 21–3 ahead, and left Woodward facing a team talk which made the problems of Wales and Western Samoa in the World Cup seem tame in comparison. Shortly after the break, an unusually subdued Will Greenwood was replaced by Mike Catt, and as they had on occasions in the World Cup, England began to rediscover some of their previously absent cohesion. Barkley and Yachvili swapped penalties, only for the French to make a pig's ear of the restart and allow Catt to spiral a long pass into the hands of Ben Cohen, who slid over in the corner.

Barkley missed the kick, and as the French pack continued to dominate, it appeared that the moment had been no more than a false dawn, but there was still time for French nerves to suffer more torment. Barkley's penalty eight minutes from time offered the visitors a chink of light, and then, with just four minutes left to play, it developed into genuine hope. Josh Lewsey rounded off a fine counter-attack to score close to the right corner, and eventually a conversion found its target to leave the French with just a three-point lead.

That they were forced to live with hearts in mouths to such an extent, having dominated for so long, seemed slightly absurd, but even taking into account the Ireland game, England had spent too long refusing to countenance defeat to go out with anything less than an almighty fight. Ultimately, however, it was a French victory, and a deserved one, as Paris rose to acclaim a Grand Slam claimed with flair, imagination, and a host of other admirable attributes French sides have made their own over the years. Four months after they stood on a podium to be crowned champions of the world, Woodward's side stood on the turf and watched as the French were crowned champions of the northern hemisphere.

It had been a truly great contest, like watching a young heavyweight destined for greatness, hanging on in the face of a brave rearguard action to claim the crown from a proud and determined champion. It had also, after years of southern-hemisphere dominance, made clear that the finest two sides in the world were very much located in the north. Had England faced anyone other than the French, they would have come out of the game on top, and there wasn't another side on the planet who would have been able to stand in the way of the French.

England, despite their second-half fight-back, had been murdered – by three points. The scoreboard might provide the definitive way of representing the result, but it doesn't always manage, thankfully for authors and journalists alike, to tell even half of the story. The English media were united in their opinion of the contest, and nobody found it within themselves to view the final scoreline as anything other than misleading.

Stephen Jones in the *Sunday Times* talked of England being 'heavily defeated everywhere but on the scoreboard', while Mick Cleary in the *Telegraph* echoed a similar sentiment: 'The scoreboard may have spoken of a mere three-point deficit. By any other name, it was a three-point stuffing.'

As Laporte revealed afterwards: 'On Saturday morning, I had good luck messages from the coaches of Australia and New Zealand urging us to finally beat the English. The whole world is fed up with England winning. Last night, we brought pleasure to the whole world.'

Woodward was well aware of the wishes of the rest of the rugby-playing planet, but equally, he knew just what an achievement it had been to make them want to defeat his side quite so fiercely. They used to affect an air of indifference about England, enjoying asking what all the fuss was about. Nobody pretended not to care any more. Every time a cheer for the French came from down under, it was an admission of how Woodward had succeeded, even if the thought did little to cheer him.

'I've got to earn my money now, look in the mirror and take responsibility. But if someone at the start of the season had offered me a World Cup triumph with two defeats in the Six Nations, then I'd have shaken their hand very firmly.'

The French captain, Fabien Pelous, maybe showing that there was some life left in the spirit of the Entente Cordiale, was quick to underline the truth of Woodward's words: 'It's good that we're champions of Europe, but they're still world champions. This doesn't change anything.'

In the space of six weeks, Woodward had seen his side lauded, rewarded, queried, criticised and questioned. I remembered his phrase about the time to head down to the pub being after a defeat, rather than a victory. After the roller-coaster ride he had endured over the course of the last few matches, someone had better get the beers in. Clive had a lot of drinking to do.

VIII

Grass roots and muddy knees

I felt like Mr Creosote: Monty Python's ever-expanding diner who finally exploded after one 'wafer-thin mint' too many. I had watched three rugby matches so far, and if I so much as attempted another one, something terrible was going to happen. A minuscule slice of blind-side run? A mere taster of drop goal? A jus of outside break? No, I'd had enough, and was ready to burst. Besides, I'd just made myself look like an idiot. Again.

It was a crisp, windy, Twickenham afternoon and I was sitting in the press box, watching the third of four consecutive schoolboy games. Alone. Completely and utterly alone, actually, without another person in the row of seating I had selected as my own. In fact, there wasn't another person in the entire block in which I resided, nor, come to think of it, in that particular tier of the stand.

Distracted by this realisation, I cast my eyes around the huge sweep of seating, wrapped around three sides of the ground in a vast, uninterrupted mass of green, flip-up chairs, all standing to attention, displaying their numbers to the world. To walk around, from one side to the other, would probably involve a stroll of almost 300 yards, every step flanked by thousands of empty seats. And I had it all to myself.

Across the pitch from me, an audience of two or three thousand people was shuffling in and out at the end of each game. They were either being replaced by others in different-coloured shirts, or performing a quick-change act once an hour to make the next set of players feel properly at home. I think, on balance, that I'd incline towards the former. Either way, the end result was that while 10,000 fans may have turned up during the course of the day, only a fraction of that number seemed to be in the ground at any one time.

I'd left the warmth of the rugby writers' centre about ten minutes earlier, simply to avoid being offered any more coffee. I was the only member of the media there, and I think someone had forgotten to reduce the numbers when the staff rota had been drawn up. As a result, I was the subject of the sort of attention and service that only minor royals or Oscar winners ever get to experience.

A crack waiting staff was, well, waiting on my every move, keen to break the boredom of a slow day by attempting to guess my next need seconds ahead of their colleagues. Every inward breath was greeted with an invitation to have 'another coffee?' and to be honest, by the time lunch-time arrived, I was already on my way to a caffeine overdose, buzzing away like an amphetamine fiend.

Unfortunately, I had neglected to take into account the effect of the wind, especially when it's blowing hard into the open mouth of a stadium which wraps around three quarters of the pitch. By the time it reached me, the gale had bent its way around two corners and, unable to escape the confines of the stand, seemed intent on aiming itself directly at anyone in its path. God, you'd have to be stupid to sit out there.

One of the other minor problems, as I discovered, was that the typhoon had a habit of picking up anything in its path and carrying it along at dizzying speeds. This appeared, in the main, to mean plastic pint glasses, dropped in their hundreds by previous visitors on occasions when the crowd numbered rather more than it did today. I sat there, eyes streaming from the swirling dust and grit, and tried to keep a careful watch out of the corner of my eye for low-flying pint pots. I don't know what was more amusing, actually – the sight of me ducking under one, like a batsman avoiding a Joel Garner bouncer, or the strangely cartoon-like 'boink' sound as I was caught unawares and one rebounded from the side of my skull.

In between this, my notes would occasionally flutter off in the general direction of Richmond, and the wind chill meant my nose began to run like a four year old with a bad cold. My numb fingers were busy dropping pens, mobile phones and loose change onto the ground under the desk, from where I emerged, inevitably banging my head on the way, as a security guard wandered over.

'Are you supposed to be here, sir?' he queried, braced against the gale, before catching a glimpse of the plastic accreditation badge on a length of string around my neck, which was threatening to take an eye out with each successive manic flap. 'Sorry,' he said, 'didn't see the pass'. He stood there for another ten seconds or so and took in the unfolding scene. I dropped my pen again and ducked under another pint glass while attempting to wipe my nose, with disastrous consequences I think it's better not to describe.

'Are you all right, sir?' he asked, with just a hint of concern in his voice. I thought I detected a fear that Care in the Community had stretched to the Twickenham press box. 'I'm fine, thanks,' I replied, with an excess of good humour I hoped would distract from my horribly dishevelled appearance. 'I'm just writing a book.'

That was the low point. I knew what I was doing, and even I thought I sounded mad. He had just stumbled along, and already he was more concerned for me than threatened by me. And the wind blew on. I remembered playing the game as a schoolboy – being cold, standing on the wing and suffering the odd stare from passers-by who worried whether you were in your right mind. It had been years since I'd experienced that sort of concerned stare, and here I was, two days into my revisitation of schools rugby, and it was happening all over again.

'I'm just writing a book,' I muttered to myself after he had made his excuses and left, shaking my head at my own stupidity, and wondering why I was ever let out on my own. It wasn't the looking like a fool that troubled me, though. Nor the flying glasses, watering eyes, freezing fingers, caffeine overdose or sticky bus ticket which had stuck to the back of my hand. What really bothered me was that I was enjoying myself. In fact, I wouldn't have swapped this for anywhere else in the world. In the circumstances, if that thought doesn't trouble you, then your problems are bigger than you thought they were . . .

The focus of my attention, and the reason behind my day-long spectating binge, was the Daily Mail Schools Cup. The final stages of this extraordinary tournament were being contested on the first Saturday of April, just as the rest of the sporting nation turned its attention to the Grand National, England's historic test victory over the West Indies and the Manchester United and Arsenal FA Cup semi-final. Such is the nature of sport, though, that no matter what is happening elsewhere, the event in which you find yourself involved tends to dominate the attention to the exclusion of virtually everything else, and rightly so.

It was certainly the case as far as I was concerned. Having turned down the chance to go and cover several different football matches, I found myself temporarily annoyed when the screen in the media centre was switched away from coverage of the game out on the Twickenham turf, and onto the clash between Arsene Wenger and Sir Alex Ferguson. Sorry, between Arsenal and United. The reason for this change in priorities, however, is rooted in the very foundations of why we watch sport – I'd found a side to support.

The tournament is divided into two age groups – Under-15 and Under-18 – with the finals day at Twickenham reserved for finals in each age group, and a Vase final, involving sides who take part in a knockout competition after losing in the first round of the Cup. The games are half an hour each way for the younger age group and five minutes more in the older. It has become, rightly so as well, the country's main schoolboy rugby competition.

On the day before the teams were due in Twickenham, I travelled to St Albans to meet with Adam Lowles, who coaches St Columba's College. St Columba's were due to meet Prince Henry's Grammar School from Otley, near Leeds, in the following day's Vase final. I'd convinced myself that the school were going to present me with a decent story about the day ahead – an angle. I wanted to discover the difference the World Cup had made to this most impressionable age group, and this was, my refined journalistic instinct told me, a school that could supply me with some answers.

Located about a mile and a half from the local station, I warmed up for my encounter by proving my map-reading skills were up to scratch, when I confidently reckoned it to be no more than 800 yards away, and downhill. Don't ask how I worked out up- or downhill from a street map, I just had a hunch – a bad one, as it turned out, and one I mused over several times as I slogged up an endless incline.

As I reached the school, I saw someone who was obviously one of the players being dropped off by his mum, about a hundred yards short of the main entrance. The reasons for the unusual drop-off point became clear when she insisted on giving him a huge hug and kiss goodbye as he stood there, checking desperately over his shoulder to see that his mates weren't watching. I mentioned it much later on to Adam, who told me that the lad was 'probably academically the brightest lad in the team'. As I imagined the stick a squad of nervous 18-year-old rugby players might have given a 'mummy's boy', I pondered that it wasn't only in the classroom where he showed his ability to think clearly.

I stood and chatted with Adam outside his office as he double-checked the kit for the following day. It was a toss-up as to who was more uneasy – he was taking his team to Twickenham the next day, and I was remembering too many tellings off from years ago, delivered as I stood outside a teacher's office. I thought I'd start with some safe ground, making consoling noises about what a dreadful game their opening round defeat must have been, when they went down 3–0 at home.

'Well, there's not much you can do when it's the toss of a coin,' Adam reflected.

'No, I suppose not,' I mused, as my brain suddenly became aware of the fact that I hadn't got the slightest clue what he was talking about.

'The pitch was too hard, you see. In fact, we hardly played before Christmas because of it. Everywhere around here was unplayable. There was one ground that remained all right, but we heard it was costing them almost £4,000 a week just in water bills. In the end, we had to go into the office there and toss a coin. We lost, so it went down as 3–0 to the other side and that was it for the Cup, we were out in the first round.'

I felt something slide out of the door behind me, and disappear across the sports pitches beyond, laughing. It was my refined journalistic instinct, my 'nose for a story', walking out in disgust. I was meeting with a side playing in the 'losers' final, who hadn't actually lost. Their PE master had called wrongly when offered heads or tails, and they were out. If the ground was hard, the circumstances in which they lost were surely harder still.

I pondered what might have happened to others in the same circumstances. Obviously, Claudio Ranieri would have been out on his ear for failing to produce the right results, but then again, even had he called correctly, they would have got rid of him for not choosing in a sufficiently entertaining manner. Sir Clive, on the other hand, would have prepared himself properly. A few weeks with a probability awareness coach, a couple of sessions with a head and tails development trainer, and Woodward would have been safely through. I opted not to share these musings with Adam, lest I followed my recently departed journalistic instinct back out into the wider world.

As the equipment was squirreled away into two bulging kitbags (does every school rugby-team kitbag include walkie-talkies these days?), I was struck by the attention to detail. More pertinently, perhaps, I became immediately aware of the tension apparent in Adam himself. His players were going to be nervous, and naturally so, but their coach and teacher was clearly working hard to maintain an impression of outward calm. This mattered to him a lot, and it was reassuring to see. Besides, if he'd pretended it didn't matter a jot to him who won, I wouldn't have believed him anyway.

Having learned the game in his native Scotland, although the accent has disappeared over the years, Adam remembers the lessons taught to him by Jim Telfer, his first coach, only too well. Given his description of the forthright way those lessons were expressed, that's not, on reflection, all that strange. Along the way, though, it seems a love of coaching has risen to the surface.

'I used to play a lot, and would still like to, but it's difficult when I'm coaching here every Saturday morning. I played at Twickenham myself once, in an East Midlands side with Steve Thompson, the year he was moved to hooker. I might have mentioned that to the lads once or twice.

'At the moment, they're fine, and I think they're going to be very bubbly today and full of things, but the test will come when they get closer to the game, and how they cope with things tomorrow morning when they've got time to kill. It's obvious they'll be excited, but I've got to try to make sure that they don't end up climbing the walls by half nine, because they'll have nothing left by kick-off.'

I got the impression he was talking about himself just as much as he was talking about the team, trying to move into a state of calmness that was, despite his best efforts, eluding him at present. Even with term having ended two days earlier, it was easy to sense the excitement in the air.

The school had given away 600 tickets for the day, and another 400 had gone subsequently, so there was going to be huge support from their friends, colleagues and families. In the life of a schoolboy rugby player, and an inexperienced and ambitious coach, this was a very big moment.

It's these times when I start to feel very self-conscious about doing my job. The competition had been running for six months now, and was just about to reach boiling point, after simmering away for that entire period. Right at the end, just before the big day, they'd had a call from me, asking if I could, not to put too fine a point on it, hang around, get in the way, have a bit of a nose about and ask a pile of questions they didn't have time to answer.

The temptation to tell me to bugger off must have been immense, but Adam, and indeed everyone I met at the school, acted as if the thought had never crossed their minds. Polite to a fault, and eternally welcoming, they were a fine advertisement for a private school system in which I'd never participated and about which I'd always harboured slightly clichéd doubts. I got lucid and intelligent answers, and people stopped to think before speaking, not through wariness, but out of a desire to give a well-thought-out response. They were much nicer people than I, in my mildly bigoted way, had thought them likely to be, and if it's embarrassing to admit it, it's worse to think that I ever harboured such thoughts.

The signs of prosperity were there all right, and you couldn't fail to spot them. Parents dropped players off in rather superior cars, and the tours they'd enjoyed as a side over the last two years had been to South Africa and Australia (I went to Blackpool for a weekend with my school side) but they were decent, welcoming people. There was also an issue in my mind as to how much of the wider social environment they saw. Adam explained that they had been national basketball champions many times in the past, and it was only later that I tumbled that this probably meant national independent schools champions. Not a tournament that brings you into contact with the best basketball players Lambeth or Moss Side has to offer, but it was an achievement nonetheless.

The '60s buildings which housed the changing-rooms were far from ivory towers, however, and it could have been, at a brief glance, a well-run state school. It was a feeling confirmed for me by the senior master, a large, welcoming man, incongruously dressed in shorts and a Hawaiian shirt, who ambled over and introduced himself as Tony Smith.

'We're a young school, just about 50 years, which, compared to the other local independent school, which has been here for more than 800, is practically nothing. We know what we set out to do, though, which is to be an old-fashioned grammar school. Once upon a time, let's be honest, you wouldn't have had to pay for this sort of education.'

He'd put his finger straight on it. It was a bit old fashioned, but only in as much as it had retained all the things that were best from the education system of that age. The kids were being pleasant and lively, and the relationship between them and their teachers was plainly a healthy one. I liked Tony, even after only the briefest of conversations. He was a rugby nut, typical of a certain type of player from a certain age, and he knew what he was talking about.

'The game's done very well in the last few years, generally as well as here at St Columba's, and it's been assisted by the way bloody footballers keep dragging their game through the mud. We're basically a basketball school, but there are lads out there who came from some very ordinary backgrounds and got involved in rugby because we were able to offer it to them.

'Tomorrow, they'll play in a national final at Twickenham, and they wouldn't have done that otherwise. I think we can look back on that and be proud, and I hope they look back on it and feel proud too, because they should.'

And he was right. The 'lads' out there on the training pitch in front of me were about to go and do something they'd remember for the rest of their lives. I instantly felt guilty about smiling inwardly at their nerves, even if it was affectionate rather than mocking, as well as taking up their time, but none of them seemed to mind. It was the sort of welcome I'd been believing rugby offered when I started my journey and, yet again, it was being proved to be true.

It wasn't all triumphs and beams, though. One of the players, a tall second row called Joe Mansfield, sat there looking straight ahead, flexing his right leg gently. He had twisted it in a PE exam a few days earlier and now, 24 hours before the biggest game of his life, it was playing him up. PE exams were a new thing to me, evidently joining the curriculum after I left the education system. Joe looked like he wished he'd never heard of the course either.

'How does it feel?' I asked, as much to break the ice created when a stranger stumbles into a moment of private despair as anything else. 'A bit dodgy,' he grimaced, before adding, 'But thanks for asking,' with a smile. By definition, I had been talking to people in the face of defeat as well as victory over the last few months, but none could have been feeling worse than Joe did at that point, and none could have been more polite. The next day, I watched him hobble off after about 20 minutes, and felt genuinely upset for him.

Adam took an hour-long training session on the pitches overlooked by St Albans Cathedral, along with two other coaches – Daniel Brown, an engaging, almost stereotypical Aussie, and Ian Devereux – who between them tried to polish a lineout that was nearly, but not quite, working properly. Meanwhile, Adam was off on another pitch with the back division, who were demonstrating the benefits of playing basketball in order to improve your handling skills.

I wasn't sure how well the basketball link was going to work, to be honest, but then I may have been prejudiced against new-fangled coaching ideas at an early age. I have some painful, personal experience of how rugby coaches love to embrace a passing trend, regardless of its suitability to the players in hand. Having started to play the game as an eleven year old, I spent four or five happy years playing classically simple rugby. The forwards won the ball, the scrum-half passed it out, and away it went down the line, until the winger ran into touch or someone knocked on, causing the whole process to start all over again. It wasn't inspired or particularly complicated, but we all knew where we stood (usually unwittingly offside) and cared little for the tactical thinking and planning adopted by other, more sophisticated sides.

As I recall, kicking was not so much frowned upon as actively barred, as the idea of losing control of the ball in any way other than a completely involuntary fashion was enough to earn a lengthy lecture from the teacher in charge. Simple was definitely best. Tales were told of props who had impressed at selection matches, without ever touching the ball – indeed, they stressed that props who actually tried to touch the ball were probably neglecting some other, more mundane part of their game. It was a different age.

Then, as the '80s drifted into their latter half, the All Blacks became the dominant force in world rugby. Our coach, evidently captivated by their success, decided we would try to ape their style. The New Zealanders revelled in the rolling maul, picking the ball from the back of one maul and rumbling into the next, mob-handed and forcing their way down the field in a series of group sorties by the pack. We, he explained as we assembled back for the start of the new season, would follow suit.

Now, the sight of Richard Loe, Buck Shelford and their ilk rolling remorselessly forwards was undoubtedly an impressive one, but we were a side of rather less daunting physical stature. The year I reached the fifth form and was allowed to play for the first team was the same year my school dispensed with a sixth form, and with it, about a dozen of the players who would have played for the side. As a result, we played against sides two or even three years older than us week in, and unsuccessful week out.

As if that wasn't bad enough, we did it in this new, All Black style, so beloved of our coach, which was about as far removed from an appropriate tactical approach for a young, continually out-muscled side as it was possible to get. I remember standing at full-back in early September, watching a number 8 pick the ball up, join forces with a flanker or two and take one step forwards and several straight back. At this point, he would get fed up of being battered and slip the ball to another forward, who would undergo a similar fate.

These days, people would describe these actions as 'phases' of play. Back then, it would have been more accurate to describe it as a succession of tired schoolboys taking it in turns to get shunted back towards their own goal line. By the time two or three of these non-drives had been expertly executed, we had generally lost about 20 yards, with the opposition never failing to marvel at our self-destructive tactics. By about December, I think I finally got a pass, as a member of the pack eventually got fed up of getting battered into reverse, and threw the ball back about as far as he could manage.

It must have been as comical to witness as it was baffling and painful to execute, but we had no say in it. This was how the All Blacks did it, and they had just won the World Cup – logic dictated that we must surely follow suit, and nobody was offered the chance to disagree. It was my first experience of a coaching cult causing sheer, unmitigated chaos, and of how a system adopted by the best, maybe wasn't always that suitable for players of lesser stature. At least at St Columba's they had physical appropriateness on their side, as I looked out on a squad all of whom appeared to be at least six inches taller than I'd been at the same age. If I reflected that policemen were looking younger as well, I must have quickly discarded the thought, aware of the premature ageing process it was representing.

Adam had tried to play down the links between Woodward's systems and the methods used in schools rugby – 'I don't know if he's so much a coach, as a man manager' – but it was looking fairly familiar to me.

One centre was squat, taking the crash ball and slipping the pass, while the other was tall and rangy, looking to exploit any gaps caused by the man inside him. The wingers and the full-back were virtually interchangeable, and the scrum-half sniped neatly around and practised moaning about the opposition back row being offside. A ringer for Matt Dawson, I thought, perhaps a little unkindly.

And the fly-half? The Wilkinson clone, and the man around whom it would all be built? He'd had to leave early, to go and have his photo taken with the other captains at Twickenham. All right, maybe it wasn't just like Woodward would have done things. I can't see Wilkinson either asking or getting permission to slide off early for a few snaps with the other side . . .

Having met them, concluded they were a fine choice as my side to follow for the day, and wished Adam well, I left them to it. I had intruded enough, taken up too much of their time and goodwill already, and felt they needed to be left to get on without the distraction of strangers. Besides, it was going to take me several hours to manage the hike back to the station.

As I trudged along, I passed a barber's shop, complete with a series of black and white photographs in the window of famous styles they could recreate for you, atop your very own head. Michael Owen was a strange choice, perhaps, and I wasn't sure how many were going to opt for the George Michael, just post-Wham phase, but it was the third option that grabbed my attention.

I could envisage it now, sitting down in the seat, exchanging niceties and describing the work you wanted done. Not the Owen, thanks, a bit passé, perhaps, and no offence, but the George Michael doesn't do it for me. No, I'll have the third one – that's the one – the Jonny Wilkinson. There in all his black and white glory, inviting you in to copy his haircut. I'd spent weeks watching kickers copy him, and now barbers were doing it too.

Add it to the list, and someone call his agent. Jonny's just become the first rugby haircut that anyone outside of Wormwood Scrubs' F Wing has ever expressed a desire to copy. Strange days indeed.

The next day dawned, and the trip to Twickenham took me back along the same route I had travelled less than a month previously, when watching England being beaten by the Irish. The same route, perhaps, but looking nothing like it did previously, divested of the throngs of people and paraphernalia of a Six Nations encounter. For a start, I claimed a seat on the train without requiring the sort of speed off the mark Jason Robinson would envy. I couldn't, it would appear, though, avoid rugby fans, even if they did take on a rather different appearance to the last lot I encountered here.

As I sat and waited for the train to depart from Waterloo, three girls got on, dropping huge hints as to their upbringing before they even opened their mouths, thanks to their strings of pearls and upturned shirt collars. I think the attire was supposed to be ironic, but the accents, unmistakably, were not. Any residual doubt as to their background was swiftly removed, as they began to talk in that desperately loud, clipped manner only those of a certain class can muster.

I can't quite claim that the following are snippets I 'overheard', as it would have been impossible to miss them, such was the volume at which they were communicated to the carriage. Suffice to say they didn't seem to be suffering from a lack of self-confidence. 'We could call Georgie – her father has flats in Barnes.' 'Have you seen Josh, he's divine, and Ryan and Jamie are just lush.' And the lasting mating call of the upper-class adolescent: 'I need a Marlboro Light.'

I was starting to reminisce warmly about the joys of having my head stuck in someone's armpit on the Twickenham train, a thought which scared me sufficiently to clamp my headphones back on instead, blanking out the rest of their conversational offerings. I left them at Twickenham station, asking each other where the stadium was, as they stood under a huge sign marked 'Twickenham Stadium'. Somewhere, three sets of parents are entitled to cast sideways glances at the geography department.

I strolled down towards the stadium, enjoying the absence of touts, looking at the empty front gardens of houses which had once been offering all manner of snacks and feasts for sale. I pondered knocking on the door of one of them and asking if the bacon sandwich offer was still on, but thought better of it. Equally, I favoured the pavements over the middle of the road, where huge hordes of people had plodded their way onwards three weeks ago. On a lesser match day, with the roads open to traffic, it's a slightly less risky proposition.

It is, it has to be said, a decidedly mixed experience, watching the very best of the country's schoolboy rugby talent, especially as you slide the wrong side of 30 and realise that you're twice as old as most of the players on display. The signs of the game's development, though, are everywhere. Even among the younger age groups, back-row moves set the platform for multi-phase rumbles downfield, while everyone suddenly seems to be adopting the same style when they place-kick.

Adam Lowles had told me the day before: 'I've not seen an under-12 all year who didn't join the hands together, hold them in front of him, and take two, slow looks at the posts before kicking. And I've not seen many who don't throw the kicking tee back to the sideline after, and pretend not to look surprised when it goes over.' He wasn't wrong, either. To the Ali shuffle, the Cruyff turn and the Fosbury flop, you can now add the Wilkinson settle-in prayer, owl head turn and quietly satisfied nod. Perhaps the name needs work.

St Columba's and Prince Henry's kicked off at 2 p.m., once the younger age group had played out their Vase and Cup finals. In the first game of the morning, St Benedict's from Cumbria, which featured players who grew up in league and union, itself unbelievable at Twickenham a decade or so earlier, eased past Lawrence Sheriff school. Lawrence Sheriff were overturned by the Cumbrians thanks to two fine individual tries – as it transpired, the first two of many.

Indeed, it soon became clear to me that individual tries might become something of a feature of the day, as schoolboys found the temptation to 'have a go' themselves, rather than surrender to the overlap outside them, almost impossible to resist. For every score I watched, at least three more went begging, as passes failed to materialise, but the sheer delight of the scorers never failed to raise a smile.

The mixture of delight and terror on the face of Marc Shackley, the St Benedict's inside-centre, as he scampered to the corner, was enough to cheer even the most hardened cynic. When Ben Bateson stormed through the middle from the back of a scrum to make the game safe, you knew you were watching one of the great moments of his young life, and the celebrations were lovely to watch.

Both players stared up into the huge, empty stands behind the posts, and for a moment, before their teammates swamped them, you knew that, in a private fantasy world, they'd just won a World Cup, deep into injury time. The Lawrence Sheriff players had blue and white shirts on, but in the minds of the scorers, they were yellow Australian jerseys, or All Blacks, French or Springboks. This was real fantasy rugby.

The roar of the crowd was replaced by a shriller, slightly higher-pitched acclaim, as schoolfriends made heroes of classmates, and memories were created at every turn. It wasn't just the kids, either – every teacher who stepped out onto the pitch was, for a moment at least, Clive Woodward. It may have been the hormones rampaging around the stadium, but it was, despite the empty spaces, a strangely highly charged atmosphere. The largest crowd of their lives was made to look tiny by the mass of vacant green seating around them, but you knew that not one of them would change it for the world.

Even the oddities seemed to be in keeping with the occasion. Everywhere you looked, there were advertisements for Tetley's bitter, despite all the players and most of the fans being too young to drink it. It acted as a sort of reminder: 'We have grown ups here too, sometimes.' Today, though, the new generation had well and truly taken over.

The next clash of the day saw John Cleveland College, a state school from Leicester, send the public school might of Sherborne School from Dorset home as losers. Some desperate tackling, two lovely tries from a full-back called Richard Durose and a spectacular long-range effort from back-row forward Matthew Lamley sent them home as 17–12 winners, in a game that featured everything you could reasonably ask for from a rugby match. So, John Cleveland and St Benedict's, both from the state sector, had overturned private schools to claim their reward. Maybe the game was opening out to a new audience more efficiently than I'd even begun to think.

Regardless of where they came from, it was where they went to, literally so, that summed the day up. As soon as the games were over, celebrations were interrupted in order that a 'tunnel' might be made for the opposition to walk through on their way off the pitch. In the middle of their highest highs and lowest lows, the players clapped each other off, the youngest players I'd seen so far, upholding one of the oldest traditions.

Throughout the course of the day, I saw neither a punch thrown nor a decision questioned. I spotted not a single piece of violence or gamesmanship, and heard not a moan or a complaint. The rugby was good – very good, in fact – horribly better than anything I'd ever played when at school, but the attitude and the discipline, the respect for the game, was even better.

And so, with Robbie Williams blaring out, offering to entertain us (is it illegal to stage a sporting event without him being played these days?), perched in my own personal wind tunnel, the game I'd come to see got underway. I remembered Adam's words: 'It'll be about how they contain their nerves as much as anything,' and found myself getting nervous on their behalf. As it transpired, with good reason.

The opening exchanges set the tone for the rest of the contest. St Columba's lost possession in the opening minute, as a previously secure and solid centre managed to knock on the most straightforward pass he'd receive all day. At the resultant scrum, the Prince Henry's scrum-half tapped the prop on the shoulder with the ball, in keeping with the well-established way of telling him it was on its way into the front row, only to lose his grip thanks to the nerves, and drop it. I watched it bounce to the floor, leaving a bemused set of forwards wondering just where it had got to. They all looked too nervous to raise so much as a smile at his misfortune, knowing that they were more than likely to manage the same thing themselves if presented with an opportunity.

The referee sensibly allowed him to have another go, and as the Prince Henry's back division shunted the ball to the wing, St Columba's made a pig's ear of their tackling, leaving a young winger called Tom Carrol to nip into the corner for the try. In a swirling wind, inches in from the left touchline, I gave Danny Care no chance whatsoever of getting the conversion attempt anywhere close, thus offering further evidence of why I'm not much of a pundit. It split the uprights, as did a penalty five minutes later, and the team I'd been an avid fan of for all of 24 hours, were having what I think we can safely describe as a 'nightmare start'.

Care, as I discovered, played scrum-half for England's Under-18 clubs side, and was stepping into a fly-half role that was relatively unusual to him. Well, you could have fooled me. I didn't see a better player all day and my admiration at his ability to squirm out of trouble and into space was complete when, just before the interval, he made the game virtually safe. Having appeared to have taken a bad blind-side option, he darted back off his right foot and cut through to touch down under the posts, sending his side into a 15–3 lead.

There was still time for memories to be made, even if the game already appeared lost, and Chris May left himself with a moment to treasure from the restart, crashing over for St Columba's to narrow the gap. The damage appeared to have been done, though, and in Care, Prince Henry's had a player who was more than capable of soaking up as much pressure as was required.

The gloriously named Boffa twins, Carlo and Paolo, kept bashing away down the middle, prop and hooker respectively and looking like they generated the sort of grocery bills that would give most people nightmares for weeks. So too did Ed Labinski, who had replaced the injured figure of Joe Mansfield, and insisted on hitting himself on the head to gee himself up. All of them were prepared to give their all to stop the trophy heading to Yorkshire and, for a brief period, Prince Henry's looked genuinely rattled. Adam and his fellow teachers must have the most physical basketball sides on the planet, if this lot are anything to go by.

It wasn't to be, though, and in all fairness, such was the maturity and composure of Care's performance, it would have been very harsh had he left on the losing side. They swapped penalties at the start of the half, but the gap refused to close any further, and despite a spirited last push, nine minutes of injury time and the sight of St Columba's forwards twice crossing the line only to be held up before grounding the ball, the Yorkshire side prevailed.

I felt for Adam and his players, but it was hard not to feel, and evidently harder still not to fall for the cliché, that the game as a whole had come out of the day better than any individual side. By the time the fourth game in a row got underway, and Colston's School began what would become a demolition of Barnard Castle, it was time to make a move – that Mr Creosote moment was approaching.

Adam and his team were down, but far from inconsolable. They'd played at Twickenham, after all, and they'd given a very fair account of themselves. There were things they could, I suspected, do a lot better, and mistakes they wouldn't repeat if given the chance to do it all again, but overall, they had nothing to be ashamed of and much from which to take pride.

Woodward and his side have certainly left their mark on schools rugby, even if some of the aspects of their play were copied more convincingly than others. The speed of the game, though, coupled with the power and size of the players, has increased dramatically since I was at school. In the space of 15 or 20 years, a faster, more dynamic and more demanding version of the sport has developed, while the spirit and sportsmanship have remained undimmed.

On the evidence I saw, schoolboy rugby, in terms of calibre if not numbers, appeared to be on the up. An England manager of the future will have some extraordinary players from which to choose. Some of the players I saw, as someone pointed out, would never play at Twickenham again. Maybe so, but the ones that do will have developed as players while watching some of the game's great role models. If success breeds success, I'd like to think I watched the earliest steps of some extraordinary careers.

If I ever recovered from my day in the wind tunnel, the future held much to look forward to.

IX

March 2004

The new month started almost as well as the last had finished as far as the Pertemps Bees were concerned, when the row over their prize money was finally resolved. Having been punished for their lack of Premiership status by having their winnings of 'up to £30,000' withheld, sanity prevailed and they were rewarded with a payment of £20,000. After his quarter-final error, Paul Honiss was not, we can safely assume, asked to make the final decision on the award.

Elsewhere, after common sense had reigned for Pertemps Bees, it was showing itself to be somewhat lacking slightly further up the scale. Rod Kafer, the Saracens coach, had been unhappy with the performance of referee Steve Leyshon during his side's defeat by Northampton in February.

Leyshon had asked Kafer to comment about exactly what it was in his performance that had caused such offence to be taken, and then, ironically enough, took offence at the comments. Leyshon reported Kafer to the RFU, and a disciplinary panel hearing the case imposed a six-week touchline ban on the coach.

'I'm disappointed that the ref has decided to make public the comments he asked me to make in private,' Kafer reflected, leaving the neutral in little doubt that 'disappointed' was too meek a word by far to convey exactly how he felt. He was backed up by his employers in a way that falls squarely into the 'half-hearted' category.

'We support the judicial process fully,' said Saracens chief executive Mark Sinderberry, 'but will seek further advice before making a decision on what course of action to follow.'

It may or may not be fair to imagine that the tribunal bore some resemblance to the court martial in which Edmund Blackadder stood accused of the horrific slaughter of Speckled Jim, the pigeon, but the suspicion lingers.

Panel chairman Commodore Jeff Blackett said, 'Verbal abuse of officials, even in private, must be prejudicial to the interests of the union and the game.

'However, we have given him credit for being the model of discrepancy [sic] in public.'

So, Kafer was discreet and got credit for it, the referee made it public, thus tarnishing the game in a way the RFU recognised Kafer had been keen not to, and Kafer is the one who ends up getting the ban. No, that Blackadder image isn't growing any fainter . . .

If Pertemps were quick, the £20,000 might just have credited their bank account by the time they travelled to Newcastle to play their semi-final. At least it would have provided a moment of consolation, as they were blown away 53–3, bringing to an end a Cup run touched with drama, controversy, romance and just about everything a Cup run requires to make it special. Newcastle would go on to play Sale at Twickenham as, helped by a Jason Robinson try, Sale had overcome Leeds 33–20 in the other semi, setting up a trip to London for two of the English game's further-flung outposts.

With the Six Nations taking up most of the attention and headlines, the domestic game was reduced, as it so often is, to a string of second teams playing each other, hoping to maintain the status quo until their established stars returned to action. Bath retained their place at the top of the table, while Leicester, after a dreadful start to the year, gradually returned to the safety of mid-table, battling through to the end of a season which would, by their own recent high standards and despite a late charge, go down as fairly forgettable.

Two failures rounded off the month, one at either end of the rugby-playing spectrum: firstly, as already detailed, the failure of Guy's

Hospital to overcome St Mary's in the UH Cup final, and secondly, what I shall refer to as the golden-boy hex.

Just months earlier, it was widely accepted that everything Jonny Wilkinson touched turned instantly to gold, before bisecting the nearest set of goalposts. Of late, though, he had remained on the sidelines as his shoulder recovered from the effects of surgery. In the end, Newcastle coach Rob Andrew was forced to utilise his talents in a purely public-relations capacity, dragging him off to New Zealand in a bid to persuade Rupeni Caucaunibuca to sign on the dotted line and follow them back to the north-east.

It wasn't the most successful trip. Caucaunibuca damaged a shoulder and needed an operation, ruling him out for as long as a year. One hoped that Wilkinson's in-built sense of confidence and optimism remained high. A lesser man could easily start to wonder whether he was becoming something of a jinx . . .

On a tragic note, the end of the month saw the horribly untimely death of young Irish flanker John McCall. Playing for the Irish Under-19 side in the Under-19 World Cup tournament in Durban, he had collapsed on the pitch shortly after winning the ball at a lineout, and was pronounced dead a few hours later in hospital. A post-mortem showed a freak cardiac failure had been responsible.

I didn't know John McCall. Indeed, I'd never heard of him, which, given his obvious ability was evidently my fault, not his, but I found myself saddened and moved by his death. A young man, doing what he loved and playing at the very highest level was taken from the world far too early. I remembered fondly a 16-year-old fly-half called Finbar Hudson, with whom I'd played at school, before his sudden and heartbreaking death from meningitis, days after a run-of-the-mill school match that none of us knew would be his last.

And then I told myself that McCall had died doing something he loved, for a country he was proud to represent, at a level he was proud to have reached, and I hoped it made things easier for his family. And I knew that was sentimental nonsense, because it was too sudden, too tragic to be diluted by something as ultimately inconsequential as sport.

I think we hope we can bear a little bit of the suffering, collectively, and make it easier for the family, just because he was playing our game when he died. And I think we mean it sincerely, but never stop to ponder the ludicrousness of our hopes. It's a great game, but while it can warm the memories and embellish the tales, it can't shield you from tragedy.

Suddenly, everyone's problems, injuries and arguments seemed far less important. Reality had come crashing through, and, with it, a bit of perspective. Probably not before time.

X

Making a difference

I'd love to pretend I was digging out tales from the unknown, finding diamonds in dustbins and spinning yarns from ever more unpromising anecdotal threads, but sometimes the story worth telling is the one that hits you straight between the eyes. This one should have arrived through the door in a large, gift-wrapped box.

I knew it was going to be interesting, from the moment Vernon Neve Dunn, guiding light of the Southwark Tigers, returned my call and came up with a suggestion for a convenient meeting place.

'Why don't you pop down and see us next Thursday? We're meeting the mayor of Southwark at the Town Hall, he's giving us a bit of a guided tour, and then he's going to train with us. He used to be an athlete in Sierra Leone, so he'll be in his tracksuit and mayoral chain. Might be a funny old sight.'

My head was spinning: 'he's going to train with us' indeed. I was reminded of the line in *The Commitments*, when Jimmy Rabbite promises a reporter that 'Wilson Pickett's going to jam with us'. For all his charm, somehow, I remembered having less faith in Jimmy's promise than I did in Vernon's. Even with the difficulties of real life, as opposed to the fantasy of celluloid, Vernon seemed like the sort of bloke who got things done. Empty promises need not apply.

The way he conducted himself on behalf of his rugby team was clear from the first time I spoke to him. He had a habit of getting things done, heading straight to the point and ensuring that his rugby team, the side he described as 'my passion', got the best deal possible out of any given situation, no matter how unusual or unpromising. For example, I asked him, not unreasonably, why the mayor was training with his team, dressed in a tracksuit and chain?

'They're doing a film about sport in Southwark, and we're in it, but I don't think the mayor got quite the profile he wanted. Got the impression he saw the rushes and said, "Let's have a bit more of me, shall we?" So, we got the call to film a bit more, and away we'll go and make the situation work to our advantage.

'This is the North Peckham Estate. Kids get involved in some terrible things here. Nobody is expected to make much of themselves and if you tell people that often enough, they start to believe it. I just thought "sod it", and decided to try something that would give the kids a chance to make a difference to their lives – to give them something to do.'

If you thought rugby was all about the Home Counties, you should go and meet the Southwark Tigers and have your preconceptions demolished. A quarter of a mile from the spot where Damilola Taylor, ten years old and alone, bled to death in a stairwell, I passed three different police signs inside the space of a couple of hundred yards. They asked for witnesses – one to a shooting, the other two to robberies – knowing that there almost certainly wouldn't be any. This is the dark end of the street – rugby on the front line.

I'd lived around here for a few years in my mid-20s, just after I met my wife. *This Life* was on the television, she was a barrister, and we lived opposite a great train robber. Well, a good one, anyway, until he got caught. I was taken in by the seedy glamour of it all, believing that somehow the air of menace didn't present a threat to me, only to outsiders, ignoring the fact that I was the biggest outsider of them all.

And then I became the subject of one of those witness appeals, which ultimately led to my decision to get the hell out. A stroll to the paper shop, and for the first time in my life, I suddenly chose to spend my change on a scratch card. Three silver coverings disappeared to reveal that I'd won £20, which makes me the most successful scratch-card player in history, to my way of thinking – temporarily at least.

I walked out of the shop, chuckling at my good fortune, to be greeted by a large man who quietly produced a knife and asked me for my money. Transfixed by the blade in front of me, I handed it over and watched him jog casually away. I'd been £20 up for about 45 seconds, and then become a victim of robbery – brief description, brief robbery. In an instant, I lost much of my enthusiasm for living in an 'exciting' part of town. It wasn't like this on the television, or when you read about it in dull, lifeless witness statements.

When the policeman came round to take mine, he shook his head as he looked around the house. 'You're living in a fool's paradise, you two. Nice house, professional people, terrible area. You want to think about what's happening around you, because it can be a jungle around here.' We didn't stay much longer. That was my second time as a robbery victim, and my illusions about my surroundings were now well and truly shattered. The knife which robbed the outsider was also the straw that broke the camel's back.

I remembered this as I walked through familiar streets, reflecting on the developments. The pub on the corner had changed – it was now an authentic old Irish boozer, built nearly three whole years ago, boasting dusty boxes of mocked-up 1950s groceries for a window display, and spicy Cajun chicken salad for lunch. Very authentic. The Greek restaurant down the road still had a signed picture in the window to commemorate its most famous customer, and as I noted how faded Lorraine Chase's image appeared to have got, I reflected that the famous don't hit this part of town all that often.

The nice old pub on the way down from the station had also been modernised, and now offered, according to the board outside, 'wood-burning ovens and DJs'. To my mind, the best DJ in a pub is one already inserted into a wood-burning oven, but maybe that's just another sign of my slide into middle age. Southwark Town Hall looked as bleak and uninspiring as ever. Nothing around here was going to leave me feeling particularly good about life.

Vernon was, as the members of his side gathered around the Town Hall entrance were quick to tell me, late, and evidently upholding a long-established tradition. He arrived with a huge bag of rugby balls slung across his back, to be greeted with an endearing combination of affection and abuse. Middle aged yet boyish in appearance, he looked much as I'd imagined, exuding the air of a man at one with the world, and among people he understood. Above all, a man with plans.

'If you get the kids, you get a chunk of the parents, and you can build it from there. I'm trying to gain interest in places like the Aylesbury Estate and the North Peckham, by doing rugby training courses at a youth club one night a week. It's on concrete, so it has to be touch rugby, but you have to try things to learn what works and what doesn't. If the kids don't like it, they won't come back.'

The realities of life: rugby on concrete, and ducking and diving around to try to attract the attention of a few parents just to keep your side alive. And all of this, all the planning and preparing, the hoping and persuading, led Vernon and the Tigers to situations like this one: trooping into the Town Hall, the most wonderfully ragtag and bobtail bunch you could ever hope to meet, to explain to a bemused receptionist that the mayor was waiting to see them.

Slightly surreal, all of it, but at the same time life-affirming. The arrival of the mayor did little to detract from the air of intoxicating eccentricity. Councillor Columba Blango became the first African mayor of Southwark last year, immediately placing the issue of sport in the borough high on his list of priorities. His sporting credentials are high – he competed as a decathlete for his native Sierra Leone at the Olympics of both 1980 and 1984, thus rather emphatically confirming that he was not quite like your stereotypical mayor. On his way to victory, Daley Thompson may have accumulated rather more points than Columba, but Sierra Leone's one-time finest multi-eventer appeared to have a touch of the showman about him, every bit as clearly as Daley ever did.

How else do you explain the sight which greeted me as I emerged at the end of a crocodile of young rugby players, heading off across Peckham High Street, led by a tall, athletic figure in a tracksuit and mayoral chain? The face of the man behind the wheel of the builder's lorry that stopped to allow this queue of people to pass defied any attempt at description.

Within ten minutes, cones had been laid out on the grass of a local park, and Vernon was putting the mayor and the young Tigers through their paces. Handling drills, balancing exercises and endless variations of relay races with ball in hand were the order of the day. He explained it to me later, when we sat and tried to digest the events of the morning over a coffee:

'All that relay stuff is quite a good staple, because they can do it at the drop of a hat, and it looks nice and keeps them competitive, but all they really want to do is play a match and get stuck in. It kept the mayor happy, though, which isn't something you often have to think about while you're organising a training session.'

It's not a situation Woodward gets asked to consider on a daily basis, I conceded, but then, awkward situations and inspired solutions are something of a way of life for Vernon.

'It's difficult to say exactly how many teams we have, because of the way we're set up and the fluctuating number of players who turn up each week. We're trying to run six teams, though, that's the aim. The youngest team are seven, and then we've got them at yearly intervals through to about thirteen.

'It can be difficult at times – this is outside the culture that they know, and very few of the parents understand anything about rugby, so my job is to get it into their face and try to enthuse them. A lot of the kids come alone, and you never see their parents, so that's difficult. If you have an eight year old coming along on their own, off the estate, then it's going to be difficult to keep them coming, because in the end the chances are that they'll just drift away from it. Without that parental support, it's very hard for kids of that age to keep involved.'

I thought back to the fleet of cars turning up to deposit the players of St Columba's at the school in preparation for their trip to Twickenham, the suit carriers, walkie-talkies and the sense of comfort and security. I pondered the number of tickets they'd dispensed to watch the side in action, the extensive parental involvement and the explanation offered to me that some of their players were from 'very ordinary backgrounds'.

It's an unbalanced comparison, of course, and not one that's particularly fair to St Columba's or their staff, but nonetheless, one which offers an insight into the lifestyle different people consider 'ordinary'. One story among all the tales Vernon recounted left me feeling quite empty, shaking my head while absorbing its impact.

We now look back on Dickensian tales of hardship and reassure ourselves that children today don't suffer in the ways they once did, that the state, and its agencies, ensure that desperate poverty and the misery of neglect are slowly being eradicated. That process may be underway, but it plainly still has some way to go until it reaches all the way into the heart of the inner city. If many of the local youngsters like to imagine themselves as featuring in some kind of London-based Tarantino film, the depressing reality seems to the outsider to be closer to a Ken Loach production, as Vernon outlines in stark fashion.

'There was one lad I used to teach – he had problems, not to go into too much detail. He was in and out of care, his mother had serious psychiatric problems, and it would be hard to imagine a much worse home background, but he was a natural scrummager. He was hugely strong, worryingly so, and he just found it came very naturally. He'd get low, and just demolish anything in front of him, and he wasn't scared or intimidated by anything, as you can imagine.

'I used to pick him up every time, drop him back, chase him up and check that everything was all right, but it was impossible to keep that up. He loved rugby, he could do it really well, and it was possibly the only thing he was really good at, and the only thing he was ever told he was really good at either. If he's lost to the game, then not only is it a huge blow to him, but it's one to the game as well, because he could go on to achieve all sorts of things.'

Somewhere, you have to have a cut-off point, I suppose. Some cases just can't be pursued, simply because the resources aren't there and to do so would detract from other worthwhile initiatives, but it seems a crying shame. If Vernon can't reach them, if the children live in such a situation that even someone with his drive and determination can't assist, then I'm not sure what the game can do. Perhaps a point has been reached where it becomes an issue about our society, rather than anything as relatively trivial as a game played by parts of our society. It wasn't the hardest case he told me about, though, as he went on to illustrate the good the game could do when it got a chance to come face to face with a seemingly hopeless task.

'There was another lad, who went to a primary school on the Aylesbury estate and played for our Under-9 side. He's always been a bit difficult to coach, but recently, when he really knuckled down, we got through to the Kent finals, which were played on a brutally cold day – windy, rainy and freezing.

'He scored in the quarter-finals, and you could see what it meant to him, and when they lost narrowly, he just burst into tears. He was a really tough kid, black lad from a really rough estate, and crying wasn't something he did easily, but it got to him. The whole team were crying – they couldn't do the three cheers business because they were so upset, and I was trying to give them the old pep talk about snapping out of it, but to be honest, it was very emotional.'

He hadn't mentioned emotion before. Emotion isn't a word he favours, possibly, in this context, because it's too vague – too related to assurances and hopes rather than guarantees and realities. For anyone quietly filing him away as a 'woolly liberal', it's an interesting aversion which gives reason to stop and re-evaluate. The frequency with which he opts for reality over dreams, for hard facts over soft focus, makes him, thankfully, a difficult man to stereotype.

'He'd turned up in the morning in his kit, no tracksuit or anything, and afterwards we had to get a load of stuff from lost property to try to keep him clear of frostbite. It took a minute, but then he was good as gold, and after he'd recovered, we got him back home again and hoped it would all be OK. As it turned out, I had to speak to his teacher about something on the Monday, and I asked how he was. She said he rarely said anything, and I explained to her what a star he had been at the weekend.

'In the end, she mentioned it at assembly, and it gave him something to be proud about. He'd been excluded from school in the past, he was often in trouble, and yet rugby had given him something to cling to, and somewhere to excel with a set of friends. I'd never even realised he was in trouble at school, because while he sometimes had his head in the clouds a little bit, he was never any trouble to me.

'The way he worked with the other kids was superb, and it shows what an opportunity we'd managed to present him with, and, more importantly, how he was prepared to seize that. If I'm being honest, that's why I probably wouldn't want to coach at a reasonably middle-class club, because I think I'd find it a bit easy. I mean, I'm sure there are kids there with issues and problems, but not on the scale that some of these have had to deal with.'

That the account ended with a positive slant on matters seems to be typical of the way the man goes about his business. Why worry about what's already done, when you could be getting on with doing something to change it? In the harsh reality of inner-city life, results and actions are what count, rather than proposals and promises. A few weeks later, I sat and spoke to Andrew Scoular, the head of rugby development at the RFU, and, during the course of our conversation, mentioned Vernon's name.

'He's a classic example of how to set about changing things in an inner city,' Scoular told me. 'He doesn't promise anything he can't deliver, doesn't do things because they look good on an assessment or because they mean he can tick a box on a form somewhere. He does things because the kids want him to, because he can see that they'll be good for the kids and good for the game, and because he won't take no for an answer, but will carry on battering away on their behalf.'

By this stage, I knew that these weren't simply empty words coming from the RFU. There may be things they've got wrong, decisions they've fudged, or intemperate stances they've adopted, but as far as the Tigers were concerned, they were firmly onside. This is probably as much down to Dunn's behaviour as anything else – he talks to them in the same straightforward way he talks to his players. He doesn't offer them empty promises, and he doesn't expect anyone else to take a similar line with him.

'The RFU have been really good to us, but I think it's time to spread the message a bit wider. It's not meant as a criticism of them, but I think, to an extent, all they're interested in is the Tigers, because we look like a nice sort of success story. If we're going to be anything in the future, though, if we're going to have prospects, develop players and take the game on from here, we need to spread the net a bit wider, and encourage those kids who aren't with the Tigers yet to come along and give it a go.'

It's easy to reach for a clichéd string of adjectives to explain what he's achieving in this neglected corner of south London, but it would be difficult to do justice to his work without them. Rugby is offering something to young people who have little else to occupy them and, as a result, the game is being embraced by those who once wouldn't have given it a second thought. Equally importantly, he is keen to instil in them something of the tradition of the game, its social side, and the off-the-field activities which provide so much of its meaning. Often, as with so many of the battles he has had to fight, this has brought him into conflict with the systems designed to make his struggle easier.

'This is the end of our third season, but we spent a year before that planning things and getting things in place. We've got a clubroom in Burgess Park, in some old, deserted Council buildings. It's a derelict room, but it's our place, and as we'd spent a year and a half without a clubhouse, having to explain to the opposition that we didn't have changing-rooms or toilets, it was a huge improvement. Mind you, it's been condemned too many times to even think of preparing food in there, without running the risk of poisoning someone.

'It's got our pictures on the walls, photos and trophies, but I've still got a bit of work to do on that front. I've tried to convince them that liberating street signs is a good, old-fashioned rugby tradition, but they just look at me strangely. Still, there you go.'

He smiles at the irony of it all. Compared to some of the events going on around these parts, stealing road signs, that good old, clichéd middle-class rugby-playing hobby, scarcely registers a blip on the police radar. People used to claim them for their clubhouses whenever they went off on tour, childishly excited at the illegality of it all. In a place where the selection of crimes on offer is somewhat wider and more serious, the prospect of it seems almost quaint.

'That's very much the heart of us, though, the clubhouse – where our home is. It's got a bit awkward, because the council have just announced plans to build changing-rooms there, with showers and the like, which sounded as if it was going to be fantastic. The problem was that I went to look at the plans, and there was no communal area, nowhere to use as a clubhouse.'

Now, there are undoubtedly those who will begin to roll their eyes, and wonder why he feels entitled to be so demanding, even in the wake of such a seemingly generous council gift horse. It seems to me, however, to be the reason Vernon has made the strides he has. The plans were fine up to a point, but that point stopped short of the one where his charges would have learned the real lessons he was trying to teach them. Of course he wants to teach them to play rugby properly, but to love the game, in order to understand it fully, he has to be able to show them all of it, not just the stuff that happens on the pitch.

Other sides talk as warmly about what happens after the game as they do about what went on during its course. Why should Southwark Tigers be any different? If this is to be more than just a social experiment, more than a proposal or a PR opportunity, if you expect it to bring young people a true picture of the sport and all it offers, you need the facilities. He isn't asking for his own sake, but because it will enable him to secure the club's future, and to help the youngsters who come to his club to understand about the game's totality.

If there's one thing that struck me about the Six Nations, it was that the whole thing is about far more than what happens on the pitch, and the same should apply to the Tigers. It's no good walking around, basking in the warm glow that rugby offers when you consider the camaraderie and the friendship, then expecting underprivileged children to understand what you mean if you don't offer them the same opportunity. He doesn't accept second best on behalf of his side, and nor should he. Thankfully, the RFU, to their huge credit, understand this equally well. Just like Vernon, their deeds have matched their words.

'I said to the council that it doesn't work like that, whether it's rugby, cricket, football or any sport, really. People need a communal area to chat in, and meet up and learn about the social side of the game. That's a large part of what we're trying to do. I said to them that all I really wanted was a slightly better version of what we had now, with somewhere to use as a clubhouse, somewhere where the kids could gather together afterwards and socialise.

'If it means going without the clubhouse then, to be honest, I'd rather do without the changing-rooms, because I want them to think of it as a social place before they think of it as somewhere they can get a shower. Then the RFU came forward, and they understood what I was talking about, and they offered £200,000 to assist with building something we needed. The council still said we couldn't have a social area, because they wanted someone to run it. We've had meetings and discussions, and I've said that we won't move unless there's a community aspect built into it.

'The council want it to be locked up at 6 p.m., and open only during the games, but that's not helping the community to get to know each other and to do something social together based around sport, which surely is what they should be aiming for? At the moment, we play on parkland, with broken glass and dogs' muck around, so it's far from perfect, but out of that there are some really positive, good things happening, and we need to make sure that they aren't lost, because they're what we're really all about.

'I've got a dream to go there, but it has to be right, and it can't be at the cost of what we've got. They're missing out on a big opportunity with the RFU offer, and we have to make sure the chance isn't lost, but it's difficult. As I said, these things, as I've learned, are rarely as straightforward as people would like to make out.'

It's a vision, no more and no less, and it's one that he refuses to accept might not become a reality. As you sit there and watch them go through their paces with the mayor, though, it's impossible not to be swept up with the same sense of enthusiasm and excitement. As Columba Blango nips through a gap during a vigorous game of tag rugby, an alderman looks on in concerned fashion, wondering whether the mayoral chain maybe shouldn't have come off after the first few pictures had been taken. Maybe, you can see him thinking, this is a gimmick too far?

The answer arrives in emphatic, if slightly slapstick style, as young Andre, all four and a half feet of him, launches himself at this figure of authority in order to prevent a try. With a swipe of his hand, the mayor is stopped in his tracks, the yellow tag tucked into the back of his tracksuit trousers remaining in place, but his chain flying off in a number of directions. The momentary silence is broken by howls of laughter, largely from Columba himself, who grins sheepishly as the suited figure on the touchline swoops to claim back the jewellery. With a couple of clips here and there, it's clear there's been no lasting damage to the chain, but lasting benefits all over the place. All things considered, not a bad day's work.

The Tigers are laughing as they leave, and Vernon is happy to sit and share his thoughts about what I've been watching and what it means, both to the locality and to him personally. Far from being demonstrative or blustering, as you might expect from someone who's achieved such things, he's quietly spoken and thoughtful. There is no mistaking, however, the sense of determination and drive which evidently underpins most of what he does. The Tigers are a young club, and his plans for expansion are, unsurprisingly, many and varied.

'As we develop, and you have to remember that we're still a desperately young side, the question of how we set about looking after the older ones is going to be something we have to consider. We began looking, I suppose, almost but not completely exclusively, at the last year of primary school, year six, because that was an age group with which I was familiar, and that was an area I felt I could work with most effectively.

'We thought, maybe a bit naively, that we could just carry on through to secondary level and develop a year-seven side, a secondary-school-age side, but it's very difficult to manage. They become aware of different things, not all their schools play rugby, there's a natural drop out anyway, and because of the decreased numbers, it's hard to attract players at that particular age group. That doesn't make us unique by any stretch of the imagination – loads of clubs have a problem among players of that age, but given our particular circumstances, it can be a bigger problem for us than it might be at other places.

'There are other problems related to that as well. Our committee at

WELCOME TO TWICKENHAM
THE HOME OF ENGLAND RUGBY

England 13–Ireland 19.
The camera work is better
before the game than after.
It doesn't take a genius to
work out why . . .

The Southwark
Tigers get involved
in a little
local politics,
mauling the mayor.

Vernon Neve Dunn puts the pride of Peckham through their paces.

Councillor Columba Blango – Olympian, teacher, mayor
and still running to keep up with the Tigers.

Guy's Hospital – as old as clubs come, and fighting to save a long and proud history.

The sights of the Guy's touchline –
a well-insulated substitute, and a
particularly flattering view
of Dave Berry . . .

Same stand, different days. A big occasion at Twickenham for the schoolboys, a bigger crowd for the Barbarians.

St Columba's prepare for their big day out
in the shadow of the cathedral.

Sir Clive in the spotlight once again, pondering the lineout chaos that was to come against the Barbarians.

the moment, who have been absolutely fantastic, are generally the mums and dads of kids who have been with us since we started, and their sides are starting to grow away from us a little bit. What I'd love to do now is to maybe start a six-year-old side, get hold of them really young and look to see if we can't bring them through as a larger group and try to keep hold of them through into their teens. That way, I think we could start to lay down plans for the future and set the course of the club for the years to come.'

The Tigers have been supported, as the offer of funding for the clubhouse might indicate, very well by the RFU, and have become something of a blueprint for how to set about running an inner-city side. If they once stood accused of concentrating on the Shires and Home Counties, it's hard to level the same accusation against the game's governing body now, at least not the development arm of it. Vernon knows them well, and through a series of joint endeavours and projects, his relationship with them goes right the way to the very top.

'The President of the RFU, Robert Horner, has been very supportive indeed, taking a personal interest and trying to help out wherever he can. This is a big sport, one of the country's biggest, and it's not going to be able to adjust to everyone's needs and fit in everyone's aims straight away, but the will is certainly there, which is half the battle won immediately.

'I've been to RFU meetings when they've discussed social development and other related issues, and they always talk about the Tigers, but as I say, I think we really have to start looking a little bit deeper if we're going to continue to grow. We've been used quite heavily to publicise the game, and when I look back at the World Cup bid, when the RFU were looking to host the tournament and failed, the Tigers were all over the promotional video. That annoys some of the parents a little bit, who want to know why they use us for publicity but won't fund us, but to be honest, while I have a degree of sympathy with their viewpoint, I can see why they do things the way they do. As I said before, these sort of funding issues are rarely as simple as they seem, as I'm learning all the time.'

I'd arrived to meet Vernon with a few preconceptions – not so much in relation to the area, but with regard to the way he felt about his side. Perhaps it was the way he'd spoken when we first discussed matters on the phone, or maybe it was just a feeling I had about the attitudes he would have to hold in order to force the Tigers to become a success.

Either way, I'd viewed him in terms that were far too narrow. The Tigers might have been his passion, but he had ideas for the development of rugby in the area that went far beyond that.

'You can start things going on the ground, regardless of the facilities or history that you've got. I'm trying to push tag rugby in the primary schools. There are 70 primary schools in the borough, and that's about 30,000 kids, of whom I'd like to get half playing tag rugby and entering festivals. That's local, inner-city primary-school kids playing the game, and that means we go on to watching those kids move up to secondary school, creating a demand to play the game.

'At the moment, we've got a lot of kids complaining that they can't play the game at secondary school, and that's an educational issue that we can do something about if we get enough children interested. The RFU have got involved and have part-funded a community coaching role, which we will have an influence over, who will go into schools, get the teachers interested in coaching, and see the game develop from there. It's planting seeds all over the place, but trying to be a little bit more sophisticated than we have been before in terms of where we plant those, in order to ensure the best return possible.'

Not for the first time, the links with the way Woodward sees the game – the joined-up thinking and the sense of planning and strategy – were being explained in a way that made it seem incredible that they hadn't been considered before. Vernon won't be hiring a visual-awareness coach in the near future, and the days of video analysis, computer simulations and highly qualified medical staff aren't quite upon him and the Tigers yet, but in his own terms, within his own area, he's building things just as methodically and intelligently.

'It's a great sport for this sort of area, because it taps in to something that they understand, and in many ways it's probably a better sport than football. We can mix it up so that all the kids can do it and all of them can find a role within it that allows them to excel a little bit, which is very important at their age.

'It's also important to go one level deeper, if you like, and look to find the next generation of kids in schools and youth clubs, and encourage them to come along to the club in the first place. This area isn't like many of the places where rugby clubs exist. It doesn't follow the same rules. If the kids are enthused, they'll come and support it and give it a go, but there isn't necessarily always the parental support or the general backup that they need in order to come along week after week and become permanent members of the team. If they stop going, then they won't decide to go somewhere else instead, they'll just be lost to the game.'

His planning reaches beyond the Tigers, as his plans for a local secondary school indicated. I might not be a television executive, and I may have had more television proposals floated towards the bin than towards the networks, but some things are too good to miss. If his next major venture doesn't persuade someone to commission a documentary, then we'll deserve the extra series of 'Home Front in the Uncovered Vets Changing Rooms' that gets made instead.

'I'm getting involved with St Thomas the Apostle school in Peckham, because they're really talented, really full of kids who can play anything. They've got the bones of a fantastic rugby side, and also have a few teachers who are really into the game. We're going to take them down to Exeter College, the private school in the south-west, and give them a game, because I've got a mate who works there.

'Exeter want to wait another few months, though, and do it next year, because they want to prepare and make sure they really put out their strongest side against us. They'll have to as well, because these lads they're going to be playing against are very tough, very quick, desperate to win, and not scared of anything. Exeter College won't have faced anything like that before, but it will be a fantastic learning experience for both sides, I'd imagine.'

The possibility of a school from Peckham heading off to the luxurious surroundings of Exeter College, and the inevitable clash of cultures that will arise, posed an interesting thought. I had no reason to disbelieve Vernon's assertions that the RFU had been anything other than helpful and supportive, and, indeed, all the evidence from other quarters appeared to support that contention. Instilling a sense of forward thinking in a governing body was one thing, but it was surely with more of a sense of hope than expectation that you waited for all their member clubs to follow the same line?

The old image of rugby may not be borne out by the more recent actions of its top brass, but lurking in the countryside, there must be those who resented 'their game' being introduced to 'outsiders'. That's human nature – it always happens somewhere. A nice piece of generalisation, maybe, but according to Vernon, who certainly has no reason to conceal such behaviour, it just doesn't stand up to scrutiny.

'Things are definitely changing, and the game is becoming more immediately approachable. When we go out to play these clubs in Kent and places like that, you might expect them to be dead posh and unwelcoming, but they're not – they're full of very normal people who feel just the same as our kids do about the game. When you speak to the coaches, there's nothing stand-offish about them at all, they're very normal, easy-to-get-along-with people, and you have far more in common with them than you thought you would have.

'I mean, it's not all like that, obviously. There are others who are a bit distant, and overall it's maybe still a bit on the reserved side, but it's making huge strides forwards in terms of accepting people from different backgrounds.

'I've never heard anything openly racist either, certainly not directed to anyone's face. The only time I did hear anything, actually, was when one of our lads got called a stupid black bastard by a kid from a team in Orpington. The irony was that they came from a fairly rough estate there, a bit like a watered-down version of the sort of background ours come from. It caused a bit of an issue, but I got them to ignore it, or at least overlook it for the time being, because his side were being hammered, and had been getting hammered all day at this tournament, and I think it was said more in frustration than anything else.

'That was abuse from a little hard nut from a rough old background, though, which is different from the sort of thing people think we might face. I've never had some little posh kid turning his nose up at us and saying anything even slightly racially offensive, so it doesn't tend to happen in the places you might think you'd expect it.

'Race has never been an issue among the kids, their schools are very mixed and they tend to be joined by their area rather than being divided by their race. Their sense of belonging to this part of London is almost stronger than their sense of belonging to any one particular racial group, which is quite a nice way to be in many ways, especially if you're the one trying to run a sports team.'

In fact, if anything, the welcome from other clubs appears to have been on the effusive side, rather than grudging, with small, individual gestures telling some quite profound stories.

'The other clubs have been very good to us, in a number of different ways. I remember when they put a notice in the Kent junior newsletter, asking people if they had any old pairs of boots that they didn't need any more, and if they did, whether they'd send them to the Southwark

Tigers, which made us look like a right bunch of old oiks, but was very welcome!

'We met one club at a tournament, and they handed over a great big box of boots, which was fantastic because a lot of our lads had never had a pair of boots before, and so it meant a huge amount to them. That was a typical moment, and to be honest, you'd have to go looking very hard for offence when people were treating you as well as that. There are more than enough tough things happening, I suppose, to start inventing some that don't actually exist. The more people are nice to us, the easier life is, and if it means breaking down a stereotype at the same time, then so much the better.'

Despite the obvious worth of his work, however, and the huge benefits the Tigers have brought to the local area, I still wasn't sure whether the players were falling in love with the game, as much as with their one particular club. Whether it was a bonding process which brought them closer to each other, or whether it was the development of a love affair with the sport itself wasn't entirely clear.

'They are very proud of being Tigers, and maybe that's something I take for granted. I'll give you an example, though, while I think of it. We've got two lads, aged 13, who've been there from the first training session we ever did four years ago, and as we've carried along, their particular age group has fallen away a little bit, and they're left there, really standing out from the others.

'They are truly exceptional athletes, one white and the other black, and they both hold the 400-metre records for their schools, which round here tends to mean that they've got something a bit special. I had to say to them that I thought it was time they moved on, went somewhere where they could be challenged a bit more, because they really have the ability to go a very long way.

'I sent them over to Old Alleynians, but after a few times, they came back to us and just said they didn't fancy it there any more. There was nothing wrong with the way they were treated there, Old Alleynians were very good to them, but they didn't have a sense of connection – it wasn't their side. They came back and said that they were Tigers, and that was the way they liked it. One of them lived right round the corner from Old Alleynians, and he had to get buses and all sorts to get here, but they would rather do that than go somewhere else. I suppose that's the level of connection and belonging we're talking about.'

It isn't that the game is viewed entirely in isolation, however, and inevitably, we end up discussing the World Cup, mulling over minor details and talking points, and musing about how the members of the Tigers treated it. With a myriad of nationalities within their ranks, they passed, not that any of them had ever heard of such nonsense, the 'cricket test' with flying colours.

'The huge majority of them would have watched the World Cup, and they would have understood a fair amount of what was going on as well, which would have helped them enjoy it. I used to sit them down at the end of training every Sunday and give them a little idea of who was playing in the coming week, and what they were like, who to look out for, how they played, stuff like that.

'They watched a lot of the games as a result of that, although I remember, because of the time the games were played in the morning, quite a few times when I'd be standing in the clubhouse watching a match on the television and the kids would be moaning at me to come out and get on with training. There was never any doubt that they loved playing more than watching!

'It gave them a bit of kudos among their friends, I suppose, because they understood what was going on, and there was a way they could show the results of what they'd been doing on a Sunday morning for the last few years.'

As he considered what had been done, the events and accomplishments, he occasionally broke off, almost as if gently revelling in a suddenly revisited memory. If the Tigers meant a huge amount to Vernon the person, victory in Sydney had captivated Vernon the rugby fan. Inevitably, the fusion of the two had been rather special.

'The World Cup was a huge help to me in spreading the word about the game, if for no other reason than it put the game on the back page of *The Sun* most days, where it had never been before. Suddenly, this wasn't a minority sport, but a game they could understand and one they could see being played and reported in front of them in a very big manner. That sort of thing matters to kids in places like this more than you might imagine, for reasons I don't completely understand.

'It was just great to be world champions at something – undoubted best in the world, and to hear people saying that we deserved to be the champions because we'd played the best stuff and deserved to beat the teams we did. The kids really took to that in a big way, so it was a real shame that they organised the homecoming parade for a school day, because there should have been thousands and thousands of schoolkids there.'

I had a feeling that he wasn't going to leave the tale there, and I was right. It's pointless, telling him that something can't be done. It's a concept with which he has trouble. Walls are there to be knocked down, and refusals represent the start of negotiations, rather than the end of them.

'As it was, I managed to convince people that it was an educational trip, so I got 25 kids from a local primary school, a few more from a secondary school, and took them along. The primary-school kids sat on the shoulders of the older ones, and between the lot of them, they watched a day they'll never forget unfold in front of them. Now, after something like that, you'd have a hard time convincing them that there wasn't something a little bit special about rugby.

'We cheered them as they went past, and I remember watching Woodward on the second bus, behind his players, watching them take their applause. There was something about him, a bit reserved without being grumpy, and you could see what it was that allowed him to persuade and encourage players to explore the limits of their abilities. I can't describe quite what it was, but he had "it". It was a fantastic day. Other people watched it on the television, but our kids could say, "I was there". That was their "I was there" moment, and that's what it's all about, really, isn't it?'

It's a fitting way for a man who has done extraordinary things to sign off, summing up an occasion and explaining what it meant to the young people whose lives he had improved beyond measure. It was also entirely in keeping with him that the last memory he relayed to me, before we strolled off on our respective ways, provided a lasting image. Casually thrown in, just to try to put things in perspective, it explained just what it was that made him 'tick'. If the Tigers had caused me to refer to Tarantino and Loach, his recollection, just like that Saturday morning when a pub erupted in celebration of a late drop goal, had me back with Richard Curtis and his syrupy, happy endings again.

'There are those moments when you just know you've achieved something even if you can't put your finger on what it is. I remember when we were invited by Blackheath rugby club to go to one of their league games and provide some pre-match entertainment by taking our Under-9 side to play theirs, which was a really nice gesture by them.

As I stood there, watching our kids playing in front of a big crowd by their standards, I saw one of our mums on the sideline.

'She was a large, black lady, who had recently had her afro bleached, so it stood out huge and white and impossible to miss. She was standing there on the touchline, chatting to a man in a Barbour jacket smoking a pipe, and the two of them were having a really good natter. I don't know the precise significance of that chat, and I don't know what the moment really meant, but I know it made me chuckle away to myself. I also know it was a bit of a sign that we were doing something right – we were achieving something a little bit special.'

An image to treasure, and an achievement to applaud. From the least promising beginnings, with huge problems and difficulties to overcome, Vernon Neve Dunn and the Southwark Tigers have created something quite wonderful. Long may the pride of Peckham prosper.

XI

April 2004

As memories of the Six Nations campaign gradually faded, thoughts turned to the end of the domestic season, and the prospect of the return down under. Woodward could have been forgiven for feeling like a secondary-school teacher with a class of truants, such were the motley collection of sick notes and explanations for future absence which began to fly his way.

With Leonard, Johnson and Neil Back gone, three key members of the pack had strolled off into the sunset in quick succession. In addition, the battle of Jonny's neck appeared destined to be a futile one, while Lewis Moody and Phil Vickery were also looking set to miss out as a result of injury.

Wilkinson's absence left the option of Paul Grayson, who had proved himself something of a flat-track bully through the Six Nations, pillaging the weak and being overwhelmed by the accomplished, or Olly Barkley, who hadn't actually got round to bullying anyone particularly convincingly. As yet, Charlie Hodgson was not being widely touted, which, given some of the treatment he was to go on to receive from the All Black back row, might be a situation with which, in hindsight, he was perfectly happy. For all the benefits that the much-heralded visual-awareness coach brought to the side, it was hard to argue that Sir Clive could have seen such an exodus coming.

Despite the seemingly frantic dash back into training, when perhaps a short break would ultimately have been more beneficial, it was hard not to feel a degree of sympathy with the England coach. Returning back to the scene of a triumph, given the Australian psyche and the lingering sense of Kiwi frustration at having blown it when it mattered – at the World Cup – was always going to be almost as hefty a task as winning the thing in the first place. Doing it while denuded of half your first-choice line-up was a genuinely daunting prospect.

Woodward, to nobody's surprise, chose to go on the front foot and, if anything, remained publicly bullish about his side's prospects:

'The reason we won the World Cup is because we have relished going head to head with southern-hemisphere teams. We have beaten them 12 times in a row, home and away, and it's my job now to keep that momentum going.'

Somewhere, deep in the bowels of the graphic departments of the nation's tabloids, you could almost sense the thanks at being reminded that the next game represented the 13th, as the puns and headlines were constructed ahead of time.

Just to put his mantelpiece in additional danger of collapse, Woodward went on to collect the Sport England Coach of the Year award. A team of experts has been sent out to study whether there has ever been an easier vote to predict, and despite an impressive showing from several Libyan elections, and numerous polls from Leonid Brezhnev's presidency, they are currently unable to put forward a challenger. In order to make the list of awards as exhaustive as possible, it should also be noted that c2c, the occasional train company, named one of their engines 'Jason Leonard', describing it as the 'highest tribute' they could pay him. It will run from Southend to Fenchurch Street, a route commonly known as the 'misery line', covering the journey, if experience is anything to go by, in about the same time it took Leonard to collect the 114 caps for which the honour was bestowed in the first place.

In keeping with his newly earned public profile, Wilkinson managed just two public appearances of any note throughout the whole of April, each of them hardly ideal for a man who makes no secret of his love of living life out of the glare of publicity, lurking quietly in the shadows. When his Newcastle teammates did what England were hoping to do later in the year, and won without him, to claim the Powergen Cup, Wilkinson acted as 'water boy' for the day.

In front of a surprisingly thin Twickenham crowd of just under 50,000, he spent the afternoon jogging onto the turf with water bottles, kicking tees and whatever other bits and pieces his side required. Quite what it does to the nerves, to be waiting to kick at goal in a Cup final, only to see one of the best kickers in the game's history trundling out towards you each time is a question only Dave Walder can answer. Then again, his success rate on the day suggests it wasn't too much of a burden.

It was a deserved win for Newcastle, although with the lead changing hands with ludicrous frequency, one which left even the best in the business struggling to recount it with any degree of uniformity, thus confirming the wonderful independence of rugby writing. Stephen Jones remembered 'many moments of real pedigree', before concluding that it was: 'breathtaking, perhaps imperfect, but compelling'. In contrast, Paul Ackford, in the *Sunday Telegraph* concluded: 'Either these are two of the finest attacking sides in the history of the game or their defences are rubbish. I fancy the latter.' Evidently, no huddling around and discussing what the 'angle' was to be from those two before letting loose on the keyboard, and immeasurably more entertaining and honest reporting as a result.

The following day, and Wilkinson set thousands of London Marathon runners off on their way around the capital, as he acted as honorary starter. A couple of hours later, and the BBC cameras were offering shots of him dispensing drinks at a feeding station, shortly before the finishing line. Thankfully, nobody was cynical enough to suggest that it had been done at the behest of the isotonic-sports-drink company who sponsor him, and the nation's grannies had another reason to love their clean-cut, thirst-quenching, race-starting hero.

The unpredictability of rugby's finances was highlighted by a string of interesting developments in the transfer market, and if it still feels strange to think of the game even having such a thing, rest assured, the way it operates is stranger still. Iain Balshaw announced that he'd be moving from Bath (top of the Premiership) at the end of the season, and joining Leeds (second from bottom). Heaven forbid there was a financial motive attached to the move, but at least he spared us an explanation of how he enjoyed the prospect of a 'challenge'.

Also leaving at the end of the year were no fewer than eleven Saracens players, seemingly to help finance six new signings. These included Hugh Vyvyan, who had dodged Wilkinson's water-carrying runs for long enough to get up the stairs and collect the Powergen Cup for Newcastle on that pre-marathon Twickenham afternoon.

Having just about come to terms with the gradual yet continual decimation of his touring party, in a bid to put the forthcoming tour into some perspective, Woodward was, by the end of the month, attempting to focus attention on his side's eventual defence of their position as world champions.

He had, he revealed, received other offers since Sydney, but was resisting the temptation to move away from England's helm just as fiercely as he was refusing to name the sides who had inquired as to the possibility of gaining his services.

'You get to the situation, like Martin Johnson, and say what do I do now? But I love this job. I want to move this team on and see it as a greater challenge. To see if we can go to another tournament and win it again is something I would like to do.'

Subjected to the sort of analysis with which the man himself has become so fond, the statement says precisely nothing that doesn't come under the heading of what Basil Fawlty used to term 'the bleeding obvious'. Of course he'd like to win another World Cup, and of course he'd like to do it with England. To hear a coach say otherwise would hardly be a tribute to the extent of their ambitions, but as a distraction technique, it was highly successful.

'Woodward eyes Cup Double' was the headline which accompanied the piece, when, in reality, 'Woodward tries to put a positive slant on a potentially tricky tour,' would have been a cumbersome, if more accurate option. Treated with the benefit of hindsight, of course, his frustrations were deeper than we ever imagined at the time. If the statements didn't sound like his normal, measured self, that wasn't, so we'd learn, all that surprising.

'We are at our best when we play these southern-hemisphere sides and I just hope we will have everyone fit.'

In the face of a wealth of medical, technical and scientific advice, Woodward was reduced to hoping, and nobody could blame him, or claim that they had any better ideas. Sometimes, sport favours chance above certainty, no matter how hard you try to reduce it to a string of statistical probabilities. As hard as it was making life for Woodward, it was difficult to conclude that things would be better any other way. Uncertainty is, always has been and always will be, part of the attraction of rugby, from injuries to the bounce of the ball, and if it gets more predictable, it surely gets less alluring.

To watch its most scientific and calculating coach falling foul of a hefty dose of Sod's law – what can go wrong, will go wrong – was, in a strange way, almost reassuring. The game could still surprise us, the freak happenings couldn't be legislated for, and that, even when temporarily annoying, is a good thing.

Elsewhere, the Tigers kept on roaring, St Columba's had moved onto more summery pursuits, and Guy's had finished their year in triumphant style, with victory over the eventual league champions, Lordswood. I remembered Dave Berry's account of their World Cup-final day, when they also played Lordswood.

'We had a breakfast and piss-up at the clubhouse, followed by a trip to league-leaders Lordswood RFC, which we then won!'

If ever Clive needed convincing of the beauty of the unexpected, I know a bunch of thirsty medics who could make the point rather well.

XII

Thinking ahead

It's raining. Hard. In fact, now I come to think of it, my route from Twickenham station to stadium always seems to be conducted in the midst of a shower. On match days, it's easier to ignore, what with the crowds of people jostling along and the thought of the game awaiting you at the other end. Somehow, it's almost as if the atmosphere seems to soak up the rain before you do.

Today, however, there's no match at the other end to greet me, which makes the walk feel longer than usual, and it's tipping it down – truly impressive, almost biblical rain. By the time I pour myself into Rugby House, leaving a trail behind me like a man carrying a leaking barrel on his back, I'm aware I look absurdly wet – so wet, that people's instinct to express sympathy for my condition is overtaken by their urge to giggle at the sight of me.

In the circumstances, the woman behind the reception desk who politely breaks the news that I actually need to go back over the road and into the ground itself, is doing very well to keep a straight face. By the time I've tried and failed to go through the revolving door the wrong way, I daren't turn back to face her, and instead try to bluster my way out, as if a swift change of direction was always in my plans. Cool and sophisticated – that's me.

Across the vast expanse of tarmac which circles the stands, the raindrops are creating a field of momentary, miniature stalagmites as they crash into the ground, leaping up in protest before joining the giant lake across which I'm trying to march. The security guard, tucked up in his Portakabin and far too sensible to venture outside, waves me through. I don't look much like a security threat. If I wrung myself out, I might manage to flood a few offices, but I'm clearly too wet to explode.

As it transpires, the man I've come to meet is having his own problems getting into work. Andrew Scoular is the RFU's head of development, and drives in each day, appropriately enough, from Rugby. With the roads resembling canals, his journey has taken him far longer than usual, and he's now in traffic somewhere outside Richmond, having phoned ahead to offer his apologies.

His secretary, Erin, who has also somehow managed not to laugh at the sight of my drenched frame, shows me to his neat, modern office and disappears off to fetch me a cup of coffee. By the time she returns, I've managed to stop dripping onto the carpet and am beginning to dry off, causing the glass walls around me to stream with condensation. From the outside, it looks as if I've installed a sauna, in which I'm sitting, wearing a damp suit. The hot coffee does little to clear the air. As I said, cool and sophisticated.

Andrew arrives ten minutes later, managing not to comment on the transformation of his working environment into a greenhouse. A quietly spoken Scot, he exudes an air of a busy man with things to do and plans to help him achieve them. His desk is perfectly clear and ordered, and inside a minute he's unloaded a laptop and a wealth of other communications equipment, plugged it all into a series of sockets on his desk and, with a minimum of fuss, declared himself ready to start work. Organised, unflappable and above all, dry, we really couldn't be much more different. Thankfully, it's him, rather than me, who's in charge of bringing through the next generation of English rugby players. Were our roles to be reversed, on the evidence of this morning, the future of the domestic game would be looking decidedly bleak.

Not for the first time, the signs of planning and purpose are all around me. Folders are neatly labelled and lined up on uncluttered bookshelves, while wall charts are colour coded and precisely filled in. The idea of having a structure and adhering to it, of researching meticulously and delivering intelligently has been a theme of everyone

I've spoken to at the RFU, and Andrew seems to offer the most perfect example yet.

'We've been pretty structured in what we do, and we've tried to send our resources into particular places, specific areas that will guarantee us the best return possible.'

Vernon Neve Dunn had talked to me about sowing the seeds in intelligent places, and now, the man right at the top of that particular chain, the man responsible for the development of the game, was telling me exactly the same thing. If it wasn't quite a mantra, there was little doubt that everyone was singing from the same hymn sheet. I'd heard, as had everyone else who took an interest, Clive Woodward talking about the need for a 'consistency of approach' and the need to prepare properly, because that was how you achieved success. Even through the fog I appeared to have created in his office, Scoular was confirming that this was considerably more than just a sound bite – this was actually how it worked.

'I've a salesforce, if you like, of development staff, who are out there coaching coaches, and looking to develop links between schools and clubs, among other things, but that's the most important one as far as I'm concerned. We're also out there looking at coach education and the training of individuals working with the clubs, so they can help them improve their infrastructure in order to attract and develop players.

'And then there are the key elements – the question of how we structure the development of the young players once we've got them, to make them the best that they can be. In essence, we've tried to build an infrastructure in order to be able to deliver better players – more and better players, I suppose, and also more and better volunteers. We look closely at club development, to make sure it's accessible to everybody, and make sure it's fun and enjoyable. That's the key at that stage.

'It's not all about the top 1.5 per cent of players; we want to try to grow the game, to make it more accessible for people to play. In order to do that, you've got to have a structure, because if you don't do that, you're just relying on a scatter-gun approach, and that won't work. You've got all sorts of other considerations and areas coming into play, and if you don't have a good structure, then you'll never be able to make the whole thing work as effectively as it could do.'

Having listened to others telling me about the importance of development, the insightful way the RFU was going about trying to ensure its continuing progress and the change in its approach from years gone by, I was now hearing about it from the man directly in charge. When the next generation of players break through into the England squad, while the senior coaches will get the attention for moulding them into a team, Scoular will have been responsible for getting them there in the first place. Quietly spoken and thoughtful he may be, but there is no disputing the extent of his achievement. He also exudes an unprepossessing air of certainty, best illustrated by his willingness to accept his system's occasional shortcomings.

'We've capitalised on the bulk of things, and I'm not going to pretend otherwise, because it would be dishonest to do so. The truth is, when things are going as well as they are here at the moment, you want to interfere as little as possible, and just make sure that the next tier of players are ready whenever and wherever they're required.'

Along with his team – his 'salesforce' – he provides the engine room of English rugby, discovering and nurturing the raw materials from which he hopes, and maybe expects, future triumphs to be hewn. All of this, however, as he is swift to point out, is only a part of what he does. As he says, it's not just the top 1.5 per cent of players he's interested in, but developing the size and scope of the sport among all levels.

'In a way, it is two games: what goes on in the leagues, and what happens at the bottom end, on the social side of things, and it's one of the things we need to look at. We need to analyse how people become the best they can be, but with the constraints upon them. If they want to play at the highest levels, they're going to have to train twice a day, devote huge amounts of time to it, and that's obviously not something everyone can do.

'It's changed as a game, in terms of its ferocity, if you like, its intensity. In the old days, if you look at the front row, for example, the ball always used to end up coming back to them – they certainly didn't have to go looking for it in the way they do now. There's currently a task force looking at how best to get everyone playing the game, and we've done things like encouraging the game of 10s for the Under-15s, to stop interest there starting to fade away, which is a potential problem among that age group.'

We chatted, inevitably, about Vernon and the Tigers, and the importance of moving the game into areas it had previously neglected. I wasn't expecting platitudes or sound bites, having already come to the conclusion that his methods were considerably more direct and structured, and I wasn't disappointed. If it's a specialised and technical job, bringing through the top tier of new talent, then it's no less important to be diligent about the way the sport sets about entering the inner cities, the places where it has traditionally been less than an obvious presence.

'We're making sure people in the inner city have access to the game. We've established two teams in Toxteth, one in Moss Side, one in the West End of Newcastle, and a deaf representative side – all places and people who didn't experience it before. A lot of the Under-12 sides, well, that's the issue – there's such a lot of them. We're almost at capacity.

'We look at the huge urban conurbations which offer large numbers of players and coaches, and we look to bring them through to a certain level. We look at, for example, places in and around Manchester, and we're looking to pair new sides up with established sides in some circumstances, to have them almost as satellite clubs. There's a territorial angle to going into the inner city that makes life a bit trickier, though, because that's obviously the nature of the inner city, and why the lines are drawn more certainly than they might be out in the countryside.'

The concept of a triangular league, attracting teams from Toxteth, Moss Side and Peckham, flitted briefly across my mind. If anything was more guaranteed to shake away residual thoughts of a cosy, middle-class game once and for all, I couldn't think of it. Given the careful way the message has been spread, however, it's hard to imagine it'll come to pass in such a blatant way. Along with an awareness of life outside the Shires, rugby also seems to have appreciated that it can't just bluster into these new areas and command a divine right to people's interest. The RFU, and this is a statement which once would have provoked uproarious laughter, seems to be acting with a huge degree of intelligent sensitivity.

'It's very important to us that we're not seen as people who arrive from outside, trying to force ideas onto people and encouraging certain groups, just because it looks good for us if they start playing. The key thing for us, though, has been that Robert Horner stood as president this year very much on a social-exclusion angle, and he's been very helpful in getting a lot of these inner-city programmes working. There's support from the very top for this, and that makes our job easier, because that's the way the very head of the organisation wants things to develop.

'London's interesting – it's not just Richmond, Twickenham, places you might expect – it's right there in the centre, in the inner cities, maybe in places that haven't been properly mined for talent before.'

Were it not set against a background of well-meaning assistance and involvement, and described by people who are plainly prepared to stand back and look at the bigger picture, phrases such as 'mined for talent' could, conceivably, start to sound vaguely sinister – as if young players were simply commodities, required to fuel an ever-hungrier and faster-growing machine. As with many of the other voices I heard, though, Scoular avoids falling into that trap not through some adherence to closely managed, neatly packaged answers, but by not bothering to conceal his sheer delight at the growth of the sport.

His background also helps. As a former hockey international, he isn't steeped in the ways of rugby's past, and doesn't find himself bogged down by old allegiances to the players of yesteryear. He was never in the bars and clubhouses with them, so retains the independence he needs to push through his plans. When he talks about things that have surprised and delighted him, he does so with the freshness of someone who really is seeing his designs displayed on what is, for him, a new canvas.

'One thing that really struck me was one day when I was driving past a school, and there were kids playing rugby with a football, just throwing it around to each other, really, but recognisably playing rugby as opposed to football. That's a sight I really didn't expect to see. When we were on the Sweet Chariot tour, taking the cup around the country, there were kids out there watching the bus go by, and they couldn't all have been interested in the game before, because there were too many of them. They didn't just want to watch, either, but to get involved – to engage, and that's something we'll attempt to foster and develop.

'We've seen, just as a rough estimate, a 20 per cent increase in kids trying to get involved directly in rugby as a result of the tournament. Some clubs have had an increase of 50 per cent, and that's phenomenal, but the key thing as far as I'm concerned is the retention. Now we're doing this exercise, trying to analyse things four or five months down the road, and the retention rate is amazing. They're people who would never have played the game, but they came and gave it a go, and now they're sticking with it, and that can only be a huge benefit for us.

'I couldn't say exactly, because I don't have those sort of figures, but to put it into perspective, imagine what would happen if football suddenly enjoyed a boost of those sort of numbers in the kids playing it regularly in an organised way. You'd be talking about hundreds of thousands of kids coming into the game. That's the sort of figure that makes you stand back and realise what's gone on here.

'We've retained about 15,000 players, so, when you examine that a bit, it's 1,000 new teams, 500 extra matches a week, and you start to run into other logistical problems. For example, we've not got enough pitches free to host that many extra games, so we've got to think laterally about a solution – don't necessarily hold all the games on a Saturday afternoon, play in the evenings, stuff like that. The answers are there, but you need to stand back a bit, take a fresh view sometimes, in order to get to them.'

He's nothing if not a fresh view, even if he has brought with him a wealth of experience as a sporting administrator. He has also experienced, at first hand from his very earliest meeting with the 'Powers That Be', exactly what the challenge entails.

'They were a bit naughty at my interview for the job,' he smiled, remembering what must, by any standards, have been a slightly daunting morning.

'I arrived for my interview and waited outside a room, high up in one of the stands here, before being called in to see the interview panel. When I walked through the door, they were sitting with their backs to a huge, glass wall, which looked out on the entire stadium, meaning I had to sit and talk to them while gazing out on about 75,000 empty seats. I've had less distracting backdrops!'

These days, he manages to make do with a slightly less impressive view, staring out on a sign to the Twickenham industrial estate, opposite the ground. Across the concourse, in the stadium, it's rucks and mauls, while he makes do with containers and trailers. If the businesses there go about their daily tasks with half the foresight Scoular goes about his, it must be the most lucrative patch of ground in London.

In order to properly assess the extent to which rugby has succeeded in bringing through its new talent, it is probably best to look at other, comparable sports. At first glance, tennis doesn't have much in common with rugby – not a team game, not physical, not predominantly a winter sport – take your pick. What it does have, however, in England at least, is a shared core support. Many of the people who followed rugby a couple of decades ago probably felt an affinity towards tennis in the summer months.

They attracted similar social groups, were riddled with the same sense of petty rule-making, and adhered to a view of the English class system which made the MCC look virtually proletarian in comparison. The All England Club, which governs English tennis, also claims control of croquet, a form of watered-down, horseless polo for the elderly and incontinent. Tennis and croquet – the cucumber sandwich and ginger beer of the English sporting world.

Where rugby has moved on, though, tennis has dug its heels in and refused to surrender to progress. Blatant cheating and thuggery are not, of course, accepted in either sport, but in rugby, trying everything within the law and refusing to accept that anything but a win is good enough is not just acceptable, but mandatory. In tennis, winning is a long way down the line, behind being pleasant, smiling for sponsors, humouring Sir Cliff and fawning to the Duchess of Kent.

Just after I met Scoular, Tim Henman was beaten in the semi-final of the French Open, largely as a result of losing about a dozen straight games midway through the contest. The radio commentary asked Annabel Croft – who, as a pundit, just as she did as a player, has often watched the latter stages of tournaments from the stands – to sum up his achievement.

'What a fighter he is, what a real fighter. Nobody will call him a choker now.'

A dozen lost games in a row, defeat snatched from the jaws of victory, and nobody's going to call him a choker now. It wasn't worth trying to imagine the reactions of Johnson, Dallaglio, Woodward and the others in the same circumstances. One game is surging on into the twenty-first century, while the other harks back to the nineteenth.

I met with Phil Sandilands, once the Director of Facilities at the Lawn Tennis Association (LTA), and now running his own sports consultancy business, PSA Sports. Having spent many years working towards the development of tennis, and now with two young sons playing mini rugby, he offered me a comparison from both a professional and personal perspective:

'Rugby's existing structure, when it was an amateur game, probably served the sport well. To actually fundamentally change a system, though, that's been in place for a century, is bloody hard work. The people there have been involved in the whole thing for generations and to automatically go towards trying to implant a professional, commercial approach into the counties, into the clubs and all the other things they're doing is hard.

'You only have to look at the dealings between the Zurich Premiership clubs and the RFU to see where it can start to fall down, and it's very similar to the way in which the Football League clubs and the Premiership have come to blows. There's always going to be that sort of division in sport, and that's one that runs straight along a fault line between the owners of the clubs and the governing bodies of the sports.

'For the owners of the clubs, player development hasn't always been right at the top of the list as far as expenditure is concerned. It might become more so, as they need to get on board cheaper talent than they have before, but it won't start as a number-one priority. For the RFU, it's different. They know that their main task is to make sure that players come through the ranks and become introduced to the sport progressively.'

And there lies the cause of many of the problems Woodward has experienced over the last few years, with battles over the length of time he gets to spend with his squad and the competing demands on their time. In football, the club-versus-country debate has rumbled on for years, occasionally flaring up, only to be soothed over by deals which are never fully made public. Rugby, as demonstrated by the furore surrounding Woodward's eventual departure, is still discovering just how complicated the problem can be.

I pondered briefly how serious this problem might get, and reached the same old conclusion. Woodward was a winner, a World Cup winner, as fêted as any coach in the country. In addition to the trophies, knighthood and plaudits, he'd surely earned himself a position from which he could win any battle he needed to. Those battles over access to his players were about to be consigned to history, weren't they, as he enjoyed the rewards of his success? Weren't they?

With regard to the bottom of the pyramid, however, the mini and youth rugby sections, Sandilands has huge praise for the way the game has set about its ongoing development. He also explained how the equivalent schemes in tennis had failed in so many fundamental areas. While it is tempting to always fall into the trap of comparing rugby with football, it was listening to him offer an expert and first-hand view of where tennis went wrong that convinced me that comparisons should be drawn in a different direction.

'In tennis, you've got a management structure which likes to focus on a number of clubs. Now, they're admittedly successful, but it doesn't take a genius to work out that once those clubs have been made successful, you don't keep pumping money into them, but stand back, look at the areas that are failing, and throw some money there instead. If you go to tennis heartlands, the links with the LTA are excellent, and they'll highlight those as ways in which the system works well. If you go to tennis deserts, though, and that includes huge amounts of the inner cities, it's difficult to find any evidence of them ever having been there, and that can't be a sensible way to set about trying to find the next great talent.

'The clubs at which they look closely tend to be in pretty safe areas, and when they go elsewhere, the development isn't sustained enough or backed up with enough money to make much of a difference. Clissold Park in Hackney is a good example. The LTA have put some money into that, but there hasn't been enough money to get a proper set-up, and without that, after a year, the kids it first attracted start to drift away and don't have enough reasons to hang around.'

The issue of retaining the talent of the future is one which was raised whenever I spoke to anyone involved with the junior side of rugby. An initial investment, whether in terms of finance or success, is of little use if it's not backed up and followed through. Woodward may be an advocate of learning more from victory than defeat, but in this instance, there may be more to be learned from the failures of others than anything the game has achieved for itself.

'I come from a sport which has a huge windfall drifting into it each year thanks to the money generated at Wimbledon, and yet has historically failed to achieve anything of real note with it. There's a £40 million indoor-tennis centre being built at Roehampton, but they need to go further afield than that if they really want to find someone who wasn't there before.

'We launched an indoor-tennis initiative, which was a partnership between the LTA, the All England Club, and the Sports Council, or Sport England as they became. The idea was to give the money to local authorities to build indoor facilities, because that's the only way you'll ever produce a tennis champion, because of the weather in this country.

'The idea was that they'd run them on a pay-to-play basis, like a leisure centre does, and that in conjunction with creating the facility, we'd also make it available to people who maybe didn't see it as being available before. On the face of it, it can't go wrong and it shouldn't fail, but you'd be amazed at the reaction it provoked. It wasn't part of the club system, it didn't fit in with the way they wanted their game to develop, so I just spent my whole time fighting with them to keep the thing moving forwards.'

On the face of it, a specific problem for a specific sport, and yet it tells a wider tale. The real challenge is not so much with the future, especially if you get the right people involved, but with the refusal of some of the representatives of the past to allow the journey forwards to take place in the first place. English rugby has, through a degree of enlightenment, albeit sometimes forced on it by its national coach, accepted in general terms the changes that need to be made, and seen the benefits they bring. Other sports, with tennis a fine example, have not, and will pay a heavy price.

To the experts – the consultants, the intelligent professional administrators and the like – it's a simple, if thorny, problem, with a straightforward if, to the old guard who cause it, somewhat blunt solution. The blazers can either take a step back and enjoy watching their game progress, or demand to retain control over every minor decision and, thanks to the outdated practices which inevitably follow, watch it wither away and stagnate.

The Andrew Scoulars of this world, when his office has finally dried out, can ensure a bright and expansive future for the sport, but only if allowed enough latitude to do what needs to be done. Thankfully, despite occasional teething troubles along the way, this appears to have been forthcoming. Once upon a time, the administrators of rugby and tennis could have been interchanged with minimal disruption. That is, in relation to the sport's development, at least, no longer the case.

Rugby's growth is not, it seems fair to say, exclusively down to what people did, but owes much to what people who weren't experts were prepared to leave alone, and the extent to which they let those who were get on with things. For as long as that state of affairs exists, the prognosis as far as the game's development is concerned seems very good indeed.

XIII

A day with a knight

As boltholes go, Penny Hill Park, located just outside Bagshot in the depths of a rather affluent swathe of Surrey, is a rather salubrious example. Indeed, with closed-circuit television cameras, high walls and ever-vigilant staff, stumbling is not, one imagines, the preferred method of arrival. Just inside the front gate, a machine flashes your car registration up on an electronic display, like something out of *The Prisoner*, while the last road sign before you turn into the drive directs you to Deepcut Barracks where, the MOD assures us, suicide is rife and murder is not. Secrecy is very popular in this particularly well-heeled neck of the woods.

This is the gated community to which Woodward and his squad repair before each international, every tour, and, sporadically, simply to re-acquaint themselves with each other over high-energy drinks, bench presses and video analysis. When they're not playing for their clubs, or appearing in an England jersey, there's a decent chance that the world champions will be squirreled away here, giant hamsters on a five-star wheel.

If it's secluded and quiet, it's also hard, once inside, to conceal their presence. England rugby players would make the world's worst spies, with an inability to blend in with their surroundings coming as standard, alongside big thighs, gaunt faces and a collected sprinkling of scar tissue. The hotel is doubtless thrilled to have them, just as they're delighted to be there, but they do, it's hard to ignore, stand out from the other guests.

As I stood in a corridor, peering at a wall-mounted dinner menu commemorating the visit of half a dozen different heads of state, and looking at the art and sculpture which adorn the reception area, the sound of flip-flops alerted me to the imminent arrival of one of them. For the modern professional sportsman, shorts and flip-flops equate to 'smart-casual', while team tracksuit and clean trainers are very much the 'black tie' end of the spectrum. Set among a collection of retired brigadiers and a few groups of ladies who lunch, 18 st. of pensive, brooding, flip-flopped prop is always going to stand out.

To be fair to the players, the attendant media probably weren't doing all that much for the sartorial levels of the place. A group of four photographers, all turning up for the forthcoming press conference, resplendent in their working uniform of jeans, trainers and freebie golf T-shirts, were causing the odd sideways glance from Colonel and Mrs Twitching in the corner. With the Barbarians waiting to face Woodward's men in four days' time, the morning had been set aside for a press free for all, as quotes, sound bites, snaps and opinions were sought and delivered.

Among the problems for the press, however, was a rather embarrassing one, and one which everyone seemed to have a different way of approaching. With the Zurich Premiership play-offs busily bringing the domestic season to a superfluous and potentially unjust climax, Woodward had scarcely any first-choice players available. Thanks to rugby's odd desire to make the league champions win a Cup competition before they might truly be crowned league champions, the top four teams in the country were busy, and their players otherwise engaged. Woodward was picking from a very new and inexperienced squad, many of whom were failing to generate too many gasps of recognition from the assembled press.

On a raised patio overlooking the golf course, with the birds twittering and leaves rustling in the background, the fourth estate were pondering a suitable plan of action, while gathering enthusiastically around a breakfast buffet laid out for their benefit. I asked Mick Cleary, rugby correspondent of the *Telegraph*, which members of this relatively anonymous squad he planned to interview. 'God knows,' he sighed, while sporadically returning to the buffet table in the hope of lessening its burden somewhat. 'I think I'll just lurk a bit, see what's said, drink too much coffee and eat lots of bacon sandwiches.' On the evidence I saw, regardless of whom he ended up writing about, his day was a success on one level, at least.

The man from Five Live was facing a similar problem: 'I hardly know any of this bloody lot,' he admitted, with a resigned smile, 'which could be a little bit of a problem.' I chuckled back, sympathetically, and suggested that, as nobody knew their faces, nobody was going to know their voices either. Just interview away, and then attribute it to whoever came to mind when he looked through the team-sheet back in the studio. A jokey solution, perhaps, but better than no solution, if only by a fraction. 'Don't think that hasn't occurred to me,' he said, strolling off to gather his thoughts. In the unlikely event that Lord Hutton reads this, I don't think he was serious.

Outside, on the terrace, the photographers were doing their best to live up to the finest traditions of their profession, by marching around, mobile phones clasped to ears, trying to offload Euro 2004 tickets they seemed to have acquired. 'You can't sell it on, because it's come from, well, just don't sell it on, all right?' A couple of local businessmen sitting at a nearby table glanced at each other, before pretending not to have overheard us, so as not to sully the decorum of the location. 'They're good seats, so don't bring fucking lunatics along with you.' As the language cut through the refined atmosphere with all the subtlety of a low-flying jumbo jet, try as they might, they couldn't pretend they hadn't heard that one. They shifted in their seats and tried to continue their conversation, while simultaneously pretending they weren't continuing to eavesdrop.

Eventually, the assembled crowd made their way back into the building, while Woodward, as if stage-managed, succeeded in following along behind them, all the way to the top table, unnoticed until they actually reached their seats. On his right, sat Andy Robinson, who looked as if he'd rather be undergoing root-canal work than enduring another press conference. He displayed slight, almost imperceptible signs that he'd rather be getting on with training – like carrying his boots around with him, putting them down on the table in front of him and saying not a single word until it was all over. You didn't need a body-language expert, trust me.

In a dark, wood-panelled room surrounded by modern, white advertising backdrops and spotlights, Woodward started to go through his paces. I remembered the story about W.G. Grace refusing to depart the crease after being given out, explaining to the bowler that 'they've come to see me bat, not you bowl'. Woodward, with a smile and a polished air, operated a similar system, from time to time choosing to answer the questions he would have liked to hear, rather than the ones actually uttered.

'Is this a great coaching challenge for you?' asked one scribe, mindful of the new selections forced upon the England coach. There are, I suppose, two options here – you either say yes, and tacitly admit that this lot aren't as good as your usual squad, or you say no, and look like a liar. A simple question, but potentially tricky. Woodward chose option C, and answered the question he would rather have been asked.

'It's a great opportunity for the players, a really great opportunity. We're going to have a packed Twickenham, and we'll prepare together and get ready together and make sure we make the most of what's going to be a fantastic day out for everyone, I'm sure.'

Nobody raised an eyebrow. It was an answer – a neat, flick off the legs to a slower ball, and things were underway. Nobody mentioned that the answer and question didn't tally, and nobody seemed to mind. I was impressed. Admittedly, the lacklustre nature of the fixture, whatever Sir Clive said, meant this wasn't the most savage or hungry press pack, but with a bit of delicate handling, they were rolling around as if their collective tummy was being tickled and the doggy chocs were raining down.

And so it continued, in exactly the same way as every press conference I've ever attended. It's an odd feature of these events, and of the media in general, that in order to attempt to produce a story that is fresh and interesting, we feel the need to go through precisely the same, tired and formulaic routine, every single time. The truth is, that with the developments to the media over the last decade, the birth of the internet and the increase in sports coverage elsewhere, everyone's so scared of giving away a tale to the 'opposition', they prefer not to ask anything in the first place.

The radio reporters eye the journalists suspiciously, concerned they'll blurt out a query of their own during an otherwise unsullied answer, thus buggering up a neat, editable recording. The journalists know that any answers they get which come close to revealing a story of any note will be carried, discussed and dissected by the radio stations long before they get to print, leaving them with decidedly old news on their hands. The only unifying factor tends to be an annoyance with the representatives from the television companies, who will try to take over, waltzing around the event as if it was being held just for them. On top of this, they'll ask questions every bit as banal as anyone else, but in an inappropriately upbeat manner, stopping just short of reminding the interviewee to 'have a nice day'.

Then, just as the whole thing comes to an end, it springs into life – every time, without fail. The key to the start of a press conference, the way you can tell that it's really come to life, is when a press officer stands up and asks if there are any more questions. There is a mumbled 'no', a communal shake of the head, and the subject of the gathering stands up and retreats back from the table, ready to make his or her escape. As one, the journalists will try to walk out alongside them, attempting to pose a couple of questions in the guise of polite, trivial conversation. I've seen people come close to blows, it was so polite and trivial.

This might yet be the angle they'll take – their 'line' – and it will be something that wasn't covered in the conference and hasn't, ideally, been mentioned at all. It'll annoy the radio and television crews as well, because this is the print media's revenge, the equivalent of the smoky corridor or the judge's chamber, where it's all off the record and on the record at the same time – where no rules get broken, but all rules get bent. Too informal to be used in a broadcast, an unguarded comment has often formed the bones of a back-page lead. In the hands of the inexperienced, it can see the entire contents of the recently completed conference disposed of in favour of one, throwaway line to a bloke who seemed to be asking mainly about the weather, or some other piece of trivia.

Woodward, however, is far from inexperienced, and his press officer, Dee McIntosh, a calm and authoritative figure, saw off such attempts with a quizzically raised eyebrow and a tilt of the head, leaving transgressors, publicly at least, appearing ashamed at having tried something so underhand. 'Clive will do a separate one for the Sundays,' she promised, ensuring that those who published on the day of the game would have something original of their own to report. Assuaged, the pack desisted, grudgingly aware that they weren't going to get a loose word out of their target in any event, but content that their attempt had ensured convention had been followed.

As everyone retreated to their respective corners, Woodward was taken on a guided tour of each of them, stopping to discuss matters and answer the same questions, time after time, for the benefit of different media, who filmed, recorded or scribbled his responses. First, however, he had a photo opportunity to fulfil, with a mental health charity. A young girl with Down's Syndrome sat with an arm around the England coach, while they chatted to each other as the cameras snapped away. And then the cameras stopped snapping, and the conversation continued. It might have been essentially a photo call, but Woodward was polite, interested and welcoming, and just because they'd got their pictures, it didn't mean he'd finished his conversation.

He galloped off to claim an England rucksack for the girl, full of bits and pieces, and got a hug and a kiss by way of thanks. It was ten minutes out of his day, but it gave the charity a huge boost and a delighted little girl the memory of a lifetime. It also left everyone with a smile on their face, as things slid gently back into perspective.

An hour later, as we sat in yet another splendidly plush wood-panelled room, I mentioned the episode to him.

'I apply a general rule to everything I do as a coach, and that is to ask myself if it's going to cost me a Test match. If there's the slightest chance it can cost a Test match, then I don't do it, but if it's not going to, well, I think people get a bit carried away sometimes. They get scared of the media, and I think that's just nonsense. Like today, a little girl comes down, it's a charity thing, and they want a few photos. Is that going to cost us a Test match? Of course it isn't, and it's madness to suggest otherwise. Let's do it, let's try to be helpful and take the photographs. It doesn't put anything at risk, so let's try to be reasonable about it and do it.'

When faced with a bunch of questioners, he might well play the percentages, but one on one, it would be very unfair to suggest he was anything other than direct. It's an interesting contrast, but is it all an attempt to develop a bit of an air of mystery around himself – to bolster an image as a slightly reserved planner and thinker? Did he think of his press encounters as a bit of a game, leaving people guessing as to what he was really thinking? Apparently not.

'It's not that I've purposefully set about trying to cultivate an air of mystery, or anything like that. The only thing I would say is that I've never done a newspaper column or anything like that, and I've always said no to all those things. I've just written a book, but that's different

– it's not something that involved breaching confidences, because it's not that sort of book.

'It's not just about coaching, or the detail of what's happened here, but about how to create a winning environment. I would never, ever write a book about all the tittle-tattle that goes on behind the scenes here because that would just be totally, totally, I don't know, wrong. You can't possibly expect to run a high-performance sports team or have any trust if you think the guy running it is going to go off and tell tales out of school.

'I've never done that and never would. The only thing I do is this sort of stuff – interviews. Whenever I've been asked to do an interview, I've done it. The only time I don't is if it's actually impossible for me to do one, but I don't turn them down. I'm also very conscious of the fact that, in my opinion, England had never really achieved anything until after we won the World Cup, so I wasn't going to stand up on a pedestal and tell the world what I thought.'

In the eyes of the coach, being straight and telling it how it is are all-important. Besides, as he was keen to observe, he's only obeying certain ground rules that exist within the squad. If the rules apply to a minor squad member, they apply just as stringently to the coach, even if the circumstances have changed over the course of the last year.

'Now we've won it, I find myself in a different position. I haven't purposefully gone about setting out any sort of image for myself; I've just gone about doing my job with a bunch of young and incredibly talented people, the same as all the other coaches who work with me here.'

The need to praise the coaching staff around him, and to ensure that they get mentioned whenever the achievements of the side are detailed, is evidently something about which he feels very strongly. It's a generous gesture, and clearly symptomatic of the way the squad set about pulling together in pursuit of a common cause. It's also a compliment that is dropped in with typically precise planning.

In the same way sporting greats are often described as reading the game several moves ahead, Woodward had ticked off a mental box as the question was asked, as if noting to himself that the opportunity to commend the backroom staff was about to appear. It didn't make it any less meaningful or sincere, quite the opposite in fact, but it seemed perfectly in keeping with the precise way he goes about all aspects of his job.

Just as I made to move the discussion on, however, he surprised me by warming to his theme and discussing the issue of privacy and confidentiality further. If the England rugby team were aware of the importance of keeping their own counsel, not every group of well-known, influential people in the country appeared, in Woodward's view, to achieve the same standards.

'I think it's absolutely critical to keep it the way we have. I'm amazed when I look at the government, for example, because they have problems in that department that we don't. The first thing I said to the players was that when I walk through that door, and we all get down to work, I want to be able to be myself. I'm going to say what I want, what I think, and along the way I'm going to make a few mistakes, because that's how it is in the real world, and that's how you run any business.

'People have to be allowed to be themselves and get on with things, because that's the only way you can do it. The only thing that would stop me doing that is if I thought people were going to go away and write about it, because things do happen, and they do kick off sometimes. People seem to think that the England camp is this cosy environment where everything is always perfect, but things do get heated occasionally.'

For a split second, I wondered if the line about the government had been a slip of the tongue – a criticism that, on reflection, Woodward hadn't wanted to make, which he was attempting to bury amidst a string of further examples. Before I had the chance to steer him back to the subject myself, however, he was heading there of his own volition. Letting things slip really isn't his style.

'If you want to be the best in the world, you've got to have standards that are set higher than any other team. That's why I mentioned the government. The same thing happens in a way, they all fall out with each other, and then Clare Short writes a book, Robin Cook writes a book about things they should never be writing about.

'How can you work in an environment when you look at people around a table and you know that if things kick off in the future, they're going to disclose private conversations and things that happened? We're playing a sport, but these guys are ruling our lives, making life-changing decisions, and they seem to accept it. It's very strange to me, but we seem to have accepted it as a society now.'

I recalled something Stephen Jones had said to me months earlier, which reinforced what I'd just been told. Jones had asked Woodward about the ideas he introduced which didn't work quite so well. Woodward replied, 'Yeah, I've made a few mistakes, but we realised them and built from them, so they didn't really do us too much damage.'

'That's the thing,' Jones reflected. 'You can't get a name out of him; he's totally loyal. There's a complete sanctity about the team room, and nothing ever comes out that's said in there. The only one who ever came out and said anything outside the team room was Richard Cockerill, and he never played again.'

Despite all the theorising, though, the guesswork and the jargon (which comes, to be fair, from the man himself as much as those trying to understand him), Woodward's methods are, on close examination, disconcertingly simple. Everyone has a job to do, and everyone has certain standards with which they are expected to comply. Having ensured these basic foundation stones are in place, the coach just keeps stoking the fire, making sure that everyone remains equally and totally determined to keep improving. It can't be as easy to manage as we like to pretend, I asked, and found the answer centred once more on the issue of standards and levels of professionalism. It didn't take a management guru to spot a trend emerging.

'This is a passionate environment and players have got to know that they can say things to me when the moment arises. I know, speaking for myself, that I've said things to players that I bitterly regret, but I've never ever read about them, nobody's ever gone to the newspapers about them. One or two players have said things to me, but I'd never betray their confidence, and that's the way it has to be done, and that's the secret behind creating what we've done.

'You shut the doors, everyone sits down and is free to say what they want. When we open the doors again, though, when we go back into the outside world, everyone is as one, we're a team. We've had a history of doing that, and that's helped us hugely to do what we've done.'

The fact that the environment is passionate was hardly revelatory, given the nature of their ambitions and the physicality of the game, and equally, the idea that players adhere closely to the rules came as little surprise. Interestingly, though, it clearly means something to the players after they leave the confines of Penny Hill Park, and retire back to 'ordinary' life.

'When I read Martin Johnson's book, for example, he could have written a lot about the behind-closed-doors stuff, because he's been there through a huge amount of it. It's a brilliant book, but it follows the rules we set out. Me and him have had our moments, God, over the strike for example, but he's not written about that, and that's why I respect the guy so much, and I trust him implicitly – I'd trust Martin Johnson with anything. To his grave, I know he'll take stuff that we've talked about and keep it to himself.

'That's not just the captain, either, that's the whole team. I know Martin would have been there as the figurehead, but it filters down through the whole team, and we've hardly had an example of anyone letting us down. I've now got Lawrence Dallaglio as captain, and he'll adopt, and does, exactly the same standards. That's why we can operate in the way we do, and that's maybe why people think I'm a bit of a mystery man in some regards. If there's a bit of mystique, I know what's probably caused it, and I think it's a good thing, because it's as a result of something we've very deliberately set in place.'

Having just sat through his press conference, though, and witnessed the clandestine discussions among the scribes about the best way to approach a decidedly mundane international fixture, it was clear that people were going to try to find out what went on behind those closed doors. Ultimately, it's a story, and a good one too, and if passions are running high, and England players are being 'frank' with each other, sections of the press are going to want that in their paper. His solution is, it seems, a very effective halfway house, involving complete honesty about certain matters, and declaring others out of bounds. Some may quibble as to the extent of the honesty, but the end result is a media entirely congratulatory in relation to the World Cup, and broadly sympathetic as regards his future plans. On any view, it's not a bad position to be in.

'I see the media as a partner, and I try to work with them whenever I can. Like I said, if I can do an interview, I will. I understand how it works, and if you take the pats on the back when it goes well, you should expect to get the arrows when it doesn't. I accept all of that. I mean, they've said some pretty horrendous things about my coaching and my selection, but that's fine. They've never said anything personal, though, and we've tried to keep it very professional on both sides, I think.'

Indeed, even his dealings with the press seem to provide an opportunity to impress – to put into effect a well-considered and structured plan. The desire not just to appear, but to be constantly professional borders almost, one feels, on the obsessive.

'At the World Cup, we had journalists from plenty of other sports with us, and it was interesting to see how pleased they were with the way we worked in relation to the media. We are professional in the way we deal with them, and that was appreciated.

'There's no change in the way I talk to non-rugby press, compared to the conversations and interviews I give to the rugby press. You can't change things because of the person talking to you, you've got to be straight with them and consistent. When I first started in this job, people said I was naive, and I don't think I was. I decided from day one that if I made a mistake, the only thing to do was put my hands up and say so. It just seems to put everyone on the back foot. If you've made an error, there's no point bullshitting the media or trying to cover it up – just say so.'

I was still less than convinced by all of this – whether they intend to or not, managers and coaches either blatantly lie, or (more usually) bend the truth all the time. It's their protection against the media, and given the treatment they occasionally get, it's hard to blame them. Woodward, however, maintains firstly that transparency is the only policy which works, and secondly that it's the approach he adopts above all others.

'I'm also very big on not speaking off the record, because I don't believe in it. When I speak, it's on the record, this is on the record now, everything else today has been, and that's the way it is. I know you'll write this up, others will write up what I've said to them, and that's the way to do it. You've got to concentrate when you speak to the media, but you do that when you know you're always on the record. If you've made a mistake, then say so. What can they do? Shoot me?

'When players ask about how to deal with the media, we always tell them the same thing – just tell the truth. Be up front about things, while obviously using a bit of common sense and keeping the team-room conversations private. Whenever they write a book, or write for a newspaper, all we ask is for them to remember that, and they do. They're the rules we work under, that's how we do it, and everyone abides by the same code.

'I got to know some of the football journalists quite well during the World Cup, and they all seemed genuinely surprised at how we operated, but that's how we do things. It's not rocket science.'

Having worked alongside some of those football journalists, I would imagine their surprise was all too genuine and occasionally bordered on the shocked and staggered. It may be that he was choosing to forget the odd detail or moment here and there as he explained his methods with the press, but the fact I was sitting talking to him, alone, with no media minder lurking at his shoulder, rather confirmed what he'd been saying. It couldn't really get much more honest than this. I tried to imagine a similar scene with the England football manager or cricket coach, and was forced to conclude that imagining was as close as I'd ever get to it.

The fact that this chapter even exists is a testament to just how much more media-aware the RFU are now than would have once been the case. It also says a huge amount for the willingness of a man with considerably more urgent demands on his time, to sit and chat with someone he had never met before, answering questions he had probably been asked upwards of a thousand times. If proof were needed as to the extent of rugby's increasing professionalism, the time Woodward set aside from a manic schedule to comply with a request from an unknown isn't a bad example to cite.

As a player, Woodward showed few signs of being particularly predisposed to enter the world of coaching – a loss of concentration in a crucial game against Wales was relayed to me by several people as an example of how far he had come in sharpening up his act over the years. To be fair to him, though, he doesn't try to recreate his playing career through rose-tinted glasses, any more than he tries to afford it undue weight when considering what makes him the coach he is today.

'Being a player helps, of course it does, but without a shadow of a doubt the best background for me, the most important thing to me in allowing me to be a better coach, was what I learned in business. I worked for Xerox for seven or eight years, and that was a huge multinational firm, but more importantly, I ran my own business, a leasing company, for eight years.

'I made mistakes along the way, but I developed what I'd call a small-business mindset. I had about twelve people working for me, but when you're in charge, when you're responsible for people's wages and livelihoods, your mind takes shape – you just get things done. I'm very proud to say that when I walked into the England job, I had that small-business mindset, and I was prepared to change things and move them forwards.'

From his demeanour as he discusses it, the way he sits up in his seat and looks you in the eye, it's plain that this sense of ordered drive and achievement stretches beyond just coaching, to the point of shaping the person he has become. The sense of responsibility, combined with the process of problem solving and goal setting is what makes him tick. What the outside world thinks of him is less important than it might like to imagine.

'I had no fear at all about saying to people in the media what I was going to do, and that was looked upon as being quite naive. They didn't necessarily think I was being naive on the rugby side, but just because I was prepared to tell people what I intended to do – that was seen as a bit unwise. I just thought it was an open and intelligent, businesslike way of doing things, and because of my background, that just seemed to be the best way to go about the job.

'I don't think it's any coincidence that the last two people to have won the World Cup – myself and Rod McQueen – have both got similar CVs. We both came through the amateur ranks, where we had to run our own businesses. We've now both got high-profile coaching careers, but we've come through the learning process of running a business, making mistakes, with people, media and all sorts, and that's a huge boost to doing this job.

'All of that process teaches you how to manage people, and that's a huge part of being the England coach, knowing how to get the best out of people, individually and as a unit. At the level we play, the coaching role is very important, and I've got absolutely world-class coaches around me in Andy Robinson, Phil Larder, Dave Alred and others. These are the very best in the world, the absolute peak, and their job is solely to coach the players and get the very best from them. My job is to make sure that they're not distracted by anything, so that process can run as efficiently as possible.'

He may have drifted into discussing coaching, as opposed to the media, but the central planks of his approach are still perfectly clear, as he focuses on the importance of things being right, preparations being perfect and attitudes remaining correctly adjusted. He is generous with his praise for the coaching team who surround him, probably for a couple of reasons. Obviously, with a World Cup victory to ponder, there's the fact that the praise is genuinely merited and deserved. You just can't quibble with what they've achieved, and when the winning players keep telling you it's largely down to the coaching they've received, you really don't need any further proof.

In addition to that, though, it's hard to resist the idea that he is having to intermittently set the ground for the next leap forwards while trying to convince a few residual blazered individuals that he was actually right all along – this was the way to do it. For all their good work elsewhere, and despite all his successes, the game's top brass and its most senior coach were not seeing eye to eye as far as the next step of the journey was concerned. In due course, the issue was to raise its head rather more prominently, but as we spoke, the smooth transition from boardroom to training pitch showed how, in his head, the two environments remain closely linked.

'One of my real passions is coaching, and I do get involved, but I also stand back and let them do what they do best. I manage the whole process, and I keep those distractions at bay, because I'm not there to interfere. This is a big organisation. What goes into creating a champion athlete, a champion team, is more than just a guy with a whistle and a tracksuit. Take Dave Redden, for example, our fitness and nutrition guy. He's been approached by loads of other sports, and he's the very best in the world in my opinion. It's no accident that we arrived at the World Cup fitter and stronger than any other team.

'You've got to surround yourselves with the very best there is, the leaders in their fields who can help drag that bit extra out of the players. I'm also helped, I suppose, by the fact that I did a Phys Ed degree at Loughborough, which had a lot of sports science in it, so I know the components, the bits and pieces that go together into making it all happen. Each of those bits is imparted to the players by the very best in the business, very aggressively and that's why it works. We're here to get results. Nobody's here for the ride, because that's not the way things are done in the England camp.'

The meticulous planning and precision, however, seem to paint an occasionally dour picture of Woodward. Even those who admire him aren't entirely sure what he's like – the issue of mystique again. Television cameras rarely fail to capture the moments when he leaps to his feet in an international, and the image of him punching the air and hopping about in the Twickenham stands is now very familiar. Is this a moment of surrender to pure, uncomplicated excitement, though, or, in keeping with his approach, a celebration of a plan finally falling perfectly into place? Does he cheer the instant, or the work which went into creating that instant?

'It's when a player does something that's totally unexpected, that's what gets me out of my seat. We're there to coach the team, to give them every chance of winning – that's our role. When you see the team out there on the pitch doing something that you haven't coached, something spontaneous, some tremendous bit of skill, that to me is what makes you stand up and say "wow". I'd behave like that if I was sitting at Twickenham as a fan, because that's the reaction it provokes.

'That's why you love the Jason Robinsons of this world, because they are so special in that regard. They can do something that makes you look twice, and that's such a wonderful thing to be able to see. To find players like that, and know they're going to go out there and do things like that, well, that's when I get very excited.

'That's what gives you the most joy in coaching, when you see them do things that you've not coached them to do. I think we've got to be very careful as coaches, because we could make rugby union a totally regimented, very dull game, but still win. There's a balance to be drawn.

'If we prepare properly, and all do our jobs, we tend to win. If we don't, we lose, and that's what happened in the Six Nations. We lost a few players, we didn't prepare as well as we could have done, we had two great teams tearing at us and we lost. When that happens, though, you know why it happened, which is a major point, and you have to smile, not overreact, and get back to work. We know why we won the World Cup, we know why we lost those two games, and both were down to preparation.'

The credit, as so often, gets handed straight onto his players, the blame apportioned where he sees fit – too often, I suspect at his own front door, in the interests of taking pressure off others. For all his plans and programmes, the science and the strategy, he doesn't attempt to elevate the role of the coach to anywhere especially lofty. Other people do it for him, admittedly, and he hardly suffers from a deficit of praise, but even when talking about the system he has created, Woodward goes out of his way to laud the players who pass through it.

'We've maybe created an environment in which these spontaneous things can happen, but it's the individuals that make the moment. You've also got to remember that it's not just Robinson, for all his talents. Take Trevor Woodman, for example, a prop forward who can really run with the ball, catch and give, do things that make you excited. It's about seeing players move out of the comfort zone of what English rugby always used to be about and do things we never thought they could do.

'That's the attitude and the work that's put us ahead. That's the key thing, not only to get ahead, but to get it into the players' heads that we're in front, because then they're going to do these things, play this sort of rugby, and it's going to be very exciting. This is, and there's no doubt about this, a very exciting environment to work in, but it's also very challenging. The moment we stand still, we know they're going to be very hard on our tail.'

One of the problems with interviewing someone like Woodward is trying to find something different about which to ask him. Rather like one of Elizabeth Taylor's husbands on a wedding night, you're left doing something the other person has experienced many times before, but somehow trying to make it feel different. The explanations as to his way of working, and his motivation for coaching the way he does, are fascinating, but have been delivered, in one format or another, many times before. As hard as one tries to shine a new light on the subject, it's difficult to do much more than cover familiar ground in a marginally different way.

Mindful both of this, and the fascination he had provoked among almost everyone I met during the course of my journey, I tried to move him on to fresh ground, to a subject he maybe hadn't been quizzed about previously in quite such detail. I tried to paint a brief, thumbnail sketch of the Southwark Tigers, explaining what they were about, where they were, and how they looked up to an English rugby side they would once never have known or cared about.

'It's very warming, genuinely, to hear about things like that, and if that's happening, it's fantastic, but to be honest, we're all so busy, and things come around so fast, you don't get a chance to get involved. I'd love to go down to Peckham, for example, and meet the people, see what's happening, and soak it all up, but you have to rely on people telling you.

'I speak to the development people, and they tell me these stories, which are wonderful to hear, and I know kids are playing in places they weren't before, and I know all the kickers stand like Jonny Wilkinson, and all that's great, but we've got priorities. I believe very strongly that sport works from the top down, and my job is to look after the bit right at the very top. If we can produce superstar players in a superstar team, people will play the game.

'We're still way behind football, but rugby's not quite so simple a game to learn. Football's a very simple game, so we've got to look at making our game a bit simpler if we're really going to get up there and compete alongside it.'

For a minute, he'd stopped and maybe, just maybe, been a little thrown by the fact that he didn't know as much as he'd like to about this angle, this part of what his side had helped to achieve. He had no need to be – as he said, coaching England is a full-time job, and other people are detailed to look after development – but the praise, coming as it did from an unexpected direction for an unexpected reason, almost seemed to embarrass him. The speed with which he turned the conversation around to the systems needed to continue this progress, and the way he mentioned the roles others played in developing the game struck me as further evidence of a man passionate about creating order, making plans, and running projects. But that's not all I saw.

There is a huge amount of modesty about Clive Woodward, and it probably doesn't get commented upon as much as it should. The accusations of arrogance are offensively simplistic. From the moment he walked into the room and introduced himself, as if to presume that anyone should automatically know his name was somehow unforgivably self-important, to the point where he was briefly struggling, working out who deserved praise for an unexpected area of questioning, it hit me. He struck me as a modest man – modest and measured. Now, there are lots of modest people in the world of sport, but to paraphrase Churchill, many of them have much about which to be modest, a condition which cannot be applied to Woodward.

He was happier praising the system than allowing himself to receive the praise for something which genuinely merited it. As astute and precise as he is, he knew as well as I did that, having delivered the system and watched it work from the top down, he, as the man who looked after the top, is entitled to receive praise for that which happens at the bottom. His reaction, in deflecting praise off onto others, was as telling as his decision to develop the point was inevitable.

'You hear these things are going on, and if they are, then that's fantastic, really, genuinely fantastic,' he said, repeating himself to buy a second to gather his thoughts. 'But it's also, not to sound too remote from it, a bit of a by-product. I've always said, and I've had lots of discussions about sport and sports development, but for me, it's got to come from the top down. If you create superstars, if you create teams that win World Cups, if you create Tiger Woods, Wilkinson, Beckham, then kids will play the sport. If you don't, they won't.

'I've said from the day this game went professional, I want these guys to become multi-millionaires. If the sport can afford it, then that's what I want for them, because they deserve every penny they get, and that way, kids will look at the game, look at what it's brought to people, and decide that it's something they want to do for themselves.'

The conversation was, slowly but surely, developing a life of its own, in the way these things do, and drifting around to football. I attempted briefly to steer it back to rugby, but Woodward had things to talk about concerning the round-ball game, rather than the oval. I let it go – the football stuff was never going to become relevant, but he was happy to chat, so why risk ruining the conversational flow? Just a casual chat about a game in which he had a passing interest. As I said, my journalistic instincts really are quite impressively sharp sometimes. Unwittingly, I had strolled into the eye of the storm, and I hadn't even noticed it was raining.

'I look at football and rugby as the same, apart from the fact that one's played with your feet, the other with your hands. I want to see kids playing touch rugby in the street, as well as football. That's what we'll get across to them. You don't need scrums and lineouts, it doesn't have to be dangerous, and it doesn't have to be on grass. Kids can play touch rugby on any surface they want, and if it gets them into the game, that's an achievement. Don't get me wrong, I love football, but they're two different games, and we can go about promoting rugby in a certain way.'

Different games, and, sometimes, capable of demonstrating their differences in very distinct ways. A few days earlier, Millwall had reached the FA Cup final, and failed spectacularly to deliver the giant-killing act they had threatened, losing 3–0 to Manchester United. The first goal had broken their spirit, so it seemed, as Millwall's player–manager Dennis Wise failed to pick up his marker in the penalty area, allowing Cristiano Ronaldo to head home from close range.

At the end of the game, Wise was interviewed on the pitch and asked about the goal. 'I got a bad call from Neil Harris,' he explained, passing the buck with a finesse he had been unable to produce with the ball. In an instant, he had, as far as I could see, dealt with the situation as differently to the way in which one might have expected Woodward to react, as was possible to imagine. As a coach, he had made public a detail which should have been kept behind closed doors, publicly spoken out against one of his players without talking to him privately first, and flagrantly tried to distance himself from blame, at the expense of a bit of public humiliation.

It hardly fitted into the Woodward way of doing things, but then again, Woodward's own choice of football team seems a strange one for a man in love with firm foundations and proper, established preparation. How did he end up cheering for Chelsea, with their treatment of their own coach and the dubious benefits accrued from being bought by a Russian billionaire?

'I'm a Chelsea fan, and was long before all the money came flooding in. My dad was born in Battersea, and supported them before me, so I always have. They're my team, and that's the way it is. Even when he was moving around in the air force, I followed all the results, supported them from afar, and now, they're still my side and I go and watch them whenever I get the chance.

'It's interesting what's going on there, because it poses the old question about whether money can buy success. What they've shown is that it can get you closer, quicker, but as for tipping you over the edge and turning you into a winner, of course it can't; undoubtedly not.'

And there endeth the lesson. It's hard to find so much as an inconsistency in his football team of choice, let alone anything more meaningful. Clive Woodward may provoke a myriad of emotions in a number of different people, but you can never take away from his achievements, just as you can't deny his place in history. You also, I pondered, as he went off to consider the threat of the Barbarians, probably won't find many people much more personable in the highest echelons of international sport.

As I clicked the tape off and folded up my notebook, three middle-aged women came wandering through the room, passing Woodward on the way, in search of a spot of lunch and a bit of social climbing.

'It's the rugby chap, he's on the television. Seems very pleasant.'

I left them to it. We wouldn't agree on all that much, I suspected. Better to leave while they were expressing a sentiment upon which we did.

XIV

The last day of term

Sir Clive may have been determined (or at least, contractually obliged) to predict that the event would be 'a wonderful occasion for everyone involved', but like so many other sporting promises, it was made with fingers tightly crossed. For the 2004 Staffware Challenge Trophy, a title absurd enough to make football's very own Freight Rover Trophy sound prestigious, he had, from an international perspective, nobody of any note in his side. Strictly speaking, he wasn't telling lies about the day being a 'wonderful occasion' for his players, but that doesn't make them deserving candidates, or capable of competing in an exciting fashion in front of a Twickenham full house.

I can think of any number of men of roughly the right age who possess a knowledge of the rules and a pair of boots. It would be a wonderful occasion for any of them to play for England, but that, unfortunately, is a million miles away from it being any sort of memorable event for the paying spectator. As John Pullin had said as England captain, after a Dublin international more than 30 years ago, 'We might not be very good, but at least we turn up.' Three decades on, and another England skipper could have uttered those words with complete honesty and sincerity, and without even beginning to cross his digits in defiance.

This was, in effect, the last day of term. The senior boys were getting ready for a very tough school journey in the forthcoming holidays, and had played in a superfluous, end-of-season competition the day before. As a result, they had notes from their housemasters, excusing them from games. Most of the second XV would be taking their place as the whole school turned out to watch, on the Sunday of the Bank Holiday weekend. It was doubtless, as the school had been told all week, a chance for them to shine, but the Old Boys side who were coming to play them were looking very good indeed. This could very easily backfire in spectacular style.

If the game promised little, the associated delights of a Twickenham match day were as entertaining as ever, even if the people who caused the biggest laughs didn't always do so intentionally. Take the man from Tavistock RFC, for example, whose bid to generate a bit of patriotic fervour fell at the first hurdle. Full of loyal intentions, he ended up trying to disentangle himself from a nylon cross of St George, as he stood at a Waterloo urinal. Strong drink may already have been taken, but his wailed, 'Oh God, I've pissed down my flag,' delivered with a straight, if slightly panicked face, may yet become an unlikely cause célèbre for republicans everywhere. The accident, which might once have rated alongside arson in the Queen's dockyards, simply caused a gentle ripple of laughter as people concluded that, for this sort of entertainment, 20p for a pee isn't such a bad deal.

As the slowest rugby special train ever took a warm and weary 55 minutes to wend its way to Twickenham, a group of eight men boarded, slightly unsteadily, and with songs to sing. They were all wearing T-shirts with their nicknames on, in the same way Paddington Bear used to wear a label around his neck in case he got lost, and were rather enjoying being the centre of attention. I spent the day waiting for the Tannoy announcement to come out, asking for the friends of 'Thunder Chunder' to come and collect him from lost property, but it never arrived.

The tout count at the station was a rather paltry 12, but was more than compensated for by the suggestion from one of their number that you could 'save some money' if you bought from him. Not since Norman Lamont presided over the economy has anyone chosen to define the word 'save' in such an original fashion. I crossed the road, to be reprimanded by a policeman standing next to a man asking if people needed to 'buy or sell your Twickenham tickets', for failing to stay on the pavement.

I pointed out, cheerfully enough, that I was doing something legal, the tout wasn't, and just possibly the forces of law and order might think they were looking in the wrong direction? He told me not to be 'a smart arse', thus confirming to me that we'd come a long way since *Dixon of Dock Green*. Looking back, I think we both probably had a point . . .

The crowd and the coach had come, so common opinion held, for two different reasons. Woodward was keen to point out that he needed to see what players like Marcel Garvey and Paul Sackey could do 'on the big stage', while about 71,500 others had come to say goodbye to Jason Leonard. It took Leonard precisely three minutes to ensure the journalists had their story for the day and the crowd had something to discuss in the pub afterwards, as he crashed over from a yard out to claim the opening score of the game. One try in 114 attempts for England, and he'd now scored as many against them as for them. The crowd told the story of what he meant to them, by raising the roof every time his picture appeared on the giant screen.

From that point onwards, it was one-way traffic. Michael Horak made it a debut to forget by fumbling Brian O'Driscoll's kick four minutes later, allowing Shane Horgan to slide in for the Barbarians' second, and midway through the half, Bruce Reihana tore onto an inside pass from David Humphries to crash over for a third try. England were reduced to taking pot shots at goal when the chance arose, and four swipes of Dave Walder's boot were an unspectacular but effective way of narrowing things to 17–12.

The crowd were predictably unimpressed, not so much at the direction in which the result was heading, as the way England were playing. Having set the bar high with running rugby and interchangeable forwards and backs, dull rolling mauls and penalty kicks were no longer what Twickenham man expected from his white-shirted heroes. England, the next generation, were playing strangely like they used to in a previous incarnation, about a decade ago – before, not to put too fine a point on it, they were any good.

Indeed, as the spectacle became less spectacular by the minute, some of the best entertainment available was born out of the exchanges between Nigel Whitehouse – a Welsh referee with a lovely line in dry humour – and the players. Through the wonders of technology, you can plug in some headphones and listen to him talking the players through the game. More interestingly, you can also, when they stand next to him, hear them talking back. If you thought politics was about planting seeds of ideas, stabbing other people in the back and casting continual subtle aspersions at the opposition's honesty, believe me, it's got nothing on international rugby.

Midway through the first half, Hugh Vyvyan, drafted in as England captain for the day, wandered over for a chat with Whitehouse. 'Watch them slowing down our ball, eh?' he asked, innocently enough, to be met with a blank look, and, 'Will do. I don't want anyone slowing down anyone's ball.' Undeterred, Vyvyan tried again, 'Neither do we Nigel, neither do we. Keep an eye, and we'll keep it moving for you.' What had started as a request, had been met with a platitude, before descending into a bit of ingratiating brown-nosing. Vyvyan wandered off, trying to work out if he'd actually advanced his cause any. I don't think he had, but I was hooked on the idea of listening to the referee.

Just before the break, I tuned in to another gem. Robbie Morris, the Northampton prop, was about to scrum down, when Whitehouse spotted that the England bench wanted to make a change. 'Number 3, they want you,' he announced, as Morris, understandably not keen to depart, looked for a way to remain. 'No, they're just talking, let's get on with it.' It was a decent bid to stay, but Whitehouse was not to be dissuaded. 'No, son, you're off.' There was a brief delay, before, almost as an afterthought, the official called 'sorry' by way of consolation to the figure trudging his way to the sidelines. One short conversation had justified the existence of this magical little device, and as the game drifted into nothingness, I was increasingly grateful.

Given his insistence of the importance of watching his two new wingers, Woodward would have been as frustrated as anyone else at their lack of involvement. Sackey had a brief run, a chip ahead charged down, and was replaced nine minutes into the second half, a minute after Garvey got his first pass of the day. We'd learned something, though. We now know that if the coach waves at him, Sackey trots obediently off the pitch, back to the warmth of the bench, and that Garvey has a good enough memory to recall what the ball looks like despite having not seen it for the best part of an hour. Not the most crucial information, you might think, but hopefully they learned more about Twickenham than Twickenham learned about them.

Leonard departed the scene with a quarter of an hour to go, to a huge ovation, as the Barbarians began to stretch away, driving England backwards in the sweeping rain and increasing cold. The English pack had done little to impress, and the lineout in particular had been a disaster, a troop of uncertain giants, trying to catch a greasy balloon in a gale. At international level, as everywhere else, ball retention is everything, governing how much of the game you dictate and how much is imposed upon you. England played as if they had fallen out with it before the kick-off, and couldn't bear to be seen near it again.

Woodward's side eventually surrendered 32–15, and it was already hard to avoid the thought that it was one game too many at the end of a long and successful season. It was, to be honest, a horrible anti-climax. The stadium announcer, sounding as if he felt much the same, tried half-heartedly to persuade everyone to go home.

'There will be courtesy buses running from the stadium to Twickenham and Richmond stations, and we would ask you to use these to help us cut down congestion.'

I'm not sure how this helps – if you've brought your car already, you're hardly going to leave it there and take the bus, and if you were planning to walk, you're not exactly causing congestion, but I'm sure they had a cunning plan. Or at least, I was, until the second part of the message came thundering through the PA.

'The stadium bars, located on the concourses, will remain open for another two hours.'

Several thousand people, initially considering the bus, took one look at the rain and headed straight for the bar. Woodward's precise planning plainly doesn't permeate right the way throughout the RFU.

Before the pub beckoned, though, there was a story brewing, and the press pack shuffled around the stadium to the room where the press conferences are held, conveniently situated on the opposite side of the ground to the press box.

That morning, Woodward had appeared on Five Live's *Sportsweek*, and was asked by Gary Richardson whether he was convinced he'd get the support he needed to mount a proper defence of the trophy in four years' time.

'I'm convinced that myself and a few people know exactly why we won it. The only thing I'm a little cranky about is that there are one or two people in influential positions to make things happen for the England team who possibly, and rightly so, don't understand why the team won. We've got to increase the number of training days, increase the investment, but it's my job to make sure people understand that.

'Sometimes you have conversations with people and you walk away

THE LAST DAY OF TERM

shaking your head, as they seem to think we won the World Cup because we had a few good players. Well, we've got more than a few, we've got world-class players, but they'll be the first to admit you don't win World Cups because you've got good players, you win them because you prepare properly.

'I'm making it quite clear that England won because of the investment, and that's fantastic. Everyone invested hugely in me and the team and that's why we won, but we can't just expect that to happen every four years. It has to happen every year, and I'm determined to keep driving that investment through. I'm here to represent the players, and people like Johnson and Dallaglio have created huge role models, and we want people to step into those shoes and win. To do that, though, we have to understand why we won.'

The press, sensing a story rather more interesting than the game which had just occurred, asked him about his 'controversial' remarks, and whether there was a rift between him and the RFU members he had mentioned. It received the flattest of bats, as he denied that any such spin could be put on his remarks.

'I wasn't trying to cause any controversy this morning, and both myself and Dee have listened to it and can't see how you reach that conclusion. I just said we have to look at the way we won, how we prepared, and see if we can move on from that. I'm perfectly happy with the number of days I have with my players.'

Dee, to her credit, was standing, staring straight ahead, and keeping decidedly quiet. It was an interesting tactic from Woodward, claiming support from someone else for his unlikely contention, in the safe knowledge that she was going to remain a silent ally. She was unlikely, after all, to become the first press officer in history to turn to her boss in front of a crowd and say, 'Actually, I did think it was a bit controversial, and the bit about the players is utterly inconsistent with what you said this morning.'

They tried another tack: 'Would you be upset if you never had to play this fixture again?' Woodward pondered for a second, and asked for a few minutes to think about an answer that wouldn't cause offence. The press chuckled, and on we went. True to form, a few minutes later, he interrupted himself to announce that he'd formulated an answer.

'I think it's a wonderful fixture, providing I can play it with a full-strength side. It's hard to get excited about a game with a decimated squad, but you'd have to talk to the people who arrange the fixtures.

Now, this press conference is suspended for, oh, 12 months, which is fantastic. Goodnight, gents.'

Another marker had been set down, to go along with the one he wasn't admitting to but everyone knew he had planted on the radio that morning. I might have underestimated the extent of his annoyance with the RFU, but there was no doubting that things had come out precisely the way he had wanted. I don't think he suffers from slips of the tongue, and I'm not sure he ever speaks without thinking first.

Having won one World Cup, he was setting his sights on winning another, and the groundwork for that started now, shifting a few attitudes, making life more convenient. I didn't doubt, from his post-Sydney position of power, that he could win the internal battles he needed to progress his plans, which, at the time, made me feel that I had some degree of insight. Unfortunately, I neither thought, nor even considered, that he'd get so fed up with the infighting that he'd decide it just wasn't worth the bother. So much for insight. Unknowingly, I'd just watched his last post-match Twickenham press conference as England coach.

For today, though, Woodward had made his point and, press conference over, courtesy bus or not, it was time to make a move. The performance on the pitch might have been poor, but the tactical manoeuvrings the coach had pulled off through the media had made it a decent day's work for him.

The seemingly perpetual season was finally approaching the last lap. The story, however, little though we knew it at the time, had a hefty old kick left in its legs.

XV

May 2004

As the amateurs finished off their sevens tournaments, held their
end-of-season dinners and pondered the possibility of some pre-
season training – in itself a testament to the new influences on the
lower reaches of the game – so those at the top set out on one last,
weary lap. The Zurich Premiership continued on with its determination
not to allow logic to stand in the way of an end-of-year finale, as a
compelling league competition mutated into the lottery of a play-off
skirmish.

Bath, who had led the way for months on end, found themselves
stranded, waiting for Wasps to overcome Northampton to book a place
in a Twickenham final which, natural justice demanded, didn't need to
be played. The standard old hoary chestnut about knowing the rules
when they entered, was trotted out, but it couldn't justify the inherent
unfairness which surrounded the format.

If the London Marathon competitors were informed that the race
would be settled by a series of sprints between the top four, over
Westminster Bridge, regardless of finishing positions, all would
equally be aware of the rules, but few could suggest it made much
sense. Knowing the rules doesn't automatically make them sensible.
With sponsors to satisfy and stadiums to fill, however, rugby was
ignoring the obvious and ploughing ahead.

By the time they arrived at Twickenham for the final, Bath had gone three weeks without a game, while Wasps had been in action on a weekly basis. Indeed, that marathon analogy falls a little short – I meant to mention that the leader would have to hang around, getting cold, before waiting for his challenger to show up for the sprint. Surely, the tournament has to have the courage to nail its colours to the mast – any mast. It's either a league, or a knockout, but it can't be taken truly seriously until it stops pretending to be both. Football has been guilty of mucking about with one of its promotion places in much the same way, but even that historically mal-administered game doesn't dispense league titles quite so illogically.

In the event, it reached a predictably muddled conclusion. Bath won the league, lost the play-off final, and ended up with nothing. Wasps lost the season-long slog, won the final, and were crowned champions of a league they didn't win. The complication arose largely because Bath opted to play in so negative a manner, reliant on penalty goals and counter attacks, that it was hard not to cheer Wasps on. Taken in isolation, it was a fair result, but looked at over the course of the season the competition was meant to represent, the 10–6 win served the sport little. Just one try in 80 minutes, a Stuart Abbott scamper after a midfield mix-up, afforded this particular cake about all the icing it deserved.

The win secured Wasps a fine Double, having conjured up a far more dramatic and deserving 27–20 win over Toulouse in the Heineken Cup final a week earlier. Robert Howley's last-minute chip, chase and dive somehow saw Clement Poitrenaud left grasping at thin air, as both the ball and the trophy were snatched from his side's hands. It also handed an extra Heineken Cup place to an English side for next season, with Gloucester suddenly qualifying as of right, and Leicester and Sale left to slug it out on the undercard of the play-off final. In due course, Leicester sailed through, and anyone who claimed to understand quite how the whole competition worked was awarded a sponsor's anorak on their way out of the ground. It's hard to imagine that too many were disposed of.

The trend for last-minute drama had commenced the day before Wasps' victory over Toulouse, when Harlequins conquered Montferrand in extraordinary fashion, with, literally, the last kick of the game. Jason Leonard had come on for the last seven minutes of his club career, with Quins trailing 26–20, and his first action of real note was to get punched by Raphael Chanal with just a minute left, earning Quins a penalty and Chanal a red card.

With the cause looking hopeless, Quins refused to surrender, and swung the ball from side to side, ruck to maul, until finally, deep into injury time, a hole opened up in the Montferrand defence. Simon Keogh darted through, had the presence of mind to get under the posts, and tried not to watch as Andy Dunne attempted to turn a one-point deficit into a one-point victory, with one, usually straightforward, conversion. A deep puff of the cheeks, and Dunne stabbed the ball between the uprights, to ensure that Leonard went out with a trophy.

Dramatic enough, but it took the Sky reporter just seconds to take us into the wide, blue, hyperbole-laden yonder, as he drooled at a distinctly bemused Leonard afterwards.

'Jason, I knew you could do it, we all did, I could feel it in my juices,' he twittered. Leonard played a very good straight man. 'You could feel it where?' Our intrepid man in the field, mindful of the fact he had just asked a truly absurd non-question, decided the best way out of this hole was to dig yet further. 'I'm sorry, Jason,' he chuckled, 'it was something my mum used to say!'

And as he finished the question, and tumbleweed drifted across the camera, Leonard was truly lost for words. Mr Sky Sports was now opting for silence, backtracking so fast that he was barely still in the stadium when the answer finally came. 'Well, having not met your mother, I can't comment on that, but I am obviously really thrilled that we've won.' You had to turn off at this point – it wasn't that it was emotional, but it made me cringe in a way that only David Brent had previously managed.

In keeping with the trend for end-of-year nonsense, Worcester's promotion to the Premiership was delayed, as Rotherham, in an extraordinary outburst of bad grace, threatened a legal challenge. Having finished bottom of the league with just three points to their name, a mere 34 points from safety, one might have imagined that they would have been analysing their own playing failures, as opposed to another club's alleged stadium deficiencies. Instead, they complained that Worcester's ground wasn't capable of staging top-flight rugby, in much the same way, crueller observers might note, that Rotherham evidently weren't capable of contesting it. As it transpired, the threat came to nothing. Rotherham slithered out and Worcester, who won all 26 of their games en route to the title, marched in, after a week-long delay.

On the international front, England won the Laureus World Team of the Year award, and presumably picked up the trophy without uttering the words 'Who the hell are Laureus?', unlike everyone else who heard the news. Whoever judges these things had deemed the England rugby squad to be a better team than the Australian cricketers, AC Milan or Ferrari, and the rumour is that the award itself is in line to collect next year's 'Best Effort at Pompously Comparing Totally Dissimilar Sporting Teams' shield. Just to underline the award's pedigree, an Australian surfer won the 'Best Alternative Sportsperson' prize, although Eric Bristow is believed to have lodged an appeal.

While he wasn't collecting awards, Woodward was back into his all too familiar routine of collecting sick notes, as his squad withered away like a Sunday morning pub side after a heavy night out. With Wilkinson now confirming what everyone had long suspected – namely that he wouldn't be making the trip thanks to his shoulder injury, Paul Grayson's decision to step back from international rugby probably wasn't quite what the coach needed to hear. Having been thrown in at the deep end at the start of his international career, Olly Barkley's 'sink or swim' process of education looked set to continue for a while yet, as Charlie Hodgson's name began to get mentioned in international circles once more.

With the awards season drifting on, Simon Shaw won the Zurich Premiership Player of the Season title, while Barkley won the Young Player's crown. At least the two of them were fit to tour, which set them apart from just about anyone else who had received any form of praise or plaudits in the preceding 12 months. Just to keep the tradition of blindingly obvious award-giving alive and well, Martin Johnson won the 'Zurich Outstanding Contribution Award for Service to Rugby', only previously, so the press release boasted, given to Jason Leonard, and presumably why nobody had ever bothered thinking up a catchier title. Cabinet makers all over the Midlands were reported to be deluging the former England captain with quotes, as his collection of silverware grew every time a group of a dozen or more rugby people put on a dinner jacket.

Finally, with time ticking down before the plane left for New Zealand, tradition was maintained, as Woodward indulged in what cynics might suggest were a few mind games with his opposing numbers. In addition to this, coupled with the comments he made at the time of the Barbarians game, the suggestion that he was setting out the rules of engagement for his next scuffle with the RFU top brass became harder to resist.

'It's been a long season and it was a tough Six Nations, but we haven't been together at all since March and the first time we've trained as a team was on Monday,' he said, in a decidedly 'make of it what you will' manner. Retreat and acceptance of anything other than perfection was not, you sensed, high on his list of priorities.

Captain Dallaglio, equally characteristically refusing to take a backwards step, either on the pitch or in writing, insisted that England would take a strong side on tour, regardless of the fact that players were 'dropping out by the second'. It wasn't quite as much of an exaggeration as it could have been. Iain Balshaw had joined the injured list, while Jason Robinson, Will Greenwood and Ben Kay were being 'rested' and would be staying at home. At home, the fans were trying to pick their side by subscribing to games of 'fantasy rugby'. Deep in the depths of Penny Hill Park, Sir Clive was doing much the same thing, privately, you suspected, viewing it as more of a nightmare than a dream.

XVI

Back down under

Woodward was putting a brave face on it, the players were talking brightly about proving themselves and, in general, the RFU were doing all they possibly could to make it sound like a fair contest, a good idea and a worthwhile venture. And if one, single soul was convinced by it all, they weren't troubling themselves to say so too loudly. As far as anyone who was in a position to be able to admit to it was concerned, England's summer tour to Australia and New Zealand was a classic example of one trip too many.

Never afraid to travel overseas with ample provisions, coaching staff, technical staff, barristers, cooks and the rest, this time, Woodward and his men ventured forth with an additional ingredient – fatigue. Having crammed the best part of two seasons into one, someone, in their wisdom, had decided that a three-week jaunt down under was the perfect way to round off an exhausting season.

Even if the limbs held up, something was destined to crack somewhere, simply because of the glut of rugby the squad had endured over the last year. Jason Leonard, better positioned than most to know how they were feeling, was in little doubt as to the effects on them:

'It's not that they're not big enough, fit enough or strong enough, but they've come to the end of a desperately long season and it builds up.

It's really hard to keep that focus and stay as sharp as you'd like to be when you're playing that much rugby over such a long period of time.'

Superlatives and plaudits had been launched in their direction for the previous six months since winning the World Cup, but even before the already-depleted touring party flew out of Heathrow, it seemed a tour destined to see the season culminate in an anti-climax. Granite-jawed and chiselled they might have been, but this was asking for blood out of a stone. Tired and in need of rest, they were heading off to their sternest southern-hemisphere opponents and giving them a chance to even the score a little. Like a boxer taking on one fight too many, two facts seemed to stand out above all others. Firstly, it was destined to end in failure, and secondly, pride and habit left them unable to acknowledge this inevitability.

When Woodward had been asked, in the run-up to the Barbarians game, how his side would prepare, he delivered an answer designed to demonstrate the seriousness with which he was approaching the game.

'We'll go about it like any other Test match. There will be no difference between this and the way we prepare to play the All Blacks in Dunedin in a few weeks' time.'

Little did he know how similar the pre-match setting would be, surrounded once more, as he eventually was, by players unused to top-flight international rugby, wondering whether they were about to get horribly exposed in the 80 minutes which awaited them. Rather grandly, some would say absurdly for a mere sporting venue, known as the 'House of Pain', Dunedin has been an All Black stronghold for as long as New Zealanders have been playing the game. Going there with a full-strength side, it would have represented a fearsome start to any tour – with this one, the writing was on the wall right from the outset.

As match day arrived, Woodward was not in the mood, one suspected, to deal with trivialities or daft questions. Unfortunately for him, our chum from Sky, freshly recovered from a verbal mauling from Leonard, was on hand once more to offer his best shot. Tom Voyce, originally on the bench, had been dropped in favour of Olly Barkley, as the wet and windy conditions led England to conclude that an extra kicker, rather than a runner, might be a better proposition to have in reserve.

As it transpired, someone with a red cloak and his underpants outside his trousers might have been better still, emerging from a phone box when required. With little else to go on, however, Sky focused their pre-match pitch-side questions on the upset this must have caused Voyce – the uncapped Voyce, as he was described. Woodward saw a momentary opportunity to end an interview in which he plainly didn't, despite his desire to remain polite, have any wish to participate.

'Oh, he's been capped before, I think. I think we capped him in Canada. I might be wrong . . .'

It was an intriguing phrase, 'I might be wrong', coming as it did from a man who knew he wasn't, thus rendering it less of a concession than it might have appeared at first hearing. You could see the interviewer mentally taking a step back, aware of his previous experiences of asking daft questions to rugby personalities. The interview didn't go much further – Woodward had things to do.

The New Zealand side had gone through its own traumatic labour in the week before the game, before being delivered as a healthy and bonny hybrid of the 'probables' and 'possibles' sides which had gone into the trial game. The major piece of information to have been confirmed from that match seems to have been that the All Black selectors had, in the first place, little or no idea who their best side might be. By the time the game was done, the 'possibles' had claimed a victory, and the entire 'probables' front row, among others, had shunted its way into the line up for the first Test.

On a freezing, wet night, with mist and rain taking turns to sweep around an open and exposed Dunedin ground, the home side went through the ceremonial motions which now precede even the most meaningless international. It's as if mumbling through a couple of anthems confers otherwise absent significance on the most ill-advised and mis-matched of contests, and over the course of the last three or four seasons, it seems you can't escape from it. It's not enough to just have a band, either, you've got to have a singer, armed with a microphone and a fixed smile, deliberately keeping either half a line ahead or behind the rest of the crowd. It's an unwritten rule, and if this sentence was sung at such an event, you'd be hearing the words 'finished reading' just as you finished reading this, still rolling down from the stands.

Doing the honours this time was a Perma-tanned Kiwi, thick of jaw and orange of skin, called, I kid you not, Jud Arthur. Had Jud hit the high notes with the same frequency he appeared to hit the sunbed, it would have been great, but he didn't and it wasn't. Ironically, in an age when people try to tell us we live in a more secular world, the addition of a ball leaves everyone asking for a bit of celestial assistance, as God was implored to save first the Queen and then defend New Zealand. Thankfully, the Haka reminded us that pre-match ceremonials don't have to be a dismal dirge.

Within ten seconds of the kick-off, the requirement for the aid of the almighty became rather more specific – the Queen would have to look after herself for a minute, because England's right flank was calling. In the first of a string of tactical decisions that didn't survive a first viewing, let alone any form of video analysis, the ball was sent away from the packs, deep to the opposite flank, and into the arms of Joe Rokocoko.

For much of the previous week, England had talked about the need to avoid kicking the ball straight to the New Zealand back three of Rokocoko, Doug Howlett and Mils Muliaina, blessed as they were with a combination of pace and vision unmatched by any other unit in world rugby. As the kick-off floated gently to the most lethal of the trio, the tone for much of the following fortnight was set. Rokocoko sailed through tackles, returning the ball 50 yards upfield, setting in motion an attacking movement that should and would have, were it not for a poor decision from Kees Meeuws, the prop, resulted in a try before Woodward's men had even touched the ball.

New Zealand, black and menacing, out of the blocks and intent on destruction, played like the rugby equivalent of a young Tyson dispatching an older, less worthy challenger without so much as a sniff of sentimentality. Suddenly, the boxing analogy looked horribly prescient, as did the vivid and violent reality of the manner in which they were to be dispatched.

Danny Grewcock was reduced to throwing silly, spiteful little swipes on the fringes of things, while each ruck and maul saw the ball returned from black-shirted depths, ready for the next sortie to begin. By the end of the first four minutes, England had missed five tackles. By the end of the fifth minute, they had 'enjoyed' 4 per cent of the possession, at least half of which appeared to have been taken up by the initial kick-off. As baptisms of fire went, this was a beauty. An All Black beauty.

Daniel Carter sent over the first of a string of kicks after six minutes, and despite a levelling strike from Charlie Hodgson shortly after, when the All Blacks next went ahead, through a stunning Carlos Spencer try, it was a lead they never surrendered. Indeed, such was the majesty with which it was claimed, had it been the only try of the contest, you couldn't have argued that it was an undeserved winner.

Throughout the course of a torrid opening quarter of an hour, England had been taunted and bullied by Rokocoko, who had reduced James Simpson-Daniel, a man rumoured to be marking him, to head-shaking bafflement. In one particularly incisive surge, Rokocoko had simply left the Gloucester man grasping at thin air. To steal the famous old quote, he went inside Simpson, outside Daniel, and the hyphen never had a prayer of stopping him.

When it came to their first try, however, the home side went off in the opposite direction. Matt Dawson had an aimless kick charged down, Howlett launched the counter attack, and then drifted out, ready to play a continuing role further into the drama. Slipping the ball to Xavier Rush, Howlett watched the back-row forward create space for him, before receiving the ball back, stepping inside and guiding a perfect pass into the arms of Spencer, who slid into the corner for the score. All of it done at high speed, with perfect judgement and in the face of a freezing, wet wind. They might be arrogant at times, especially when laying the accusation at the door of others, but New Zealand, and especially this current incarnation, play the game with a mixture of simplicity and purpose that, at its best, is impossible not to admire.

Hodgson, who proved himself to be one of the few bonuses of the tour, kept his head despite the best decapitation-based efforts of the New Zealand back row, but was having a torrid time. Jono Gibbes was enjoying, in every sense of the word, one of the great debuts, and time after time, Hodgson had the opportunity to do little more than dispose of the ball by whichever means was quickest, whether by hand or boot, before the All Black flanker hurtled into him. When Gibbes wasn't terrorising Hodgson, Richie McCaw took a turn, forcing an England back line already looking short of cohesion and imagination into yet further chaos.

Midway through the half, after a passing movement which went through more phases than David Bowie, Rokocoko moved from creator to finisher, surging inside through a seemingly thick wall of white shirts, before striding under the posts. Simpson-Daniel was left looking around, bewildered, asking if anyone had seen the man he was supposed to be marking, as a mother might inquire after a lost child. It was a pose he was to re-adopt twice more before even the temporary sanctuary of half-time was reached.

As the visitors restarted, Carter's inevitable conversion having sent the All Blacks 17–3 clear, they finally put together a sustained period of pressure, driving the ball to the New Zealand posts before being awarded a penalty by South African referee Jonathan Kaplan. Awarded, that is, for a total of maybe three or four seconds, before Ben Cohen came careering off the wing (and you didn't get to write that often on this tour), to berate the official for failing to spot a late tackle.

In an instant, the penalty was reversed, the pressure was off, the fight-back was aborted and the pendulum had swung back firmly towards the home side. Several weeks later, at the end of the tour, Cohen expressed his approval for a plan to cut the number of games played by the country's top players. If he didn't get away from the mental side of the game soon, he explained, he'd 'burn out'. As England retreated from the All Black line, never to return, one imagines the coach, momentarily at least, was fully prepared to accede to his winger's request to play fewer big games in the future.

Just minutes later, and the result, as everyone knew deep down was already the case, was put beyond all doubt. Muliaina, Rokocoko and Howlett combined out wide with a stunning display of interchanging and space creation to claim a beautiful score in the corner, inevitably converted by the imperious Carter, sending their side 24–3 clear, and, on a wet night, home and dry. In a game when most experts predicted reasonably enough that passing would be difficult, England had been sunk by a display of swift and deadly handling to which they had no answer.

If they were to have any chance of regaining even the faintest of footholds in the contest, reaching the break without conceding further was of primary importance, but even this proved too much. Cohen missed touch, the counter attack was illegally smothered, and Carter swept home a kick to extend the lead yet further, before Steve Thompson conceded a penalty in front of the posts to ensure another followed on the stroke of half-time. Trailing 30–3, there was nothing Woodward could do or say to his troops, other than to try to ensure the margin did not get any more embarrassing than was already the case.

'Simpson-Daniel hasn't even touched the ball yet,' someone moaned to me, looking for reasons to explain the onslaught. The ball? I wasn't sure I could identify a moment when he'd touched his opposite number. Lawrence Dallaglio, who managed to emerge with credit for his sheer refusal to surrender, had referred to the side as 'battle-hardened' before the game. In truth, they looked shell-shocked, as all the fears about the endless season came to life in front of our eyes.

Still the kicks were fired aimlessly down the throats of the All Black back three, and still the threat from the men in white shirts failed to materialise. By the end, despite a brave rearguard action which limited the home side to just two second-half penalties, it was one-way traffic, with a scrummage against the head right at the end adding insult to injury. England's set-piece play had been woeful, their defensive play in the back line conspicuous by its absence and their attacking options utterly impotent. New Zealand were good, and in places, particularly when attacking with ball in hand, they looked spectacular, but it was a difficult contest on which to make a meaningful judgement. The fears about it being a tour too far, a Test match too many were proved to be absolutely spot on, and with two matches still to come, even if she wasn't singing yet, the fat lady was clearing her throat and taking a deep and ominous breath.

Dallaglio's performance at the press conference which followed was as uncompromising as his performances on the pitch had been, as he appealed to the passion of his colleagues in a bid to drag one, last effort from them. He knew the scale of the task that awaited them, and the chances of success, but having never ducked a challenge, he wasn't intending to start now. Somehow, he was determined to find something to carry them through the two remaining games. A plea for some emotional soul searching was all he had left.

'I think the most important thing is for people to go away and contemplate – to think just what pulling on a white jersey means to them, because we can play a lot better. I firmly believe we can put things right.'

In sporting terms, at least as far as this particular tour was concerned, it was the equivalent of the captain of the Titanic standing on the deck just before it slid under the waves and announcing his firm intention to relaunch at first light. As impassioned and determined as he sounded, as much as he was prepared to lead by example, the task was simply too big to be completed. Besides, there were other problems to consider.

So long heralded, and rightly so, as a model of disciplined, regimented defence, England were having to face up to the fact that the reputation they had worked so hard to attain was starting to suffer serious damage. Cohen's ill-considered bleating was maybe a sign of the pressure and frustration he felt, as much as anything else, but Grewcock's squabbling, especially when there was so much conventional work to be done, was a more worrying symptom. Nobody was going to be surprised that being on the end of such a drubbing had left them rattled, but displaying it in such a public way was a huge bonus to the opposition, especially on a tour when baiting the English has long been an accepted pastime.

The pressure was mounting from all directions. Even Warren Gatland, the Wasps coach, had suggested publicly that the English players were bored of too many meetings, suggesting that the back-up staff were justifying their existence at the expense of the well-being of the squad. Nobody from the Wasps contingent within the England party was commenting publicly, leaving Woodward to condemn the suggestion as 'total nonsense'.

'Warren is an outstanding guy and an outstanding coach and I think he will be a bit embarrassed when he reads it. Certainly, the Wasps players are.'

In the stark, carefully worded response, there is certainly room to interpret that things were not running as smoothly as they might be in the camp. Why were the Wasps players embarrassed, if they hadn't said it? Wouldn't they be angry, rather than embarrassed? Surely embarrassed suggests being 'caught out', rather than being wrongly quoted? In any case, once the statement opened with the phrase, 'Warren is an outstanding guy,' we knew we were in the world of PR. As events were to show, Woodward's relations with the various Premiership coaches didn't always tend to leave him in quite so complimentary a mood.

Yet it was understandable, as the lunacy of the tour and the inevitable exhaustion of the players and coaching staff must surely have been showing through somewhere. It seemed, however, that someone at the International Rugby Board (IRB) and the RFU had chosen to believe that just because players were professional, they were exempt from ever getting tired – that wages made tired legs magically fresh. As had been proved once, this was total nonsense, and it looked set to be highlighted twice more in the next fortnight.

By the time the sides emerged in Auckland, nobody was left in any doubt as to the effects of the previous week on Woodward. No fewer than six changes were made, an almost unheard of amount of tinkering for a man who prides himself on not suffering from knee-jerk reactions, spread evenly between forwards and backs. Simpson-Daniel, Mike Catt and Dawson made way for Tom Voyce, Stuart Abbott and Andy Gomarsall, while in the pack, Steve Thompson, Grewcock and Joe Worsley were replaced by Mark Regan, Steve Borthwick and Chris Jones in an attempt at curing their lineout chaos.

Major changes, perhaps, but in all honesty, despite a braver, more committed performance than the previous week, nothing much else seemed to change very much at all. The start was more aggressive and structured, and Hodgson's two early penalties suggested that the beginnings of a remarkable turnaround might just be in sight, but a judicial intervention, vital and absurd in equal parts, suddenly changed not just the path of the game, but the tone of the tour.

Just ten minutes had elapsed when Keith Robinson, the All Black lock, 'found himself', for which read 'put himself', on the wrong side of a ruck, lying on the ball, killing it dead and stopping an England attack in its tracks. Simon Shaw, standing over Robinson and staring at a black jersey where the ball should be, gave him a nudge, nothing more, with his knee, and 20 seconds or so of handbags broke out, with half-hearted punches and threatening glances and shoves aplenty – in the grand scheme of things, hardly a bar-room brawl.

As the scuffle petered out, however, the Welsh referee, Nigel Williams, was called over by Australian touch judge, Stuart Dickinson, and a fevered debate broke out between them, complete with much finger pointing and nodding in the direction of the English pack. Dallaglio was summoned over, Shaw was told to accompany him, and a verdict and sentence were swiftly dispensed.

'White number 4.' A quick check to see if he'd got the right man, which he had – to a point. 'Touch judge reports deliberate knee – red card. Off you go.'

And with a flourish of the red card, England were down to 14 men, a stunned and understandably upset Shaw was forced to trudge off, and the crowd, who had been chanting 'off, off, off' from the moment Shaw was summoned, cheered themselves hoarse. It was an absurd decision, for an offence that merited at the very worst a yellow card for overreacting, and even then, one which should have included Robinson as well, for killing the ball in the first place. That would have been sensible and uncontentious, which may, just possibly, be why it seemed to Stuart Dickinson like such an unattractive idea.

To be fair to Williams, he had, once Dickinson had made out his case, very little option but to take the action he did. The fact Dickinson was 30 yards away and obscured by a pile of steaming bodies, that he had to check Shaw's identity with the video replay official, and that the description given to Williams evidently hadn't matched the act committed, appeared to trouble him little.

In the aftermath of the contest, which was now, in effect, ruined, Woodward was admirable in saying what he saw and what he thought – that Dickinson was influenced by the crowd into convincing Williams to make an unfair dismissal. Steven Tew, the deputy chief executive of the New Zealand Rugby Union and evidently a man who had long since conquered his fear of appearing self-important, complained to the IRB about the comments. The row blew up and rolled on, and every little bit of it was more serious and more damaging to the game than anything poor Simon Shaw did on that pitch.

From that moment onwards, Woodward's side were doomed, despite a performance with more character and resolve about it than had been shown at any single point in the first Test. Carter chipped away at the lead with yet another penalty, but England somehow clung onto their lead for 20 wearying minutes, conceding a man in the pack, space on the flanks and burdened by a merited sense of injustice.

Abbott was forced off with a shoulder injury, Tindall with a bad hip, and still the less than menacing and hastily constructed midfield trio of Fraser Waters, Olly Barkley and Hodgson stuck to their task with admirable courage, if insufficient bulk. Gomarsall was genuinely impressive at scrum-half, especially with a pack liable to lurch backwards at a moment's notice, as their depleted ranks struggled to hold an All Black eight intent on pressing home their advantage. Eventually, the try had to come, as Rokocoko, to nobody's surprise, teased open a hole among the white shirts to send Carter tumbling over the line, despite Voyce's desperate efforts to stop him.

Only the profligacy of Justin Marshall, taking bad options in all directions despite having as easy a ride as an international scrum-half could ever expect to enjoy, looked likely to stop the score mounting, and as he regained some composure, the inevitable began. Cohen shipped a suicide pass to Josh Lewsey, who put the ball straight into touch from a yard outside of his 22, allowing Rokocoko to slide into the far corner as the resultant lineout fed the ball wide. In case anyone retained any doubts about the extent to which English composure had been dented, Barkley put the restart out on the full and New Zealand started to win more than their share of lineouts.

Richard Hill, one of the few remnants of the World Cup final to start the game, was now too battered and bruised to continue, and he duly limped off. With England stretched, Rokocoko ghosted over for another, before rising high to claim a cross-kick and hat-trick. The resistance, brave as it was, had crumbled. Carlos Spencer slid home late in the day to make the final score 36–12, with a ravaged England side looking glad for the shelter of the dressing-room. Dallaglio, a warrior to the end, looked furious, Woodward looked genuinely bemused, and all eyes turned back to the tenth minute, and began to consider once more the Shaw sending off, which had played such a large part in the game.

Make no mistake, England were well beaten once more, but this was a performance worlds away from the sorry, shambling nonsense they had produced in Dunedin a week earlier. Outclassed, perhaps, out-refereed, certainly, but they had shown character and courage to keep plugging away at opponents superior in terms of freshness, form and numbers.

The following day, the disciplinary hearing, held in the All Black team hotel, no less, heard from Richard Smith QC, Woodward's erstwhile travelling wigged wonder. On the technicality of Dickinson having consulted with the video referee, Shaw was cleared. The fact remains, however, that he is the third English player ever to receive a red card, after Mike Burton and Danny Grewcock.

As Shaw lived to ruck another day, so Grewcock – poor, misunderstood, volatile Grewcock – took his place in the dock for a stamp on Carter, picked up by the video referee who had just played a part in clearing Shaw. Grewcock would have been dismissed there and then, in the 59th minute, moments after coming on as a substitute, had the referee seen the incident, leaving his side to battle on with 13 men.

Grewcock has been sent off for England before – in fact, he's been sent off playing for a number of sides. Having been received back into the fold once, whether he is offered another shot at repentance remains to be seen. To many, stamping on a grounded opponent who is unable to evade a flurry of studs is as bad as it gets, and even the most forgiving fan must be finding their patience sorely tested as far as he is concerned.

By the time the team had staggered out of Auckland and landed in Brisbane, it was surely only old habits dying hard which left Woodward and Eddie Jones sniping at each other, as everyone else seemed too weary and too fed up to care. Just play the game and get the hell out – everyone was shattered, form had been left far back down the road, and the Webb Ellis trophy seemed to be getting more tarnished with each successive outing. After his previous visit to Australia, Woodward had freely acknowledged, even in the wake of triumph, that there would be rebuilding work to do. Nobody seemed prepared for the ferocity with which the old structure was being torn down, though.

Young players were being introduced to the international stage in such ferocious and desperate circumstances that you half expected them to turn around, announce they'd made a big career mistake, and go off and do something less dangerous – lion taming, or tightrope walking. The older, more experienced members of the side were looking jaded as the circus trudged on to its final stop, unable to produce anything like the form which had served them so well seven months earlier. As a learning experience, it was an exercise of dubious merit. The only thing most people seemed to have learned was that touring can be dull, and being beaten out of sight is depressing – facts which most of them probably already knew.

The eighteenth international game of a monster season awaited them first, however, against an Australian team who were anything but jaded, coming into the contest at the opposite end of their season and looking for fresh-legged revenge. Woodward was, once more, searching for an interpretation of events to encourage his men to one final effort, insisting that there was no pressure on England, and all of it rested on the green and gold shoulders of the opposition. 'It's the last game of the season – a complete one-off,' he insisted, although he probably had to call Twickenham and check, just in case they'd lined up a few more on the way home.

In the sense that the last game is always a one-off, because there's only one of them, it was hard to disagree, but true one-offs don't have 17 other internationals preceding them, with all the wear and tear that entails. After the events of the previous two weekends, nobody was expecting a miracle, and as such, nobody went home surprised.

Wendell Sailor managed to pull a hamstring in the last knockings of the warm up, leaving Clyde Rathbone to fill in as such a late reserve that he played the first half in the number 21 jersey he had been wearing in preparation for a night on the bench. As with everything else that happened to him, things could scarcely have worked out more perfectly.

We were once again reminded of the onset of the commercial era, as the stadium announcer asked us to welcome the 'Qantas Wallabies' to the field, rather than 'Australia', and the pre-match rituals showed every sign of being as obscure as ever. God was asked to save England, fair Australia were advised to advance, and Adam Harvey, looking like Elvis at the end, rather than the start of his career, strummed his way through 'Waltzing Matilda'. On the pitch, England made a decent start, yet found themselves six down in as many minutes as Joe Roff punished a couple of indiscretions among the forwards. Hodgson narrowed the margin, and the visitors were managing to offer a decent account of themselves before, as in each of the two previous games, an injection of pace saw them cut to pieces out wide.

The Australian backs conjured up a sublime passing movement, sending Rathbone into the corner to increase the margin, with Roff converting. Three minutes later, Cohen failed to release in a ruck, and Roff again struck to extend their margin to 13 points. Richard Hill's crash over in the corner, midway through the half, was notable for two reasons. Firstly, it represented England's first try of the tour, after a mere 188 minutes of rugby, and secondly, it was about the first time they'd retained the ball through more than four phases of play. A modicum of face-saving had been achieved, but nothing more. Like Monty Python's knight on the way to the Holy Grail, they sneered that their wounds were little more than a scratch, as limb after limb was hacked off.

As if to emphasise the point, Rathbone found himself on the end of an overlap in the last minute of the half, diving for the score to leave his side 21–8 ahead. Paddy O'Brien, the normally inscrutable New Zealand referee, had done England few favours, with a strange decision to penalise a delayed lineout, despite Mark Regan, the hooker, being treated for an injury at the time, but it was hard to lay it all at the door of the official. For the tenth time in two and a half tests, England had conceded a try thanks to either a miscalculation or missed tackle in the back division, leaving an extra man on the flank. I make no claims to be a coach, but something was going badly wrong, and it didn't take a genius to locate it.

To their huge credit, England struck back in the second period, as Dallaglio crashed over at the end of a sustained drive, undoubtedly, regardless of the score, the most deserving try-scorer of the day. For a moment, the vaguest possibility of a fight-back appeared, only for Rathbone, complete, since the break, with correctly numbered shirt, to make things safe. As the ball was moved wide, he chipped, shimmied, surged, kicked on and regathered, to effect a moment of wizardry at high speed, and claim his third score. Number 21 may have got two and number 14 one, but the hat-trick was the property of one man alone.

From then on, it was one-way traffic as Roff carved the back line apart yet again to feed Jeremy Paul, before the reserve hooker claimed another, getting on the end of a passing move to score, virtually unopposed in the corner. By the time Lote Tuqiri danced through the middle of the pitch, drifting between tacklers as if playing against schoolboys, it was almost over. England could only hope for no further damage, and I was seeking divine inspiration, wondering how many different ways there were to describe a team conceding a try because their back line had failed to defend properly. The final blow was left to Roff, asked by George Gregan to land a kick from distance to bring up the half century of points. To nobody's surprise, he did, and the final curtain came down on a dismal tour, with Australia romping home 51–15.

If the plane home had managed to land in the stadium at that very minute, you sensed the England players would have gladly boarded and escaped. In the aftermath of their last victory on Australian soil, seven, long months earlier, the RFU opted to take the trophy on a celebratory tour of England and send the World Cup-winning side on a bruising tour of the southern hemisphere. It's not difficult to assess who got the better deal. Dallaglio, impressive to the very end, was dignified and generous in defeat, but his face betrayed both the hurt and the fatigue.

It had been a tour which highlighted many things. Some, such as the length of the season damaging the players, were always going to be obvious. Others were not so easily anticipated. With key players either rested or injured, the England back division is not the weapon it was, and indeed, fails even to rank as competent when put against the best the world now has to offer.

Torn apart by flair and pace, some degree of fighting fire with fire must surely be introduced if England are to compete more evenly when the sides next meet. To keep the ball close, and play the game tight, against either of these two sides, is inviting disaster. It used to be said in footballing circles that it only took a second to score a goal. A tired old cliché, maybe, but with the pace of Rathbone, Rokocoko, Howlett, Tuqiri and others, these two sides are bringing ever closer the day when you can also say it about rugby.

The last time they returned to England from Australia, the side had been bearing gifts, and were greeted by thousands at Heathrow. Suddenly, it was all very different, and memories of last November had faded still further. Nobody was better positioned than Woodward to reverse the slide and nobody would have set about the challenge with as structured and single-minded an approach. Equally, nobody knew just how much of an effort it was going to take to recreate the background from which he had benefited in the run-up to the last World Cup. Fewer still, as it was to transpire, realised quite how wearing that battle was proving to be.

For the moment, though, it's back to expectations and hopes once more and, after some rest, planning and preparation as the long slog recommences. It was sad to see England humbled, even when it was deserved in the face of such stunning displays, because there's always something bleak about watching a champion bow out – watching them hang around just that bit too long, and losing the mystery they once enjoyed.

'There's no mystique,' Woodward had told me, back at Penny Hill Park. He was talking about himself, but now, unfortunately, he could just as easily have been describing his team. The demolition ball had done its work, and while the Webb Ellis trophy rested safely in their grasp, England were left to look out at the ruins of what had once been invincible.

If the structures and schemes meant anything, and the training and grafting were to be justified, the journey to the next World Cup started here. Stripped of all but their title, England had to recover and rebuild, and in the process show character beyond which, arguably, had been demanded of them before. Never had they needed their coach and his visions of the future quite so badly. Never, however, as we were about to see, had things gone from bad to worse at quite such dizzying speed.

I cast my mind back to that conversation at Sydney Airport, days after the trophy was secured. 'The blazers could still bugger the whole thing up,' the voice had warned. He was about to be proved right in the most dramatic of circumstances.

XVII

Knight of the long knives

The end, when it came, generated different responses in different people, depending on how close they were to the Woodward 'camp'. To his trusted few, the coaches, advisers and confidantes with whom he had discussed the fine details of his plans over the years, it had an air of inevitability. It was the logical result of asking a man to fight one battle too many, against people he didn't expect to be fighting in the first place.

To others, those who followed it from a slightly greater distance, including the vast majority of the rugby-loving public and almost every other habitual devotee of the back pages, it was a genuine bolt from the blue. On the surface, it had all the classic ingredients of a 'silly season' story – a tale that crops up when there's nothing much else to fill the sports sections. The Olympics were over, it was a Premiership-football-free weekend, and England's football international against Austria was still several days away.

Coupled with the fact that when it first appeared, in the *Daily Mail*, it was accompanied by a few paragraphs promoting Woodward's forthcoming book, it didn't take a cynic to conclude that it was a convenient bit of publicity. For once, however, the cynics were wide of the mark, as the following few days were to prove.

The distracting feature of the story, as far as distinguishing the likelihood or otherwise of its accuracy, was the claim that he was leaving rugby to enter the world of football. This seemed far-fetched, desperately so, and with the FA having recently gone through a crisis, and people still questioning the role of Sven-Goran Eriksson, it all seemed just a little too convenient.

Added to the fact that Woodward would have to spend a couple of years obtaining the appropriate qualifications to manage a professional football team, it was an angle that caused many observers to lose sight of the real thrust of the story. Maybe he wasn't about to swap the world of the oval ball for that of the round, but the suggestion underpinning the whole tale, that he was about to walk away from rugby, seemed to be slightly overlooked as a result. The story didn't have to be entirely correct, not for the moment, anyway, for Woodward still to be walking away from Twickenham. Half-right would be perfectly sufficient to end an era in English rugby, and as the day wore on, it became increasingly clear this was the case.

At the heart of his dispute with the RFU was the amount of time he got to spend with his international squad. Woodward had wanted between 22 and 24 days a year in order to rebuild a side decimated by retirement and injuries to a point where a serious defence of the World Cup could be contemplated. He got, through an agreement drawn up between the game's governing body and the Premiership clubs, just 16.

A failure to increase access, in the light of his achievements, would probably have still been unacceptable. A decrease, having just led a tired and bedraggled touring party through the southern hemisphere on a jaunt that saw chunks of gilt flake from his glittering successes, was always going to lead to a stand off. Woodward's mind, knowing that the decision had been made and signed, the deal done and dusted, was set. He wasn't acting in a fit of pique, rather than letting his head, as so often before, rule his heart.

The news didn't so much leak out, as flood. Once the tale blinked its way into the light of day, it generated its own pace. By the following morning, the papers were full of the story, and the rather clipped, curt statements offered by the RFU, redolent of a past age in their tone, when even journalists were meant to behave with a degree of subservience, smacked of an organisation trying to quell a forest fire with a thimble of water.

By the end of a long day of negotiations, Woodward left Twickenham explaining that he was 'still England coach', knowing the statement meant only that the fine detail of the severance agreement had still to be formulated. The RFU explained that, 'Sir Clive has not formally tendered his written resignation,' which hardly caused the attendant scribes to pack up their notebooks and shrug their shoulders at the lack of a story, either.

Even at this point, there were small details, oddities perhaps, that may not have helped the swift resolution of the discussions. Woodward was represented by his solicitor, Peter Baines, who also happens to sit on the management board of the RFU. This board is chaired by Graham Cattermole, who, along with RFU chief executive Francis Bacon, was effectively heading the negotiations with regard to the settlement. Given the rancour which was to become all too publicly evident between the two sides, it appeared to be a somewhat curious state of affairs.

By the early evening of Thursday, 2 September, however, the negotiations were done, and Woodward made a statement confirming that his written resignation had been tendered and accepted, with immediate effect. Andy Robinson would take over as acting head coach, and amid a string of reciprocal thanks and tributes, none of which fooled anyone, Sir Clive was gone, pending a press conference the following morning. It was over, and now we awaited the explanations.

The fact that Woodward made 'no further comment' in his Thursday evening statement was, everyone agreed, neither here nor there. He was going to sit down the following morning and spell out his reasons for leaving the job he had described on numerous occasions as 'the best in the world'. Even though nobody was expecting glad tidings all round, what was to come was still enough to command another day of back-page headlines.

Held in the 'Spirit of Rugby' suite, it soon became clear the location was only chosen because the 'There's no argument here' lounge and the 'We're all still the best of friends' conference room were fully booked. It was the spleen of Woodward, fully vented in several directions, rather than the spirit of rugby, which attracted the attention, as, not for the first time, the now former England coach conducted a controlled and enthralling 80 minutes at Twickenham.

The placement of the RFU chief executive between Woodward and Cattermole at the top table may have been accidental, but it didn't take long to see the wisdom behind such an act of segregation. Just as they do while waiting for events to get underway at Penny Hill Park, the rugby writers spotted a Bacon sandwich, and prepared to get stuck in.

Firstly, however, the chief executive opened proceedings, going through the fine detail and the formalities for longer than anyone really wanted or needed, in the manner of a compère suddenly fallen in love with the limelight.

'Ladies and gentlemen, in a minute, Frank Sinatra, but first can I just take you through the rest of the programme, and maybe offer you one or two thoughts of my own.'

Finally, however, the insistent glares of the press pack became impossible to resist any further, and the main event took to the microphone.

'This is not a spur of the moment decision,' Woodward announced, drawing breath just long enough to confirm that we were about to get something juicy, 'but something about which I've thought long and hard in order to put my thoughts in line.' This was already shaping up nicely.

'It's not just one thing, but a combination of matters.' Hold on, he was going to offer us chapter and verse. People started making sure that they had a spare pen, enough sheets left in their notepads, and that the batteries in the tape recorder were going to last. It was not going to be one to miss.

'I signed a contract an hour before getting on the plane to go to the World Cup, knowing that it had a 12-month clause. Coming back from the World Cup, I was going from an environment in which I was totally in control, and since then, it's been disappointing.

'From the moment the plane landed back in England again, in fact, I've been disappointed, because the control we've had has been watered down. I've ended up staggered at the number of meetings I've had to endure with the same old people, going over the same old discussions.

'We'd proved we could win the World Cup, but we only won it by a fraction, in the 20th minute of extra time. The discussions should have been about what we needed to make sure we won it again, but they weren't.'

Normally, other than in the most extreme circumstances, the press have to step forwards and light the blue touch paper themselves if they want to see fireworks at an event such as this. Not today, though. Woodward sat down, in control but smouldering, and then went off in a shower of sparks without a moment's assistance from anyone.

'I said to Francis that we'd have to agree to disagree on what's going on here. I think England can still win, but people are asking us to dispense with a proven, successful formula. I don't want to keep moaning about access time, but look at Kelly Holmes, the rowers, the Olympic gold medalists – they win by inches. We won by an inch, and in order to do that, you need every advantage you can get in terms of preparation.'

It wasn't the nature of the conflict that was causing raised eyebrows, so much as the directness with which Woodward was willing to discuss it. Frustrations which had simmered for a long time were rising to the surface, and with no reason to keep his thoughts behind closed committee-room doors any more, he was giving his grievances a very public airing.

So, the first half of the original story was well and truly vouched for, and already, just a quarter of an hour or so into proceedings, there was no going back now – bridges were being burned in all directions. That left the slightly more exotic aspect, concerning Woodward's footballing intentions. It wasn't quite a denial, but then, it wasn't quite an acceptance either – what it was, though, possibly more by design than accident, was enough to keep the story running for weeks to come.

'I've applied to do a grade-two coaching award at the FA, not the England job! Having said that, I've met with people and players recently, and I've learned a tremendous amount from them. I'm not about to get involved in first-team football, though, and I doubt I ever will be. Besides, I'm 100% committed to the Lions, and I won't be taking on any other paid work until after the end of that tour. As far as football's concerned, it might be that I never end up doing anything more than coaching Maidenhead Under-9s.'

So far, it was all classic Woodward, if a more unfettered version than previously heard, on account of his new-found freedom to express himself. People had hardly accused him of being a 'yes man' before, of saying things just because they were popular, but suddenly, the frustration and the anger were being expressed more clearly than ever.

'I'm being asked to compromise, and you don't win things by compromising. I'm amazed and saddened that the RFU and the people at the clubs haven't had the vision to do what needed to be done. This is the greatest job in world rugby, and it's a huge wrench to walk away from it, but when you see what's going on, how tired the players are getting, then it's time to call it a day and leave someone else to take up the challenge.

'If we won the World Cup by 50 points, then fair enough, but we didn't. You can't run the game through the directors of rugby [at Premiership clubs], three quarters of whom are foreign, and the other quarter want your job anyway.'

Ears were pricked up now, all right. Having a dig at the RFU was one thing – people had expected that – but to attack the clubs quite so directly was a different matter altogether. He wasn't finished yet, either.

'I know what's going on; I hear what's said. I've heard what [Warren] Gatland and [John] Connolly have said, for example, and I'm meant to be working with them. There's nobody here, though, sadly, who has the teeth to deal with them. There are also some very strange people running rugby clubs in this country.'

In a matter of seconds, things had gone from intriguing to impassioned. Marking out his territory and stating his case was one thing, but attacking the directors of rugby, the club owners and the RFU all in one answer was quite an assault. Even by Woodward's own, impressive standards of speaking his own mind, this was powerful stuff – powerful enough to leave Bacon interjecting to talk about the positive steps he felt the RFU had made in the last few years. As a diversionary tactic, it fell slightly short, as Woodward observed what a 'joke' the agreement they had reached with the clubs was. It wasn't exactly convivial.

Bacon even tried to backtrack, accepting that he had of course known that this 12-month option had been open to Woodward. Given that it was negotiated, on behalf of Woodward, by a member of Bacon's own management board, this wasn't quite the masterstroke it might have been, but the chief executive still seemed hopeful that he could restore a degree of good humour and calmness to the proceedings. Unfortunately, the previously silent Cattermole decided it was time to offer a few thoughts.

With the air of a slightly pompous local councillor making a pedantic point of order at a planning application, Cattermole was a stiff-collared public relations disaster waiting to happen. The occasion needed an increase in tension about as much as it needed a bomb hoax or a lightning strike, but he blundered on regardless.

What he wanted to say, you suspected, would have been uncannily similar to the mutterings of Henry II, shortly before Thomas Becket met such an untimely end. 'Who will rid me of this turbulent ex-head coach?' might not have quite the same historical ring as Henry's outburst, but it wouldn't have been much less heartfelt. Instead, he managed the extraordinary feat of sounding blustering and prissy at the same time.

'We're going in the right way. It might take longer than Clive would like, but if you're going to change things overnight, then you're going to have major problems. As for some of the things Clive has said, I think you should know that he prepared a report before the World Cup which I sat and discussed with him in Brisbane for almost three hours and we agreed certain things. For example, I gave him access to the management board – regular access on a quarterly basis, to speak to them directly.'

It took a sarcastic retort from Woodward, thanking him for access to the management board, to ensure that the frost between the two men developed into something genuinely glacial. In one, brief exchange, though, it became clearer than ever what Woodward had been up against. The implication that he was lucky enough to get three whole hours of Cattermole's time told its own story.

The fact that Woodward was expected to be grateful at the granting of an audience with the by now fabled management committee 'on a quarterly basis', however, was far more revealing. Throughout its structure, the RFU, as I had witnessed, had done marvellous things. It had let those who knew best handle the development of the game, and it had been sensitive and intelligent in the way it went about much of its business. Then there was a man, sitting in front of the national media, a Captain Mainwaring in civvies, expecting thanks for allowing the man who delivered the World Cup to speak to a room full of stuffed shirts once every three months.

I remembered what Woodward had said to me a couple of months earlier: 'It all starts from the top and works downwards.' He was talking about success, but watching this display, it was plain that damaging public relations worked in much the same way. The people I'd met from the RFU, the ones who worked 'on the ground', had been aware and committed, yet their organisation's image was still rooted in a bygone age. Millions of television viewers were now going to be forming their opinions of the organisation from a man who gave the impression that he thought he was running the Twickenham branch of the Territorial Army. So much for the corporate facelift.

It was, in many ways, a depressing end to an uplifting journey, and one raising just as many questions as it answered. The rift between Woodward and the clubs seems destined to grow ever wider, despite a retraction he issued a few days later. It's hard not to argue that they haven't got good reason to feel angry, having been publicly lashed without access to an immediate reply.

They're not the villains in this particular drama, any more than Woodward is. They pay the wages, provide the new talent, play the finest club rugby in the world and deserve a say in how often their players are made unavailable to them. Woodward, even with decreased access to his international squad, enjoyed more of a say over the clubs than he ever would if the touted move to football eventually came to fruition. It's hard to imagine Arsene Wenger or Sir Alex Ferguson ceding too much ground to him, and as for his own dear Chelsea, coaches can rant and rave, but only money talks.

By the same token, it wasn't the clubs who brought a million people out onto the streets of London on a chilly December lunch-time, to cheer a collection of burly men in suits, perched on a bus. It wasn't a club game which filled the Southwark Tavern, and a thousand other pubs besides, with nervous, excited, crack of dawn drinkers on that famous morning. It wasn't the clubs who generated the interest that brought a 50 per cent increase in children turning up at their grounds and asking to learn to play the game.

The truth, and with it, the answer, falls somewhere between these two, understandably entrenched, standpoints, and the blame for their failure to find common ground must fall at the door of those given the task of delivering an agreement. It's impossible, using the exclusive perspective of either the Premiership clubs or Woodward, to reach an agreement – the former are driven by business motives, the latter is simply driven.

The real sadness is that it couldn't be resolved in some way before the issue got to the point of resignations. There are, of course, some who suggest that Woodward got out at the right time, that his methods were tired and his days were numbered. A few of these even put together a convincing case, while some appear to be settling scores for one of a myriad of slights Woodward may or may not have delivered over the years. Not being famous for tact when in pursuit of an ambition, he's responsible for a fair few of those.

There are others who point out what he achieved, what he built, and the plans he put in place. They talk of a team being rebuilt, rather than one in meltdown, and mourn the disappearance from English rugby of a man who caught its imagination like no other before him. Maybe they never fell foul of the man the way others did, or maybe they just happen to share the same vision, and the same unapologetic way of going about things. History waits to prove the correctness or otherwise of both camps.

Personally, I was left with a sense of frustration – frustrated that the man who delivered such a dream had been made to feel so fed up with the whole affair that he walked out on it, unable to take any more. I felt frustrated that his final blast at the clubs was so poorly judged, not least because it deflected attention away from his real target – the people who left me feeling more irritable than anyone else.

For all their willingness to change elsewhere, the RFU emerged from the whole saga looking like the sort of sporting body casual observers had always imagined them to be. I'd had my own preconceptions about them when I first approached them several months ago, yet had been forced to re-evaluate dramatically, as they exceeded my expectations in department after department. In so many areas, they are a dynamic, progressive organisation, and yet when it most mattered, when the world looked on and made a character judgement, those at the top played right up to a dated stereotype.

I felt a bit sorry for Woodward, but it's hard to get too worked up about a millionaire knight of the realm who's grown tired of his job, having delivered a World Cup, trousered a handy pay-off and set himself up financially for life. I had admiration for him, I thought he was incredibly personable and polite, and intrinsically decent, but I suspect sympathy isn't a sentiment he requests or expects. Besides, being due to manage the Lions having told the world that football, not rugby, is his first love, he's already got fresh battles on his horizon about which to muse.

Similarly, I didn't feel sorry for the clubs. They had a better agreement in place, from their perspective, than had been the case. They had more people coming through the gates than ever before. They had a television contract, excellent media exposure, and the signs of future growth were all around them. Everything in their garden was rosy.

No, as I tried to put my thoughts into order after a turbulent few days, it was, to my amazement, the RFU I felt sorry for – or, to be more precise, the vast majority of the people I met at the RFU. They had seen their organisation been made to look foolish, and by default, they were made to look foolish too, and they didn't deserve that. They had been let down by those who sought to lead them. The blazers had buggered it up.

As I strolled along from the stadium, I pondered some of the phrases I'd heard. From the feudal roots of 'on a quarterly basis', to the sulky tones of 'of course, Clive wants more' it had been depressing stuff. Then, to cap it all, there was Bacon's hopeless attempt at managing the situation, as he spluttered, 'I don't want to, you know, sort of indulge in debate about things that myself and Clive didn't agree on,' when it had already raged for almost an hour. What sort of debate did he think we wanted? It wasn't really the occasion to ask him for his desert-island discs.

From the midst of an incredible achievement, a moment of sporting history that would remain in the memories of all who saw it, things had descended to this. It was probably always destined to end in tears, because that's the nature of sport, but so soon? Hardly anyone had emerged looking terribly good, and some looked considerably worse than others. It didn't have to be like this.

It wasn't the depths they'd reached that depressed me, as much as the distance they'd fallen to get there.

XVIII

Journey's end

My timing, on balance, was rotten. After years of gradual, steady improvement, culminating in the capture of the World Cup, I'd managed to meet up with the England rugby team just as form and triumph once more became a stranger to them. You don't have to take my word for it either, as the statistics alone make out a compelling case.

In the run up to the World Cup, they strung together 14 consecutive victories, slipping up only when fielding a weakened side against the French in Marseilles. To put that into perspective, a week later, their full-strength line-up beat the same opposition 45–14. From that point onwards, they swept aside the world in Australia, and breezed through against Italy and Scotland at the start of the Six Nations, before finally falling to Ireland.

Had it not been for that defeat by the French, and then by a solitary point, they would have won 25 times in a row. When I arrived, though, they lost five of their eight post-World Cup Test matches, including their last four of the season. Before I came along, they hadn't lost at Twickenham since October 1999, winning no fewer than 22 games on the trot. I watched them play there twice, and guess what? They lost them both. I couldn't get to the Wales game, and was forced to rely on the wonders of television – they won, of course.

I was a hex – a bad luck symbol, the sort of person a team really doesn't need following them around. I became aware of the effect I was having on them about halfway through my journey, but opted to keep quiet about it, despite beginning to feel distinctly paranoid.

When I sat down to chat with Sir Clive, I fully expected his chair to mysteriously collapse midway through my first question, or a fire alarm to go off and the interview never to recommence. At the very least, I'm sure someone must have been pinching his car stereo as we spoke. If he'd run under a ladder while breaking a mirror over a black cat, it couldn't have been worse than what I'd done to him and his side. By the time his resignation was announced, the paranoia was in its more advanced stages. Every time I heard the word 'rugby', I looked over my shoulder, wondering what fresh piece of chaos I'd inadvertently caused.

Having begun my journey in the wake of a post-election high, I was leaving them with the mid-term blues and a leadership crisis. In keeping with the best traditions of politicians, however, Woodward was able to point to a record of success. Unlike the best political traditions, he was telling the truth. By the time he'd explained his lifelong affection for football and left his job to spend more time with his family, however, the political parallels were impossible to ignore.

Much had been written about the quality of the young players England had to fall back on during the course of their recent adventures down under, and little of it had been particularly flattering. On the face of it, on the back of a row of defeats, and with the sheen fading from the Webb Ellis trophy, they weren't generating very much about which to be positive.

It was bleak and anti-climactic, and if the world was to be judged by headlines alone, English rugby was in a state of disrepair. Many of these headlines, as I'd discovered over the course of the previous nine months, were nonsense. When Woodward had asked us not to get carried away by a string of positive results, he was, in the most part, ignored. England were much better than he was prepared to admit, and we weren't playing any part in his game of bluff.

Now, after a brief period of disappointment, where results had failed to raise the spirits and race the pulse, he had once more been asking people not to blow it out of all proportion. Again, just as they did when it was going well, people ignored him – they weren't taking part in his games.

211

The only logical conclusion to all of this is that the public at large, certain sections of the media and anyone else who cares to voice an opinion, know more about the workings of the England rugby team than Woodward himself. Unfortunately for those who like their arguments simple and uncomplicated, that's even more nonsensical than the notion that the game is crumbling before our bewildered eyes. Somewhere, there exists a middle ground, a way of showing that while things have doubtless gone off the boil since Wilkinson's drop goal delivered a dream, the systems which made it possible are still in place.

England had, over the course of the previous 16 years, become renowned for their ability to peak between World Cups, saving their best for the years where it was never fully tested. What Woodward managed, in order to achieve the heights he did, was to tease the very last out of the legs of an exceptional group of players, taking them to their absolute limits in order to land the ultimate prize. As ever, it's all a matter of opinions and viewpoints, but it seems short-sighted to the point of being contrary to blame him for the collapse of a side, rather than to praise him for his ability to take its previous incarnation as far as humanly possible.

Several of the players blooded on the last tour would obviously have benefited from having enjoyed an earlier introduction to international rugby, but to have done so would have meant fielding a side insufficiently savvy and streetwise to have brought home the Webb Ellis trophy. Suddenly having to deal with a glut of inexperienced international players is just the price you pay for draining every last drop out of the old stagers, and keeping them together as a unit for as long as possible.

Given what they achieved, few complained at the result then, and few, if they thought it through, should complain now. Rebuilding and developing is a cyclical process, and if you want to hit the heights, you'll inevitably have to experience the depths to get there. Woodward departed because of a disagreement about why the players were having to call it a day so soon – arguing over the prospects for the future, not the failings of the past.

The challenge now, however, despite the background of success, is possibly greater than at any time since Woodward took command. He raised the expectations, and it was those as much as anything else that caused his disenchantment. The first time you pick up a golf club, just getting the ball into the air is a feat of which to feel proud. After a while, though, you expect more – the ball has to go further, straighter and closer to the target. For a long time, English rugby fans celebrated whenever the ball left the ground – now, having seen the fundamentals mastered, their perception of what is acceptable has altered. Having won a major, they want more.

So, having delivered a dream, where to now? With two talismanic captains announcing their retirement in quick succession, and a new side needing to be constructed by a new coach in order to defend the trophy, where does the game as a whole go from here? Is it more difficult to reach the summit, or to stay there?

England's triumph undoubtedly validated Woodward's blueprint for the direction in which the game in this country must develop. As a result of his success with the most spectacularly fit and well-conditioned bunch of players ever to emerge from this country, thousands of rather less well-prepared players are about to try to follow in their tracks. Whether they are quite up to the challenge, and quite how the extraordinary dynamism of the England team is suited to being adopted by lesser physical specimens has been something worth witnessing.

The game of rugby is about much more than just the finest athletes disputing massive contests in front of huge crowds. To the vast majority of its participants, it's about muddy pitches, forwards who can't run, fly-halfs who can't catch and wingers who can't be bothered. A delicate balance has developed through the years, where a handful of the elite act as a counterbalance for the great majority of the less talented, and any alterations to that must be sensitive and careful.

In the wake of this triumph, has English rugby changed at all levels, though? Are flagging back-row forwards, dreaming of a post-match beer, going to accept being bellowed at by coaches demanding an eleventh phase? Are players happy with the idea of forwards and backs being virtually interchangeable? It might have been wonderful to watch England doing it, especially with a pint in your hand and no personal risk, but has the game reached a level where it is moving away from its core audience?

Once upon a time, what the international side did was almost capable of being copied, if at a slower pace and with smaller people – has this gone for ever? Can you only play their way if you're super-fit, hugely brave and powerful and prepared to train every hour of the day? Where does this leave the average club player?

On the evidence of what I've witnessed, and having spoken to people from all levels of the sport, the answer is, almost inevitably, inconclusive, but the manner in which it was delivered to me gives huge reason for hope. At the highest levels, the game is being played better than it ever has been before, and the briefest glance at a video of club rugby from ten, perhaps even five years ago, confirms that contention.

Players have been given a glimpse of what can be achieved with sufficient work and dedication, and those that wish to pursue a path to the very top know what is expected of them. The structure Woodward helped to lay down has provided a route map to the top, even if the journey is beyond all but a few truly exceptional athletes. In this regard, even if the first steps of the new breed of England internationals have been faltering, made under huge pressure and in difficult circumstances, the uncertainty as to the direction they need to take has been removed. Having succeeded once, the way to repeat that triumph may involve minor alterations, but the days of radical structural change and revolution seem to have passed.

The squabbles continue, though. I witnessed Woodward's requests for further time with his squad, for greater reserves to be directed their way, and while those were made from a position of strength, it wasn't strong enough to force them through. The day-to-day tinkering, the political infighting which went hand in hand with his achievements, won't alleviate the possibility of further, minor conflicts for his successor somewhere down the road.

What I have learned, however, is that for the majority of lovers of the game, the biggest headlines don't always reflect the biggest issues. As important as these arguments were, and as crucial as it may have been to Woodward to gain another four or five days a year with his squad, the battle is more important to those writing about the game than it is to most of those who play it. It's just a small piece of a larger jigsaw, and while it impacts, along with a thousand other factors, on the success of the international side, to the average player and fan, it's ultimately just another one of those critical non-essentials.

Therein, I think, lies the point. The individual pieces of preparation, the little bits of jigsaw Woodward hoped to bring together to produce another triumphant picture, were too far removed from the lives of ordinary players and fans to actually mean anything. They were happy to let the man who showed he knew how combine these together in order to produce future days of glory, but personally, they have no time for the minute detail. The risk was always that the coach emerged looking like someone who always wanted one extra little bit to add to the mix – that his record became subsumed by what were seen as his constant demands.

This is where, though, it seems to me, his belief that success comes from the top downwards may yet reap its true rewards. Whether it was Woodward himself stressing the importance of a solid structure, Jason Leonard offering his blueprint for how junior clubs can develop themselves, or several others, there are a few people at the top of the game who understand how it works at the bottom of the pile. Some of them may still be in relatively subsidiary positions, but they are there, they are talented, and they are not scared to speak their minds. If the RFU was recruiting the wrong people, limited of vision and conservative in nature, the future would be bleak, but it is not.

The demands, as I've said, are different – drastically so – but rugby has an acceptance running through it of the difference between bottom and top that other sports maybe do not. Wherever I went through the lower levels of the game, there was an appreciation for what Woodward had done, and a respect and fascination for the man. The national side may live different lives to the rest of the game's participants, but there's no sense of unfairness or jealousy, other than the most natural kind. They not only see, but appreciate the importance of the bigger picture. People went to the victory parade to celebrate with their heroes, not to cheer at people with whom they had nothing in common, but admired all the same.

Whether it was Dave Berry and the medics of Guy's, who admired and applauded, while realising that their own careers were, by definition, going to head off in different ways, or the kids in Peckham, with the problems life threw at them, there was a pride that their game was played better in their country than anywhere else. Crucially, the work of Andrew Scoular and the development staff at the RFU seemed to be ensuring that the links between the bottom and the top remained strong, thanks to a structure which made the route to progression crystal clear.

Not everyone is destined to take that route – few are capable, in keeping with the nature of any competitive sport, but all are made aware of how it can be done. It's easy to mock Woodward and his systems, his desire to chase tiny details until they fit perfectly into place, but without it, the broader picture would never have been painted.

As I sat down, trying to pull all the pieces into place in a bid to summarise what the journey had showed me, I got a call from Vernon Neve Dunn, with an update on the Tigers' progress. The Kent tag rugby festival finals were being held, and Peckham and the areas surrounding it were providing four different teams. No other club in the country had managed to host more than one qualifying competition, but weight of numbers meant that Vernon had staged four of them.

When he told the kids that he needed a couple of weeks off in the summer, having trained them solidly for much of the last eleven months, they responded by turning up regardless – 50 of them. Before the game was introduced to the area, and before England won the World Cup, the suggestion that you could have gathered together such a number would have been laughable, but now it was very much a reality. Success had trickled down from the top, and through careful planning and inspired coaching and leadership, here it was, proving that the theory worked.

Quite apart from the social value of the game in such areas, the process of turning up players where nobody had previously bothered to look could only bode well for its future. The words and phrases, the non-essentials and the schedules can become almost a matter of amusement, until you go and see the reality. As Scoular pointed out, a thousand extra sides a week is an amazing feat, and from those players, who is to say what gems might yet be found lurking?

Among the schools, too, the development is clear. I first watched St Columba's, new to the game at this level, wondered how far their dedication might take them, and couldn't imagine there were many sides better equipped to succeed. I then watched them defeated by a side playing with flair and wit, marshalled by a little midfield general, and realised how far the game had come on since I left school, barely 15 years earlier. I then watched the senior final, and amended my judgement once more, as Colston's took the schoolboy game to a new level. By the time they move up the pyramid, it's hard to see their alumni failing to make their mark on the highest tiers of the game.

All around me, though, and it was something that shone through more brightly than anything else, was the impression that, despite becoming more focused, the game had lost none of its basic sense of fun and mutual respect. People remain as much in love with it as ever

216

they did, whether a young fly-half looking forward to life in front of huge crowds, or an ageing prop, playing out his days behind a huge stomach. The art of coarse rugby is as much in evidence as ever it was, but the art of good rugby is being embraced with equal enthusiasm.

Everywhere I had gone, I had enjoyed the company of people who enjoyed the game – loved the game. Whether over coffee with Clive and Vernon, or beers with Dave and Rick, whatever their personal standing, the affection for their sport, their very special sport, was impossible to ignore. It's one thing to look, and even to try to analyse the top strands of English rugby, finding reasons for its successes and failures, but it's a far more meaningful trip if you go via the minor roads. Through the lower levels and beneath, where the phrase 'for the love of the game' actually comes to life, things seem to get put into perspective in a way that doesn't happen as easily at the highest level.

If this is beginning to sound like a hymn of praise to English rugby at the close of the Woodward era, while I make no apologies for reporting it exactly as I found it, the intention, or at least the expectation, wasn't initially nearly so positive. Before I'd taken a step of the journey, watched a game for this book or spoken to a player, I anticipated discovering the extent to which the game had squandered its inheritance – how it failed to make the most of the benefits the World Cup could have brought. The dangers of pre-judging something were never brought home to me more clearly than over the following months.

It didn't take long to see that the story was going to head off in a very different direction. Within weeks, I was acutely aware that I'd been horribly wrong in my assessment of the situation, so wrong, in fact, that even had I tried to chop and change things to support my faulty contention, I couldn't have done so. The post-World Cup international results were poor, but that wouldn't have created the problem. Trying to demonstrate that the underbelly of the game was falling apart, that the fabled structure was, in fact, built on quicksand, would have been impossible.

Not just that, it would have been dishonest. Prior to the World Cup, the state of the game at its lower levels had been declining – on average, one club a fortnight was folding, and the number of people interested in the sport was sliding ever downwards. The crowds watching Premiership rugby were increasing, but the numbers actually participating were dropping steadily. It was getting richer at the top, poorer at the bottom, and a damaging fragmentation seemed inevitable.

Through a marvellously maintained and conceived support structure, that divorce between top and bottom hasn't happened. The numbers entering the game have grown dramatically, and a fatal trend has been reversed. The seeds for this revival weren't sown in the wake of that Sydney victory, but several years earlier, in time to make the most of the glut of players and interest thrust suddenly at the sport. If the RFU squandered their opportunities in the wake of the 1991 tournament, the same mistakes weren't being made twice.

Everyone who played a part in turning that around was prepared to talk to me, taking time out of busy lives to explain what it was they were trying to achieve. Uniformly, rather than boasting about how far they'd come, they described how much further they had still to go. The transparency was across the board, the willingness to be held up to scrutiny and query, whether from Woodward himself, or any of the staging points below. It's a stance that can only be safely adopted when there is nothing to hide and much of which to be proud.

I turned up, anticipating a few months as a critic, and instead becoming something of an admirer, for which there's no apology. Often, and rightly so, you'll hear journalists and writers talk in disparaging tones about people becoming 'cheerleaders' when they refuse to see fault in a favoured subject and applaud every move and utterance without question or doubt. I questioned everyone I came across, arriving with a sense of impending doom, yet found myself forced to drastically amend my opinion. Having someone praise you after they've questioned you is surely more meaningful than when they cheer you out of habit, regardless of what you've done.

Yes, I felt let down by certain individuals when the resignation affair came to a head, but I'm not sure how well they represent the organisation they manage. I heard from many at the RFU about the importance of living up to your promises, of achieving things rather than just talking about them. They were the real spirit of rugby, not the bickering duo who sat in the room of the same name as Woodward's endgame was acrimoniously played out.

Over the course of the next few seasons, the balance of power in world rugby will continue to shift, and England, as world champions, will be studied more closely than most. Even while bearing in mind Woodward's decree about it all working from the top downwards, however, I'll know, more surely than ever before, that the score on the pitch at the end of an international doesn't tell the whole story of English rugby. Equally, I'll know that the next four years won't necessarily be long enough for the next stage in the development of the English game to be fully completed.

Somewhere, however, and happening more often than ever before, I'll stumble across a game involving children who would once never have dreamed of picking up a ball and running with it. In parts of the country once ignored by the sport, there are youngsters falling in love with it. Equally, at the oldest club in the world, there's a bunch of young medics willing to fight for their survival, protecting the traditions they take desperately seriously, for the same reasons as those inner-city children – because they love the game.

People had said the game was dying from the bottom, upwards – that the national side was strong, but the amateur game was fading away. I looked for traces and found nothing but the fresh, green shoots of recovery. Far from fading away, it seems to be preparing itself for the next generation. Thanks to the willingness of dedicated people, a few visionaries, and an elderly organisation prepared, generally at least, to move with the times, whatever habit and history may incline it to do, the game is prospering.

I thought back to the happiest man in the world, sitting at the bar of the Southwark Tavern, knocking his pint into his fry-up in glee and declaring that it 'doesn't get better than this'. It's taken me a little longer than I expected to get back with an answer, but having emerged from a lengthy and refreshing immersion in the game, I think I can help him out.

No, despite a few stumbles along the way, it doesn't.